Genealogies of

# West Virginia Families

from

THE WEST VIRGINIA HISTORICAL
MAGAZINE QUARTERLY, 1901-1905

CLEARFIELD

Reprinted for
Clearfield Company, Inc. by
Genealogical Publishing Co., Inc.
Baltimore, Maryland
1992, 1993, 1997, 2001

International Standard Book Number: 0-8063-4692-2

*Made in the United States of America*

# Contents

# THE CAMERONS

FAMILY HISTORY OF THE CAMERONS OF VIRGINIA—BY W. T. PRICE.

But few if any names are held in higher honor, or in more affectionate remembrance than that of Major Charles Edward Cameron, Warm Springs, Bath County, Virginia. He was a son of Dr. John Cameron, who was the first of the Cameron clan to come to America, so far as known to us. He was a son of Evan Cameron, of Fassifern, a younger brother of Lochiel, who led the Camerons at the battle of Culloden. Lochiel and Evan were sons of " John the Tanister," who was the son of Sir Evan Dhu Cameron, according to W. and A. K. Johnston's " Scottish Clans and their Tartans." The term " Tanister" signifies land owner or governor. In Johnston's book this is recorded:

"An eminent native of Kilmalie was the famous Sir Evan of Lochiel, who was born in 1629 and died in 1719, and was a famous cavalier in his time. From his swarthy complexion he was named Evan Dhu. At the head of his clan Sir Evan is said to have made no less than thirty-five armed forays into the territories of his enemies."

Evan Cameron of Fassifern married Lucy Campbell, of Barcoldane, the mother of Dr. John Cameron, the American immigrant, and immediate ancestor of the Virginia Camerons. Lucy Campbell's father succeeded to the estate Glenmore, on the death of his brother, who was shot at the Ferry of Ballachulish in Appin by Allan Braec Stewart, otherwise known as Vic Jan VicAlaster, a crime for which the Laird of Ardshiel was judicially executed by the Duke of Argyle at the Castle of Inverary.

In the period of the Scottish civil wars the Camerons were ever loyal to the house of Stewart. One of the poet Campbell's more

1

hrilling poems is about Sir Lochiel just before the battle of Culloen.

Popularly he was known in his clan as the gentle Lochiel, while
1 the histories he is written of as the "Great Lochiel." It was
,ochiel, who in his loving, ardent way exclaimed to Prince Charles
Come weal, come woe, I'll follow thee!"

Lochiel Campbell's steel Highland pistols, found on the bloody
nd fatal field of Culloden, marked with his initials, may be seen
1 the museum of antiquities at Edinburg.

In their religious proclivities the Camerons of that period were
'atholics, and eagerly sided with the cause of the Pretender, who
'as the son of James the Second of England, born after his father
ad been dethroned. After his father's death in 1701, the Pre-
ender was declared by the King of France the rightful King of
Ingland. In France he was called the Chevalier St. George; in
Ingland the Pretender. Parties in England, more especially Scot-
and, espoused the Pretender's claims from time to time. Many
ives were sacrificed and many grievous calamities occasioned. It
'as in the reign of George the Second that the Pretender made his
ist effort, being then an old man. His partisans the Jacobites put
orward his son Charles Edward, known as the Young Pretender
nd the Young Chevalier.

The Scotch Highlanders favored the young Pretender and when he
oined them there was a Scottish uprising to make him King, where
pon many noble and gallant men lost their fortunes and their lives.
n the battle of Culloden, April, 1746, the Scotch were sorely de-
eated.

The defeated Pretender found it hazardous to make his escape
broad with such tempting rewards offered for his head. True to
heir character the Scottish partisans were very true to him and
fter many romantic escapes he reached France.

Dr. John Cameron, the ancestor of the Virginia Camerons, bore
he colors of his clan on the field of Colodon and after the loss of the
,attle many of his relatives along with a number of other promi-
ient persons engaged in the rebellion were carried to London and
xecuted. Dr. Cameron, the color-bearer, made his way to Spain
n a Spanish warship. From Spain he soon found a way to the
Vest Indies, Cuba probably, and was there a short while, thence he
vent to New York City. In New York he met the widowed lady

2

who afterwards became his wife, **Mrs.** Margaret Murray. Her maiden name was Margaret McBarron. She was a native of Ireland, of Scottish ancestry, and a Presbyterian in her religious preferences. Mr. Murray, her first husband, was a wealthy merchant of New York, and a native of Liverpool, England. There were two daughters by the first marriage, Sarah and Mary Murray.

Dr. John Cameron moved from New York soon after his marriage and located in Norfolk, Va., where his two children, Charles Edward and George Hugh, were born. The eldest, Charles Edward, was born February 22, 1853. Hugh was several years younger, but the date lost.

Charles Cameron was named for the young Pretender. At first he was named George Hugh, but when he was several years old his father, Dr. Cameron, now of Norfolk, Va., gave a dinner to some Scotch friends who had fought for the Pretender, and they became so stimulated in patriotic feeling of devotion to their favorite that Dr. Cameron, to please them, sent for a Catholic priest, had Charles baptized the second time and named him for the Catholic prince, Charles Edward, the last of the Stuarts, who claimed the crown of Scotland.

Dr. John Cameron resided in Norfolk until Charles was six years old, and then moved to Staunton, Va., about 1760. In the course of time amnesty was accorded rebellious Scottish subjects so they could return to Scotland and repossess their property. Whereupon Dr. Cameron sailed for Scotland, hoping to recover his property and then return and make Staunton his permanent home, but he never returned, lost at sea.

Charles E. Cameron knew that his father, Dr. John Cameron, had in his own name a large estate in Scotland, and was in the line of inheritance also to a fine property besides, as his father's uncle and many relatives had perished, so that if Dr. Cameron had lived to recover his property he would have been possessed of an immense estate that otherwise reverted to the English crown.

At the time of his father's death Charles was a mere child, and had nothing in hand to show that he had any right to the Cameron estate in Scotland. While a half-grown boy he clerked in a Staunton store, and a few years later was offered employment as bankkeeper to the Mossy Creek Iron Works, for Henry Miller, the owner and builder of the first iron plant in the upper Valley of the

Shenandoah, in the northwest section of Augusta county, twelve or fifteen miles from Staunton.

At the age of 19 young Cameron's thoughts turned to love, and he married Nancy, a daughter of his employer, a little younger than himself. In about six months after marriage the girl wife died.

On Monday morning, October 10, 1774, Charles E. Cameron and his brother Hugh were with the Virginia troops at Point Pleasant. A battle not being expected, Charles Cameron and others were detailed and put in charge of Jacob Warwick to hunt and slaughter meat rations for the proposed expedition to the Indian towns in Ohio, as ordered by Governor Dunmore. In the meantime the battle had been suddenly joined, and by the time the hunters and butchers rallied and recrossed the Kanawha the battle had virtually ceased.

Upon his return from hunting he found that his brother George Cameron and his brother-in-law, Colonel Charles Lewis, were killed in the action.

Mrs. Colonel Charles Lewis was Sarah Murray, half sister of Charles and George Cameron.

In person George Cameron was tall and of very dark complexion, with dark hair and eyes, and very high prominent forehead, bearing a striking resemblance to his father, Dr. John Cameron. While he was a child his playmates would sportively tell him that if he was ever shot by the Indians it would be in the forehead, as it was so prominent, and so it turned out, for when Charles found his brother among the slain the bullet holes were in his forehead.

Charles Cameron served through the revolution as a lieutenant, and was with the Virginia troops at the surrender of Yorktown. Colonel Peyton, in his history of Augusta county, mentions Charles Cameron as one of the "Gentlemen Justices of Augusta county," in 1790.

On December 14, 1790, the counties of Bath and Pendleton were formed from Augusta. Mr. Cameron received a grant of land for services in the revolution, and it is believed he went from Augusta to Bath about the time the county was formed. He accumulated lands in addition to the grant, and finally possessed a magnificent estate. About four miles west of the Warm Springs he selected a site for his residence on a precipitous bluff overlooking the Jacksons river, and commanding a lovely view up and down the

4

valley. He built a large and commodious house of stone, one of the handsomest west of the Blue Ridge at that time.

Major Cameron was the first Clerk of Bath county, serving both courts as such for a great number of years. He was succeeded by his nephew, Charles Lewis Francisco, who was in his day one of the most widely known county clerks in the State of Virginia.

Near Charles Cameron's residence is one of the finest of mountain springs, over which he had erected a stone spring house two stories high. In the upper story he kept the records of Bath county a hundred years ago. That house is still in a good state of preservation, and the residence is about as good as ever.

Soon after the revolution, on the organization of the militia, Mr. Cameron was appointed colonel of a regiment, and was ever afterwards known as Colonel Cameron. It appears that he was claimed by Lafayette as a personal friend, for when Lafayette visited America Colonel Cameron went with the valley veterans to welcome him, and General Lafayette presented Colonel Cameron a handsome gold-headed cane as a token of his esteem for him personally, and it was prized by him all his life, and was in constant use.

After being a widower for twenty years, Colonel Cameron married for his second wife Rachel Primrose Warwick in 1793. She was the eldest daughter of Jacob Warwick, so distinguished in the pioneer annals of West Augusta and the early settlement of Bath and Pocahontas. This lady was born March 17, 1773, at Dunmore, now Pocahontas county, but at that time it was Augusta county. An extended notice of her parents appeared in the WEST VIRGINIA HISTORICAL MAGAZINE July, 1902.

Like the home of her parents at Dunmore, then at Clover Lick, had been a place for ministerial entertainment with the best of cheer and a place for worshipping God, so Mrs. Cameron's princely home on Jackson's river was ever open for ministers and God's service. In early youth Mrs. Cameron united with the Windy Cove Presbyterian church, but at the time of her death, November 6, 1858, at the age of 86 years, she was a member of the Lexington Presbyterian church. Her remains were borne to the Warm Springs for interment.

Colonel and Mrs. Cameron were the parents of three children. Two died in infancy, and for several years they were childless, during which time they adopted two nephews—Andrew Gatewood, a

5

son of Mrs. Cameron's sister, Nancy Gatewood Poage; the other was Charles L. Francisco, whose mother was Mary Murray, Colonel Cameron's half sister, who had become Mrs. Francisco. It had been their intention for these nephews to inherit their great estate, but after these nephews had lived with them ten years, their son, Andrew Warwick Cameron, was born June 6, 1806.

Nevertheless the nephews were liberally provided for. Andrew Gatewood was educated for a physician, and was presented by his aunt with a farm in Pocahontas county. Colonel Charles Cameron gave his nephew, Charles L. Francisco, a farm in Bath county.

Mr. Francisco would say of his aunt Cameron that "her affectionate heart appeared to embrace all the children of want around her, and her home was as open as her heart for the accommodation of all who needed and desired her help."

These worthy people reared five or six nephews and nieces, besides some other young persons not relatives.

Colonel Cameron died at his home "Fassifern," Bath county, four miles west of Warm Springs, June 14, 1829, in the 77th year of his age. In personality, Colonel Cameron was of middle statue, blue eyes, fair complexion, and his hair brown until silvered over with age. His teeth were sound to the last.

This noble man deserves lasting remembrance as a brave, patriotic soldier of the revolution, a citizen without reproach, one of the best of fathers and husbands. Mrs. Cameron survived her husband about thirty years. When Mrs. Cameron was about 36 years old she came near her death by being thrown from her horse. Her hip was broken, and she was lame ever afterward and used a crutch or cane. After the death of her husband she made constant use of his cane, the gift of General Lafayette.

In reference to Andrew Warwick Cameron, the only surviving child of these worthy persons, the following particulars are given: He was favored with the best educational facilities then in reach by instructions of Prof. Crutchfield at Warm Springs; he spent some time with Dr. John Hendren in Augusta county, and then went to the University of Virginia.

His first marriage was with Margaret Grattan, daughter of Captain Samuel Miller, owner of the famous Mossy Creek Iron Works. Captain Miller was one of the more prominent and wealthy citizens of his day, and was a presidential elector on the Clay ticket in 1832.

A. W. Cameron's first marriage occurred January 25, 1828, the nuptials being celebrated by the distinguished Dr. John Hendren.

Mrs. Cameron died April 13, 1829, aged 19 years, leaving an infant daughter named Margaret Grattan Miller, who became Mrs. William Boies Cochran, of Augusta county, January 6, 1859. Mr. and Mrs. Cochran were the parents of three daughters—Maria, now Mrs. Tate Sterrett, of Hot Springs; Rachel Primrose, now Mrs. A. C. Harman, Staunton, Margaret Miller, now Mrs. Dr. I. P. Bishop, of Rockingham county.

The sons were Warwick Cameron and George Moffett. George died March 4, 1883, aged 14 years.

Colonel A. W. Cameron's second marriage was with Ellen McCue, daughter of John Hide, near Lexington, who was high sheriff of Rockbridge county, and a citizen of great wealth and influence. Mrs. Hide was Sallie Crawford, of Augusta county. There were four sons and five daughters in his second family—John, Charles, Andrew, George, Primrose, Sally Mary, Lucy and Jennie. John Cameron, the only surviving son, is a popular physician at Goshen, Va.

Charles, a Confederate soldier, is survived by his son, Wm. T. Cameron, a physician in northern Pocahontas and adjacent sections of Randolph county, W. Va.

Andrew and George are deceased. Andrew was unmarried, and George is survived by his family, who are residents of the Goshen vicinity.

Primrose became Mrs. Joseph Sherrard, Lexington, Va. Mr. Sherrard is a member of the Rockbridge bar.

Sallie became Mrs. Thomas White, youngest son of Rev. Dr. W. S. White, of Lexington, one of the most eminent Presbyterian ministers in Virginia in his day. Captain Tom White is one of the foremost business men in Lexington.

Mary became Mrs. Judge Leigh, and lives in Lexington.

Lucy became Mrs. Dr. White, an eminent physician in Lexington.

Jennie became Mrs. A. W. Harman, of Richmond, who is State Treasurer.

While he was yet a very young man, A. W. Cameron was appointed colonel of the Bath county regiment of Virginia militia, and was ever afterwards known as Colonel Cameron. He was a Henry Clay Whig, and represented his county in the Legislature occasionally, though the county was democratic, of the Andrew Jackson type. In 1840 he left the "Fassifern" princely home on Jackson's river and located on the Hyde plantation, near Lexington, where Captain Tom White now resides.

When the war between the States commenced, Colonel Cameron was broken in health, and had passed the age limit for military service. His four sons joined the Confederate army. He was oppressed with anxiety about his sons, and was heard to say that so many of his Scotch ancestors had died in battle that he had a presentiment that he would not die a natural death himself, and anxiously felt that his sons might meet death in battle. Two days previously to the battle of Manasses, Colonel Cameron rode to Lexington to hear the news from the seat of war. Many persons had gathered in front of the hotel, eagerly awaiting the mails. When the mail coach drove up, one of the passengers, in the act of taking from it a Minnie rifle, struck the gun in a way which caused it to discharge, by which Colonel Cameron was instantly killed, William McClung mortally wounded and William Smith, of the Virginia Military Institute, slightly wounded in the wrist. Thus Colonel Cameron's sad presentiment was realized July 18, 1861, in the 55th year of his age.

In personality, Colonel Cameron was of the highest type of imposing manhood, over six feet high, features regular, hair brown and eyes dark; hands and feet remarkably small, but shapely. As to traits of character, he was a loving, thoughtful, devoted husband, a judicious, affectionate father, a true friend and a kind, considerate master. While he was imbued with much family pride, he was not offensively so. He never boasted of his family's record before his visitors or other associates, but within the sacred precincts of the family circle he endeavored to impress it on his children that it was a great privilege and a blessing to have a gentle and honorable ancestry.

The second Mrs. Cameron survived her noble husband more than thirty years, living to a very advanced, yet serenely happy old age. In her youth she was admired as one of the Rockbridge beauties, and received marked attentions at the pleasure resorts, but was not spoiled. To her honor be it written that by those who knew her best she was admired and loved for her sweetly, gentle disposition and her sincerely, lovely Christian character. It can be said of her

8

with peculiar emphasis that "her children rise up and call her blessed."

The compiler of these sketches of the Virginia Camerons feels he should not lay aside his pen until grateful appreciation is expressed for the helpful service rendered by Mrs. Tate Sterret, of Hot Springs. With loving care she has gathered up all that is most valuable in the preparation of these historical papers.

---

## THE CLENDINENS.

In the language of the Psalmist—"A man was famous as he had lifted up axes against the thick trees."

Among those who stand out with great prominence in the annals of our pioneer history is this Scotch-Irish family the founders of the city of Charleston, the capitol of West Virginia.

The exact date of their coming to Virginia, or where they landed, or first settled is a matter of uncertainty. They were known to be on the Ben Burden Grant in 1755, by the records of Augusta county.

There were three Clendinen brothers who came to America, Archibald, Charles and one other, whose name is unknown to the descendents of Mason county, who settled in Baltimore. Thomas Clendinen, who married the daughter of Dr. J. Hozlett, of Cecil county, is no doubt a descendent of this brother. They had two sons, Alexander and William, both graduated from the Baltimore Medical College. Thomas Clendinen married the second time, Nancy Neice Armstrong, of Scotland, having moved after the death of his first wife to Fishing Creek, ten miles from Zirkville, S. C. Their only child, Robert, became a lawyer of reputation, in Zirkville. The only one living of this

9

branch of the Clendinens is Mary Clendinen Catching Towey, whose home is in Baltimore. She is a great grand-daughter of Thomas Clendinen. Mr. C. C. Miller corresponded with her in 1899. The name of Charles Clendinen and his sons are written upon every page of history that tells of civilization and growth of all that country now embraced in the counties of Greenbrier, Kanawha and Mason. What influenced these brothers to leave their native land and come to the new world, we know not. Perhaps, like many others that sought an asylum here, they were familiar with homes among the rocks, and caves, may have known something of the persecutions of "Ulster" or the battle of "Bothwell Bridge," or the terrors of the "seige of Derry," that sent so many across the Atlantic, to seek peace and liberty.

History tells us they came about 1761 to Greenbrier county. Archibald, and Charles, no doubt with a more restless and daring spirit than the other brother, pushed on down through the Valley of Virginia, into the wilderness of Rockbridge county, and then still farther into the dense forests of Greenbrier county.

They left behind them all the comforts of civilization and we contemplate their surrounding and privations, and stolid indifference, as to their fate, with wonder and awe. We tremble as we think of their cabins built far from any habitations, targets for the fury of the savage foe. A raid was made by the Indians, into the mountains in 1763, under the command of the young warrior Cornstalk, who afterwards became so famous, by his great generalship in the battle of Point Pleasant on Monday, October 10, 1774, even though the day was lost to him, and he was forced to retreat across the Ohio river, back to their Indian stronghold, on the Scioto. At this time the treaty was made by Lord Dunmore, with them at "Camp Charlotte," not allowing General Lewis to have any part in the negotiation, having ordered him to halt at "Pickaway Plains," but which was indignantly disregarded by General Lewis, until he had come within three miles of "Camp Charlotte." The massacre of "Muddy Creek," "Big Levels" and Kerr's Creek, makes us realize what a settlement in the wilderness meant. These Indians in time of a cessation of hostilities, came to the cabin of Archibald Clendinen, after destroying the settlement at "Muddy Creek," and without warning put to death not only the family, but about 100 of the settlers (men women and children) who had bee· invited by Wm. Clendinen to a feast of fine fat elk, he having just ·

10

turned from a successful hunt. The only person who escaped was Conrad Yolcom. Mrs. Clendinen, her infant child, along with her brother, John Ewing, who was on a visit to his sister, Mrs. Clendinen, were carried off captives. The massacre is graphically described by Hon. H. L. Holcomb, of Portsmouth, Ohio. This narrative told by John Ewing after his captivity has been preserved in the Ewing family. Hon. T. T. Davis, of Greenbrier county, W. Va., states that the Archibald Clendinen farm where the massacre occurred, is now owned by Messrs. Haynes, Scott and Persinger. The latter married a great-grand-daughter of Ballard Smith, a relative of Archibald Clendinen, The old grave-yard on the farm has long since been destroyed. Where Charles Clendinen lived at the time of the massacre or how he and his family escaped there is no record. He was married before he came to America, but the burial spot of his wife is not known. After this terrible massacre the Indians went back to "Muddy Creek" and there waited for part of their company who had gone to Kerr's Creek in Rockbridge county to make a raid upon the settlement there. Captain Hall's company from this county, was doing duty at Fort Randolph, in 1777, when Cornstalk was on his mission of peace at the fort. Among the members of his company was one of the Gilmore family, who had suffered in the massacre at Kerr's Creek. He, with a company, had gone over the Kanawha river hunting, and was killed, and scalped, by a couple of roving Indians. His Comrades, many of whom still remembered the loss of friends, in 1763, and the part Cornstalk took in it, before they could be restrained, rushed to the tent of the great chieftian and put to death Cornstalk and his son, and those with him. Cornstalk at the time was drawing a map of the country between the Shawnee towns and the waters, to the Mississippi, with chalk upon the ground. Cornstalk was first buried not far from camp, where he fell, near the intersection of Second and Main streets, but in 1841, his remains were removed to the court yard. Several years ago, at the completion of "Lock 11," Col. Munford, contractor, had his Italian workmen carve out of native rock, to the memory of Cornstalk, a monument, and placed in the court house yard.

Charles Clendinen had four sons—George, who was born in Scotland, William, Alexander, Robert, and one daughter, Mary Ellen, who married ——— Cantrell. This family of Cantrells lived on the bank of the Greenbrier river, where Major John Cantrell, their only son, was born September 17, 1780. The widow came to Mason county, when he was but 14 years of age. They settled first on the Ohio river, what is now known as "Pleasant Flats," near "Eight Mile Island." In 1802 he married the daughter of George Clendinen. In the same year he moved to the north bank of the Kanawha river. At that time there were but two settlements between Point Pleasant and mouth of Elk. George Clendinen was born in 1746. His history shows a beautiful care of his father, and other members of his home. They remind us of the Scottish clans, never separating far from one another. His strong character developed at an early age. History tells us nothing of the wife of Charles Clendinen, but she impresses one with the fact that she must have been a noble pioneer mother,

MAJ. WM. CANTRELL.

whose influence was felt in the home, and helped to mold the characters of her sons.

George Clendinen had risen in prominence in the affairs of his county (Greenbriar) in 1788 and was sent with Colonel John Stuart, of Greenbriar, to the Convention at Richmond, that ratified the Federal Constitution and voted for it, though there was strong opposition, headed by Patrick Henry. It was then he met Cuthbert Bullett and purchased the grant of 1030 acres, left him, by the will of Thomas Bullett, on the Kanawha river above the mouth of Elk, on which is located the capitol of West Virginia. Thomas Bullett was a military man, received his commission from Washington, and was held in high esteem.

12

George Clendinen speaks of him "as, a soldier like myself—sword, cannon and musket." In passing with General Lewis' army to the Ohio river, at the time of the battle of Point Pleasant, he saw this land, and no doubt was struck with its fine location. After the purchase, May 1, 1788, he came with his father and brothers, along with some others—the Harrisons, Watkins, McClungs, Harrimans, Edwards and Tacketts—and reared the walls, of the "fort" they first named "Fort Lee," afterward known as "Fort Clendinen." It was a two-story, double hewed log house, bullett and snow-proof, making it secure against any attack from the Indians. After building this, they put up a number of other rude log cabins around it. In this fort Charles Clendinen died in 1790, and was buried near by. His grave, if marked, has long since been destroyed. It is known to be on the property of C. C. Lewis, Sr. Dr. J. P. Hale purchased the old fort building, and moved it off, and made an effort to perserve it. In December, 1794, George Clendinen employed Alexander Welch, of Greenbriar, to lay off forty acres in a town with two streets, which was named "Front" and "Main," now "Virginia" and "Kanawha" streets. No name was given to the town for many years, but was known as the "Clendinen Settlement," or at "mouth of Elk." It was finally changed to Charlestown, in honor of the father of George Clendinen, when changed to Charleston there is no record. The first court was held at the "Fort," the residence of George Clendinen, October 5, 1789, He furnished the court books for 1920 pounds of tobacco. Tobacco was then "legal-tender." Those present at the court were: Thomas Lewis, Robert Clendinen, Francis Watkins, Charles McClung, Ben Strother, William Clendinen and others. The court ordered that George Clendinen be "recommended as county lientenant," Thomas Lewis as colonel, Daniel Boone, lieutenant-colonel, William Clendinen major, Alexander Clendinen ensign." Early in 1789 an alarm was sent out by "runners," of an Indian invasion. George Clendinen at the head of all the available military force of the Kanawha Valley, hastened to Point Pleasant, then known as the "mouth of the Great Kanawha." His brothers Robert, and William, and Alexander, were all officers at this time. Military organizations were in those days important and necessary for the security of the settlements, and men of courage and ability were selected to command. George Clendinen always responded with promptness and eagerness to any call sent out from the alarmed settlements which made them feel very much more secure in their cabins.

George Clendinen was one of the first representatives from Kanawha county. He was sent to the legislature in 1790, with Andrew Donnally in 1791 with Daniel Boone, 1792 with William Morris, and again in 1794 with the same gentleman, and in 1795 with Thomas Lewis. These records were burned during the Civil War, but were published in the "Kanawha Republican" in 1847, and fortunately were preserved by Dr. J. P. Hale. When the Virginia Assembly enacted, December 19, 1794, that the town of Point Pleasant should be laid off as a town, George Clendinen was one of the trustees appointed. You will find recorded in 1790 in Deed Book A-B in the clerk's office in Kanawha county, "negroes and cattle" given to his daughters, Scynthia, Parthenia and Mary, showing he was married when he came to Elk. His wife's name was Jemima, said to be the sister of Thomas Ewing of Ohio, on the authority of C. C. Miller, and Mary Clendinen McCulloch, of Mason county. He sold all the 1030 acres, purchased from Cuthbert Bullett, to Joseph Ruffner, except the 40 acre lots laid off in the town of Charleston. These sales occurred in 1795-96. May 3, 1797. Jemima Clendinen appeared before the court as widow of George Clendinen. She was appinted administrator and gave bond in 1864. His personalty was appraised at £54. On the court books of Augusta county is recorded a suit brought by the heirs of George Clendinen in 1813 and closed in 1827. His daughter Parthenia married John Meigs, son of R. J. Meigs, of Revolutionary fame, and brother to Governor Meigs of Ohio. Governor Meigs of Ohio, married Sophia Wright, of Connecticut. Their graves are the only ones in the Meigs lot in the cemetery at Marietta. Their only daughter married John G. Jackson, after whom Jackson county, West Virginia, is named. The Jacksons of West Virginia, descendents of this family reside at Parkersburg and Clarksburg ( H. B. Meigs) John Meigs, husband of Parthenia Clendinen, was born in 1771, and died in 1807. They had two children—Teresa, Charlotte, who married Rev. Fielding Pope, of Marietta, the other was R. J. Meigs, (3rd) who was forty years clerk of the D. C. He was a man of great distinction and national reputation. "The history of the Meigs' family of America" by H. B. Meigs of Baltimore gives all the different branches of this family. Many of them live in Washington and Baltimore and Mass.

The R. J. Meigs 3rd, died about ten years ago. His son is now clerk of the District and is quite an old man. His brother John, named for the husband of Parthenia Clendinen, also resides in Washington. After the death of John Meigs, husband of Parthenia Clendinen, the widow came to Mason county and in 1809 married Major Andrew Bryan, who was a farmer on the south side of the Kanawha river. By this second marriage there was one son who died young and two daughters—Mary, the eldest, married John McCulloch, who was born in Berkeley county, Virginia, in 1791, and died in Mason county, 1884, his wife, in 1901. He came with his father, the pioneer John McCulloch, down the Ohio river, it is supposed, by the Redstone route in 1792, when just a babe; his father died in "Pleasant Flats," in the upper part of Mason county, on the Ohio river. John and Mary Bryan McCulloch had three daughters and two sons. The eldest daughter, Margaret Parthenia, married P. S. Lewis, of Mason county, great-grandson of Col. Charles Lewis, killed in the battle of Point Pleasant. The second daughter, Mary, became the wife of Dr. C. P. T. Moore, of Mason county, and Sallie, the youngest, married Jesse D. Bright, son of Hon. J. D. Bright, of Indiana. The eldest son, John, married the daughter of Dr. A. R. Barbee, the youngest, Charles, married Miss Emma Chapman, of Mason county. The second daughter of Andrew and Parthenia Bryan married John McMullen, who was before the war, a prosperous farmer of Mason county. They were all, father and sons, in the Confederate army. Nine of the family are now in the county. The farm became the property of C. C. Miller. Bettie, the youngest daughter of Major Bryan, has quite a romance connected with her life. She was engaged to be married to a young lawyer of Greenup, Kentucky, but her father being old, was reluctant to give up his housekeeper, and only source of comfort, and unjustly intercepted her letters. She pined away, thinking he had proved false to her. Her father finding the skill of the doctor could not save her life, sent a messenger in great haste down the Ohio river in a canoe, and brought back the disconsolate lover, to the bedside of the dying girl in time to take a last farewell. Cynthia, the second daughter of George Clendinen, married ——— Lamb. Little is known of them, or their descendents. Mary, the third daughter, became the wife of Major John Cantrell. Their only daughter, Jemima, became the first wife of C. C. Miller, of Mason county.

George Clendinen went to visit his daughter, Parthenia Meigs, at Marietta in 1796, and there died in 1797. The place of his burial is unknown, though his wife died in 1815 and lies in an old cemetery on the Kanawha river. To appreciate what it cost the pioneer to live and hold his own, the country we now so quietly possess and enjoy, we should know something about the character of these Indians, who brought so much distress to the settlers along the frontier. They were led by skilled warriors, educated from childhood in their crafty mode of warfare. Many had made a name for themselves that would call forth envy and admiration among the natives of the present day. Historians well informed upon the subject describe Pontiac as "possessing great native talent and integrity, commanding in person, with courage and ability that would compare favorably with some of the most renowned commanders of the civilized world." Cornstalk, who was born within the limits of Greenbriar county in 1727, received his naming from his chieftain. Mr. Stuart, of Greenbriar, author of the "Memoirs" on record in Augusta county, speaks of Cornstalk "as a famous warrior distinguished for beauty of person, strength and agility, graceful and princely in manners." Col. Wilson, a British officer with Dunmore, said, "As an orator he was unsurpassed," his voice was as clear as a bugle, and at the battle of Point Pleasant, he could be distinctly heard, above the din of battle, calling upon his warriors to "Be strong. Be strong," and at the treaty of Camp Charlotte, his voice, in tones of thunder, could be heard over twelve acres. Every one is familiar with those blood-thirsty chieftans— Kilbuck, Logan, and Crane, besides many others, who were equally as cruel in their warfare, if not as famous. The people of the Kanawha Valley owe to the memory of these Clendinens some acknowledgement for their great services. By their courage and sacrifices they, along with others, equallly courageous, made it possible for the white man to possess this beautiful and now prosperous valley. No portrait is known to be in the possession of any of the descendents of George Clendinen, but we picture him in his hunting shirt and buckskin breeches, going forth with his flint-lock and scalping knife, at the front of his band of sturdy mountaineers to the relief of some far-away settlement, at what we now call "double quick time." It took a courageous man like George Clendinen to live in the wilderness at that day. He knew no fear, he was "true as steel." Well he knew his fate should he fail to disperse the blood-thirsty tribes, he had gone forth to meet. No wonder Richard Henderson and Daniel Boone, in 1755, met on the "Wilderness Road" so many returning to civilization, who would listen to no entreaties to return with them. They were terror stricken with what they had seen of the cruel Indian warfare.

When we think of what George Clendinen achieved at that early day with the small resources at his command, he seems to have lived a century ahead of the times. He stands a "peer" among men, even from our standpoint of enlightenment, and progressiveness, worthy to occupy a seat in our most honored assemblies.

MAJ. WM. CLENDINEN.

## MAJOR WILLIAM CLENDINEN.

This portrait of William Clendinen, so familiar to the people of the Kanawha Valley, long ago was taken from a miniature medallion owned by one of the Gallipolis descendents, now living in New York city. It is a handsome portrait, which a photograph cannot do justice to, the beautiful coloring on the ivory gives to the picture a soft finish, which is lost in the other art. These medallions were very popular portraits at the time this was taken, and many families now possess these rare and valuable pictures, that are so highly prized by them that money cannot buy them.

This brave pioneer was the second son of Charles Clendinen, the first emigrant of this family, as far as is known, who came over to the colony of Virginia. The descendents are numerous in the counties of Kanawha and Mason, also through the State of Ohio. The old Bible, brought from Scotland with the records of William Clendinen's immediate family, is owned by Sophia Elizabeth Walis, a great-grand-daughter of William Clendinen, daughter of James Beale Clendinen, whose home is in Mason county.

### THE RECORD TAKEN FROM WILLIAM CLENDINEN'S BIBLE.

Wm. Clendinen was born the 23 day of May 1753.
Margaret Clendinen was born the 10th of May, 1762.

#### ELIZABETH CLENDINEN
Daughter to Wm. & Margaret Clendinen Was Born The 28
August 1785
#### SOPHIA CLENDINEN
Daughter Was born the 27 March 1787
#### CHARLES CLENDINEN
Was born the 18 of July 1789
#### JOHN CLENDINEN
Was born the 18 November 1790
And died the 24 July 1793

And. Clendinen was born the 30th day of August, 1796, and died the 20th day of November, 1803.

Anne Clendinen was born the 31 day of July, 1799. Died March 3d, 1855.

The date of William and his wife, Margaret birth, also And. and Anne, are written by the same person in a good legible hand. Then follows the children of Charles Clendinen and Sophia Miller, his wife:

William was born Oct. 4th, 1808. Died Feby. 25th, 1846; aged 38 years.

John was born Oct. 25th, 1810. Died May 2d, 1857.
Sally was born Jan. 5th, 1816. Died 1835; aged 18 years.·
Emely was born June 5th, 1818. Died.
Charles A. was born March 5th, 1821. Died.
James Ed. Beale was born Sept. 18th, 1825. Died July 27, 1898.
Margaret was born Feby 25th, 1823. Died.
Rachial Letita was born Feby. 4th, 1828.

### MARRIAGES.

James E. B. Clendinen and Agnes Sterrett were married Oct. 30, 1862.

Sophia Elizabeth was born Sept. 15th, 1853.

Charles Washington, Dec. 31st, 1865.

George Walis and Elizabeth Clendinen were married April 6, 1892.

Charles Washington Clendinen and Mary Willie were married Sept. 27, 1893.

This old Bible was "printed by Mark and Charles Kerr His Majesty's Printers."

MDCCXCI
EDINBURGH
"Appointed to be Read in CHURCHES"
The first page is dedicated
To the
Most High and Mighty Prince James, By the Grace of God, King of Great Britain, France and Ireland.
Defender of the Faith.

In the old Steenbergen cemetery near Gallipolis Ferry can be seen the tomb of William Clendinen and his wife Margaret and his childrn. Inscribed on the tombs are William Clendinen died Sept. 1828 aged 76. Margaret, wife of William Clendinen died March 1835 aged 73 years.

George Clendinen always spoke of William as his "favorite brother." He was married to Margaret Handley in Greenbrier county about 1783. He fought in the "Battle of Point Pleasant," and shared with his three brothers, George, Robert and Alexander, the hardships of the march through the wilderness and over the rugged mountains, with

General Andrew Lewis' army from Fort Union, (now Lewisburg) to the mouth of the Great Kanawha, where they expected to have met the treacherous Lord Dunmore and in conjunction with his army to march against the Indians on the Scioto. Their arrival at the mouth of the Kanawha is a familiar tale, and the great victory achieved without the assistance of Lord Dunmore, stirred the hearts of every patriot throughout the colonies, and helped to fan the sparks that burst forth in a flame in 1775, that aroused such patriotism that they rushed madly to throw off the yoke that enthrawlled them, and made King George to tremble upon his throne. William Clendinen was a Captain in that battle, and well may his descendents be proud of the part he took in it; for we know he did it well and was among those who played a conspicious part in the grand victory achieved that day. Mr. J. W. Steenbergen says he has heard his son Charles Clendinen, oftentimes remark, his father's life was saved by a pair of "moccasins" he picked up while fighting and put inside of his hunting shirt, making one side broader than the other, the bullet grazed his side. This prominent pioneer came with his brother George after this battle, to the mouth of Elk about May 1, 1788, and no doubt assisted his brother in rearing the walls of Fort Clendinen. He was among the number who hastened to Point Pleasant in 1789 to repel the threatened Indian invasion. His name is among those who qualified at the first court of Kanawha county, held at "Fort Clendinen." When Charleston was laid off as a town, Dec. 19, 1794, he was appointed one of the trustees. In 1796 Major Clendinen was sent to the legislature of Virginia from Kanawha county, with William Morris, in 1801, with David Ruffner, and in 1803, with Andrew Donnally. He came at an early day to the mouth of the Great Kanawha, about 1797, then to Eight Mile Island on the Ohio, where he remained until 1802, when he purchased land from General Mercer, on the Ohio river, opposite Gallipolis, and moved there with with his son Charles, who was born in Greenbrier county, and built the first hewed log house in Clendinen District, named in his honor. The old house has long since disappeared, was torn down about 1857 or 1858, after his death. It stood near the river, about 100 yards from the present "Ferry House." The old Ferry House was on land sold off the Clendenin place to Newman, and was about 75 yards above the present Ferry House. It was torn down and the logs used to rebuild, near the Steenbergen home, and is still used as a tenant house. William Clendinen sold land, in.1795, to John McCulloch, on the Ohio river, in what is known as "Pleasant Flats," and again to John McCulloch, another tract adjoining Stephenson, and in the same year to Stephenson adjoining John McCulloch. This John McCulloch was the pioneer, who came down the Ohio river in a flat boat, with his family about 1792. John Edwards also purchased land on the Ohio river from him in 1799. In this same year he sold land above the mouth of Elk to Joseph Ruffner, and to his brother, Alexander, a small tract in Kanawha county. He bought 67 1-2 acres from John Reynolds, on the Kanawha river, and sold land (200 acres) to John Sower, in 1803. These sales are all recorded in the clerk's office, Kanawha county, in deed books A and B. William Clendinen conveyed his farm to his son Charles the 18th day of October, 1809, and was by him sold to Lawson Brooks, May 24, 1836. It was again sold to General T. H. Steenbergen (the pioneer) Oct. 12, 1838, and is still a part of this farm. In January, 1809, William Clendinen was appointed, with Jesse Bennett, along with three prominent men from Kanawha county, to locate the county seat of Cabell. Those gentlemen from Kanawha were John Shrewsbury, David Ruffner, John Reynolds.

Charles Clendinen (son of William) married Sophia Neal, of Gallipolis, in 1806, and after his father's death, moved to a farm he purchased near Henderson, W. Va., and which afterwards became the home of his son James Beale Clendinen. William Clendinen's daughter, Sophia, married John Miller, and Anna, Henry Miller, both of Galipolis, Ohio, C. C. Miller, so long associated with the "Merchants National Bank of Point Pleasant, was the son of John and Sophia Miller, and he married Jemima Cantrell the grand daughter of George Clendinen. Elizabeth married ———— Bing, of Ohio, and W. A. Cable, of Point Pleasant, is a grandson. Mrs. S. Dunbar, of Gallipolis, and Mrs. J. Downing, of Middleport, Ohio, are grandchildren of Henry and Anna Miller. In the Southern Magazine, published by Hon. Virgil Lewis some years ago, there appeared a "Journal," kept by Lewis Summers. The Hon. Lewis Summers, says a Kanawha paper long ago, was born of highly respectable parentage in Fairfax County, Virginia, November 7th, 1778. He entered upon the duties of active life during the presidency of the elder Adams. He used his influence to place Jefferson in the "White House." In 1805 he moved to Gallipolis, Ohio and served several years in the legislature and senate of that State. In 1814 he moved again to Kanawha county. In 1817-18 he served in the legislature of Virginia, and July 1819 he was chosen one of the judges of the general court, and judge of the Kanawha judicial court. In 1829 he was elected a member of the convention to revise the Constitution of the State. He had a strong and vigorous mind, which impressed him upon the events and times with which he was connected.

CHAS. C. MILLER.

He acquired a reputation which will ever cause his memory to be cherished with warm affection by the people of western Virginia. He died at the White Sulphur Springs, August 27, 1843, after having been more than 24 years judge of the general courts of Virginia. He is interred in Charleston. This "Journal" kept by one so distinguished, will give us some idea of the general manners and sterling worth and hospitality of Major William Clendinen. The Journal is dated July 1808, and is thought to have been published with some interesting notes by W. S. Summers. This "Journal" thus begins: "I went to Gallipolis, stopped at Menagers, where I met Col. Clendinen, who fully answered the account I had of him. His frank, friendly manner was a sure indication of the hospitality I was to receive at his house. On July 10th I went to Col. Clendinen's and spent Sunday with his family. His farm is fine land and his house sufficiently furnished to be comfortable. On the 11th I rode with Col. Clendinen to "Crab Creek," to Munceys and Garrets, met Col. Andrew Lewis, who is also a gentleman. This Journal is interesting. William Clendinen resided in the old home until his death, which was caused by "cancer of the face." Thus passed away the Clendinen pioneers, the great men of that day filling places of great trust with practical executive ability. They deserve more than just a passing notice from the writers of biographys. Much of their history has been lost but enough has been preserved by records to excite our admiration and gratitude.

DELIA AGNES McCULLOCH.

## HON. PHILIP DODDRIDGE, OF BROOKE COUNTY, VIRGINIA.

### By W. S. Laidley.

The ancestry of this notable man, as given by the family, is as follows:

The first of the name that came from England was John Doddridge, who settled in New Jersey many years before the Revolution, and who afterwards established himself in Maryland. His children were Ann and Joseph.

*Joseph Doddridge* married Mary Biggs, and he died in Bedford county, Pennsylvania in 1779, leaving six daughters and two sons, *Philip* and *John*.

*Philip* left Maryland in 1770, and settled near the mouth of Dunkards creek, in Virginia, when in May, 1778, a band of Wyandotte Indians destroyed his buildings and took captive three of his children, and he then removed to Washington county, Penna.

*John Doddridge*, the other son of Joseph, was born in Maryland, March 30, 1745, O. S., and he married Mary Wells, a daughter of Col. Richard Wells, Dec. 23, 1767. Shortly afterwards he removed to Friends Cove, a valley a few miles south of Bedford, Bedford county, Pa., and his father having neglected to complete his title to a settlement right, he lost his estate, and John then removed to the western part of Washington county, Pa., where he in 1773 located a farm of about 400 acres and on which he resided until his death in April, 1791, and on which farm he erected a chapel, which was ever afterwards known as "Doddridge's Chapel," and it was said to be the first chapel built west of the Alleghenies. In their native State the family belonged to the Church of England, but after coming west they attached themselves to the Wesleyan Methodist Church.

His wife, Mary Wells, died in 1776.

John and Mary Doddridge had two sons and three daughters. Joseph, the eldest son, was born Oct. 14, 1769, in Bedford county, Pa., and he died in Wellsburg, Virginia, Nov. 4, 1826. He was an Episcopal Minister and Author.

*Philip Doddridge*, the younger son, and the subject of this sketch, was born in Bedford county, Pa., May 17, 1773, in the same year in which his father established himself on a farm which was supposed to be in Western Virginia, but when the line between Virginia and Pennsylvania was established by protracting the Mason and Dixon line, their home was found to be about three miles on the Pennsylvania side of said line, in Washington county.

Philip remained at his home, working on the farm until his seventeenth year, when he went to Wellsburg, Brooke county, Virginia.

Philip and his older brother, Joseph, attended Jefferson Academy, Canonsburg, Pa., and Joseph there prepared for the ministry and afterwards became quite distinguished and was the first Episcopal minister who preached west of the Alleghenies. He was ordained by Bishop White in 1792, and he published his notes on the Indian Wars, &c.

At the age of seventeen, Philip, at Wellsburg, (then called Charlestown), attended school under the tuition of a Mr. Johnson, where he acquired a knowledge of the Latin language, and learned to render the prayers of his father into Latin, and to converse with his teacher in this language.

Philip wanted to see the world, and the only mode of transportation on the Ohio river, was by flat boats, and the chief trade was with New Orleans, which was shipped on these flat boats and floated down, and he took passage on one of these boats, rendering such services as he was able in consideration of passage for the trip.

While at Natchez, where the Spanish Governor then resided, Philip took a stroll about the place to see all that was to be seen and learned, and he met this Governor and they were not able to converse either in Spanish or English. Philip tried his Latin and found that they could make themselves understood.

The Governor was surprised to find a boy and a flat boat one at that, speaking Latin so fluently and he took him with him to dinner and was pleased to show such a scholar some attention.

After his return from this trip to New Orleans, he obtained several elementary law books, Blackstone's Commentaries, Bacon's Abridgement, Coke on Littleton and others, and began to study law and applied himself to master these works on the subjects treated.

## As a Lawyer.

The exact date when Philip Doddridge obtained his license to practice in the Courts of the State of Virginia, we are not able to give. At the first Court held in Brooke county in the spring of 1897, he was admitted to practice in that Court. He practiced in the various counties in the State and in the adjoining States, and in 1808 he was appointed the Attorney for the Commonwealth in Ohio county, and he was recognized by Hon. Joseph Johnson as one of the most prominent young lawyers at the bar in Harrison county in 1807 and 1808.

We have tradition for his ability as a counsellor, but we have history for his pre-eminence as an advocate. He was noted for his clear, rapid, comprehensive and analytical mind, he could at once grasp the controlling point of the case, and in a few sentences could so present the same that it became impregnable.

In Mr. Willey's sketch of his life, he tells an anecdote of his ability as an advocate.

Mr. Doddridge, with Mr. Ross and Mr. Campbell, both celebrated lawyers of Western Pennsylvania, were defending a landlord, at whose house a drover had stopped and while there was murdered, and an idler about the place assumed the character of an accomplice and turned State's evidence and testified that the landlord, with others, had done the murder.

While the character of the landlord had always been above reproach, here was positive evidence of an accomplice, and notwithstanding the ability and accomplishments of Mr. Ross and Mr. Campbell, they had to confess that they had not been able to make any impression on the jury.

Mr. Doddridge was appealed to, to come to the rescue, and he felt that his client was innocent, and that the accomplice was a liar and a scoundrel, and that the jury must be made to know and feel it also.

Mr. Doddridge, leaning against the railing of the bar, apparently in a careless attitude, began his speech and said:

"May it please your Honor, and gentlemen of the jury, I am not about to make a speech, but to relate a simple fact. Down in Virginia, in my earlier days, there lived a celebrated lawyer by the name of Gabriel Jones. He was of the old school of Virginia gentlemen."

Then Mr. Doddridge proceeded to describe the said lawyer Gabriel Jones, with his cocked hat, his frilled shirt bosom, and waistbands, his powdered hair, blue coat, white vest and cravat, silk stockings and silver knee and shoe buckles, &c., and dwelled upon his peculiar style of man, that the jury could but see the greatest man, and one of the most eccentric ones, that had ever made a speech in a Court House, and one whose readiness and wit was beyond controversy.

Mr. Doddridge painted this great character so vividly that the appearance of the man could not have added anything to the distinct and clear comprehension of the jury and then he added:

"Well, gentlemen of the jury, when Fauquier county was made a county and held its first court, Mr. Jones went there, with other lawyers, to attend said court, and when he arrived he was met by all the other lawyers and especially the junior members, who wished to pay him some attention and manifest their respect for his great ability and prominence. On Sunday morning these young lawyers invited Mr. Jones to go with them to church to hear a celebrated but somewhat eccentric preacher, who was that morning to occupy the pulpit. They all proceeded to the church and found that the preacher had commenced his discourse, and as Gabriel Jones walked in, followed by the other lawyers, with his cocked hat under his arm, they reverently marched up the aisle. The preacher paused and pointing his long finger at the famous lawyer, said: ' Oh, you old sinner, with your cocked hat under your arm, your hair not white enough, but you must powder it—you come into the house of God after His services have commenced. I will appear as a witness against you in the day of judgment.' Mr. Jones stood looking his reprover calmly in the face, said in response, to him: 'Yes, I have no doubt but you will, for in the course of a long practice, I have ever found that the grandest rascal was the one to turn State's evidence.' "

The effect was electric, and it had the effect for which it was told, and gave the jury the idea of the value of the testimony of the accomplice, and they sustained the good character of the prisoner and acquitted him, and saved the life of an innocent and good man.

Not only did his practice extend over the adjoining territory in which he lived, but his services were secured on important cases in the highest courts of the land. He practiced in the Court of Appeals of Virginia, and in the Supreme Court of the United States.

Justice Story in 1822, speaks of Mr. Doddridge as "one eminent for his talents at the Bar."

Chief Justice Marshall said of Mr. Doddridge "as a lawyer he was second to none at the Bar of the Supreme Court."

## His Family.

Philip Doddridge and Julia Parr Musser were married at Lancaster, Penna., April 30, 1800. She died in 1859.

There were ten children, five boys and five girls. They were:

*Jasper Yates*, born in Lancaster, Pa., 1801, and he died in 1834.

*John Musser*, born in Lancaster, Pa., Dec. 3, 1802. He was the Cashier of the Branch of the Bank of Virginia, at Charleston, Kanawha, until the bank building was destroyed by fire, Sept. 13, 1862. He then joined the U. S. Army and was appointed Paymaster by President Lincoln, Nov. 26, 1862. After the war he was appointed Pension Agent by President Johnson, March 2, 1867. His wife was Catherine E. Klein, of Wellsburg, Va. She died in 1868 in Wheeling, and he resided with his daughters, Miss Margaretta and Miss Theresa, until his death, Feb. 4, 1892.

*Benjamin Zaccheus Biggs*, born in Wellsburg, Va., 1804. Was an invalid most of his life, and died in 1872.

*Sarah Mary*, Wellsburg, 1806.

*Eleanor Sophia*, Lancaster, 1808. Married Perry Plakensburg, and died in 1840.

*Cadwallader Evans*, Wellsburg, 1811. Was an Attorney at Law. Practiced in Kanawha, and died in Charleston, Dec. 27, 1885.

*Julianna Adeline*, Wellsburg, 1814. Married Mr. Ramsey.

*Philip Alexander*, Wellsburg, 1816. Married Ellen Scott, of Chillicothe, Ohio, and afterwards Sally Hansford, of Paint Creek, Kanawha county, where he lived and died.

*Harriet Verena*, Wellsburg, 1819.

*Ann Ruth*, Wellsburg, 1820. Married William Meek and removed to Canton, Ills., where she yet resides, and has assisted in the preparation of this sketch. Mrs. Meek is a remarkable woman, for one of her age; her hair retains its natural color, her eyesight almost as good as ever, and her hearing not affected in the least, and is exempt from the usual infirmities of age, and she spends most of her time in reading, which is her greatest pleasure. She is the only surviving child of Philip Doddridge.

In the year 1822, Mr. Doddridge was seized suddenly with some disease which suspended all animation and he was pronounced dead by his physicians.

It was as if there was a wheel in the machinery of his body had "caught on the center" and could neither go forward or backward; he could not live nor could he die. He said of it. that he was perfectly in his senses, heard and knew all that was going on, but was totally unable to move a muscle or make the slightest exertion. Supposing him to have died, those in the house proceeded to prepare him for burial, and the time set for the funeral services, but his wife did not believe him to be dead, and more than once were the burial services postponed. Those around her thought her crazed with grief and yielded for some time to her entreaties, and finally she begged for one-half hour more, and she, with the energy of despair, assisted by "Aunt Polly," a slave in the family, they worked with him, rubbing vigorously with brandy, finally she saw evidences of returning life, and greatly to the surprise of friends and especially of physicians, he was slowly restored to life.

Mr. Doddridge related the incident to one of the Judges of the United States Supreme Court, and Judge Story wrote the same to his wife, and the family knew of the truth of case.

# JOHN DUKE OF BERKELEY.

Among the early Scotch-Irish settlers of Frederick county, Va., was John Duke, an emigrant from the north of Ireland, whom, it appears, came into the Valley by way of Pennsylvania or Maryland, shortly after 1753. Two years prior to this date it is found that he was living near Ballymony, in the north of Ireland, as a lessee of Felix O'Neil, one of the family of O'Neil the once powerful Lords of Ulster.

John Duke had a family of eleven children, their names were: Betsey, William, Francis, John, these said to have been born in Ireland, and Robert, Mary, Mathew, Margaret, Mary (?) James and Jane, these supposed to have been American born. The dates of their birth occuring in the period between 1747 and 1767. John's wife's name was Margaret. He died in Berkeley county in 1791, she in 1792.

These facts, with other data, are obtained from a small account book, dated 1745, which John Duke used as a family register and memoranda book. In it he had his children's record and those of his son William, as well as receipts from his Irish landlord, transactions with his neighbors in America, and various domestic chronicles pertaining to his household. There are charges for loans of money, sales of wheat, salt, linen and other necessities made to such well known persons as: John Ber Meter (Van Meter!) Edward Lucas, William Morgan, Capt. Richard Pearis, John Black, William, John and James Wright, and other names, perhaps none the less prominent, and all of which suggest that John Duke may at first have been one of the pioneer traders in that section.

In 1762 he purchased of Robert Lemon, a plantation of 164 acres located where Kerneysville now stands, near Shepherdstown, Jefferson county, W. Va., and lived here till his death. The wills of both he and his wife are of record at Martinsburg.

Of his children—I. William *m*. Mary Ann, dau. of Nicholas Lemon, of Frederick county, Va., whose widow, Christina, afterwards *m*. Rev. Henry Eaty; II. Elizabeth *m*. one of the Blue family of Hampshire county, Va.; III. Francis *m*. Sarah, the dau. of Colonel David and Hannah Shepherd of Shepherdstown. Francis was killed at the first siege of Fort Henry (Wheeling) ; IV. John was married; he, too, was killed, but it was while serving as a Virginia militiaman, in General St. Clair's defeat, 1791. He left sons; James, William and John; V. Robert, who was living in 1792, and was one of the executors named in the wills of his parents. Was he married? If so, to whom, and where are his descendants, if any? VI. Mary died in infancy; and the next VII. Mary, *m*. a Foutz, settled at West Liberty in Ohio county, and is said to have left descendants. VIII. James *m*. Judith ——; they lived at Charlestown. He died 1825 leaving these children: William, James, Sarah, Ailcey, Mark, Thomas, Susannah and Catherine; IX. Mathew was living in Berkeley county, 1792, but nothing further is found of him; X. Margaret also was living in Berkeley county in 1792, after which time trace of her is lost; XI. Jane, the youngest, said to have been a most beautiful woman, *m*. Capt. James Glenn, a hero of the western campaign of 1791-2 and she was his first wife. They had three children, all of whom died in infancy. After her death Capt. Glenn, of "Glen Burnie," *m*. Ruth Burnes, from whom are now numerous descendants.

Of Betsey, Mathew, Margaret, Robert, Mary and James, little is found beyond that here stated, but further information is needed.

A genealogy of the descendants of William and Francis Duke, is in course of preparation and the purpose is to extend it so that it may include, if possible, all branches descending from John Duke, the emigrant ancestor. Information on these lines is very much desider, and anyone having facts or traditions relating to this family, or will in any way assist in obtaining same will receive grateful acknowledgement from the compilers, Messrs. S. A. Duke, of Baxter, Deer, county, Arkansas, and S. Gordon Smyth, West Conshohocken, Pa.

SAMUEL GORDON SMYTH.

December, 1903.

## NOTES RELATING TO THE ELTING AND SHEPHERD FAMILIES OF MARYLAND AND VIRGINIA.

Prior to 1748 that part of the Province of Maryland lying west and south of what are now Baltimore and Carroll counties, and extending far into the altitudes of the Alleghany mountains, formed the extensive territory of Prince Georges county, out of which has since been carved the District of Columbia and the populous counties of Frederick, Montgomery, Carroll, Washington, Garrett and Alleghany; leaving however, a considerable area retaining the parent name. Nearly all these have the Potomac river for their southerly limit, beyond which lies the State of Virginia.

The Blue Ridge whose impenetrable fastnesses formed the frontier line in colonial days and marking, for the time—the limitations of early settlements—separate the present counties of Frederick and Washington, and intersect the Potomac where the historic town of Harper's Ferry sits enthroned amid her majestic surroundings, just within the wonderfully picturesque gateway to the Valley of Virginia. Here lay the parting of the ways: the one leading along the Shenandoah, and further west,—along the south branch of the Potomac,—to the farther south; and the other, by the waters of the upper Potomac at Cumberland, and by Wills' Creek, or other routes— to the headwaters of the streams emptying into the Ohio; and so on to the Mississippi and the seemingly illimitable west.

The head-springs of many of the water-ways of western Maryland: such as the Antietam, Conococheaque, Monocacy, Catoctin, Rock Creek and others tributary to the Potomac, rise in the highlands of Pennsylvania, at this time within Chester—afterward: Lancaster Co., but now in part comprising York, Adams, Cumberland and Franklin counties; that region forming the water-shed east of the Blue Ridge between the Susquehanna on the north and the Potomac on the south.

Each important stream in those times, marked the Indian's trail. Along its banks generations of redmen had passed north and south in peaceful intercourse, or, until trodden as war-paths in intertribal· feuds, or, as the battle-ground of contesting races, yet always and under whatever condition, remaining the primal course into which the overflowing tide of emigration poured from the eastern provinces toward the empire of the south and west, and so became the first highways into that mysterious wilderness; and over them the pioneer pushed unawed by fearsome danger and undaunted by the stealthy foe,—though sometimes checked—until his final supremacy in possessing a freeman's home in a liberty-giving land.

In the first decade of the eighteenth century stray colonists from the north made their southward journey over these forest-stream paths and continued unremitting and unceasingly until every ford, ferry and confluence along the trail, had its little village, thus marking the beginning of the triumphal progress of our imperial civilization. At first a trader's cabin gathering to itself. drifting settlers, formed the nucleus of such communities, where composite racial elements mingled in that equality of personal civil and religious liberty so long denied them in their native land. English, German, Irish, Scotch, French and Welch; Lutheran, Baptist, Episcopalian, Quaker and Presbyterian, living together in accord, yet, for the time, more firmly welded by the common interest of protection against the red foeman of the frontier. Such then, was the composition of the early settlements of the whites in Western Maryland.

The rich well-watered little valleys skirting the base of the low mountain ranges attracted the first settlers; although the Swedes and Dutch long before had ventured upon their trading expeditions to these parts; they dealt in peltries and had not stayed to claim the soil.

Extensive grants of land were first obtained along those smaller water-ways and finally extended to the shores of the Potomac.

Prince George's County seems first to have been the objective point of two migrating movements, both approaching it contemporaneously by different routes. One came down along the· foot-hills of the Blue mountains from York ("little" York, as it was then called), Hanover, Lancaster and other overland points in

Pennsylvania reached by the German, Huguenot and Scotch-Irish pioneers who had gathered in these localities from Philadelphia, New York and the east. The other movement consisted mostly of English people from the older settlements in the tide-water counties of Virginia, lower Maryland and the southern portion of West Jersey. These advanced by way of Chesapeake thence up the Potomac, Patuxent and Patapscoe toward the South mountain where the human tides met and blended, then pushing through the gap at Harper's Ferry, began possessing the almost boundless virgin lands beyond.

Along the Monocacy and its vicinity, settlements were begun at a very early period; and after 1723 the valley was known to contain numerous colonists. They were principally the younger generation of the original planters of the Dutch towns along the upper Hudson in Ulster Co., N. Y., and others were from the mixed communities in the Province of East Jersey, more particularly, those lying near the shores of New York Bay. It is known that at a very early date many inhabitants from the vicinity of the Rariton and the Passaic rivers in East Jersey, moved westerly to the foot of the Kittaning range in Sussex county, N. J., from whence they later crossed the Delaware into Bucks—now Northampton county, Pa., locating in the Minisink country where they formed settlements about "the forks of the Delaware." From this region they passed along the foot of the Blue Ridge toward the Susquehanna. At Harris' Ferry and other crossings, they struck the principal trails leading in to Maryland.

In 1755-56 the entire chain of settlements in the vicinity of Easton and southward of it, was ravaged and burnt to the ground until the whole Minisink country was devastated and made desolate, by Leedyuscang, the chief of the Lenapes. Many of the settlers who escaped this barbarism fled toward Maryland and joined her population.

John Van Meter, of New York, who prior to 1730 had been a successful trader and enjoying friendly relation with, if not strong influence over—the Indian tribes on the southern trail,—and Jost Hite, his brother-in-law, are supposed to have been for a time in the Monocacy Valley before finally settling in the colony of Va., where they opened up the Opequon region for settlement in 1732-34.

Among the families who accompanied them was one that remained in Maryland after Van Meter and Hite passed over into Virginia, this was Cornelius Elting, a relative of both and a native of New York. In 1732 Elting obtained an extensive grant of land on the Potomac, near Whites' Ferry, to which he gave the name of "Abraham's Lot." A few years later he added another tract of 325 acres naming it "Eltings' Right." I think there was still another which was located at Broad Run, in the Catoctin Valley; and on one of the streams he built a mill which continued to be in use long after he and his son Isaac had passed away. It was a noted landmark during the Revolution and was known as Elting's Mill.

These Maryland Eltings were descendants of Jan Eltyge or Elten, of Dreuthe in the Netherlands; a son of Roeloffe Elten and Stryker Lebring. Jan was first at Flatbush, L. I., but later removed to Kingston in Ulster county, N. Y., where he married about 1677 Jacomynte Slecht. Their children were: I. Roeloff, b. 27 Oct. 1678; m. 13th June, 1703, Sarah Dubois, dau. of Abraham Dubois, the son of Louis, one of the Patentees of New Paltz. Issue: Johannes, b. 3 Sept., 1704; Jacomyntje, b. 7th March, 1706. Johannes m. 15 Nov. 1730, Rachael Wittiken.

II. Cornelius, (afterwards of Maryland), b. 29 Dec. 1681; m. Rebecca Van Meteren, 3d Sept. 1704. He d. in 1754, and she d. in 1756. Issue: Cornelius, b. 18 Aug. 1706, d. 7. 1. Isaac, b. 24 Oct. 1708, d. (in Md.) without issue, 1756. 3. Cornelius (of Va.), b. 10 Nov. 1710. 4. Jacomyntje, b. 27 July 1712; m. — Thompson, and had William, Cornelius, John and Ann, who m. — McDonald. 5. Zara, b. 6 Febr. 1715; m. John Hite, eldest son of Jost Hite. 6. Ezechiel, b. 16 June, 1717; 7. Elizabeth, b. 30 Aug. 1719; m. Abraham Ferrel, who settled in Pequa, Lancaster Co., Pa., and had: Cornelius (of Va.), Israel, Rebecca, who m. David Shriver of noted Maryland family, Elizabeth and Mary. 8. Alida (or Helita), b. 3d May, 1724, (sup.) m. Isaac Hite, another son of Jost Hite and 9. Gideon, b. 13th Oct. 1728.

III. William b. 19 Jan. 1685; m. Jannetjen Lesier, and had: Elsjen, b. 9 Sept. 1711.

Aaltje and Geertje were two (sup.) children of Jan and Jacomyntje Elting. They were m. at Kingston in 1695 and 1699, respectively.

35

Cornelius Elting, his wife Rebecca and their son Isaac, died in Frederick Co., Md. Their respective wills were probated there; the parents in 1754 and 1756, and Isaacs' in 1756, also. At that time there was said to be serious mortality among the male members of the family and of others, in consequence of a malignant fever which was epidemic through the Potomac valley.

The Monocacy valley seems to have included among its early population representatives of races and creeds other than the Dutch who came mostly from New York State. Janney, in his History of Friends, speaking of the emigration of many Quakers from Salem, N. J. and vicinity, and others from Nottingham, Pa. (now in Cecil Co., Md.) to the Monocacy about 1725, says they afterward established Cold Spring Meeting in 1736. In 1732 however, some Quakers from Pennsylvania, New Jersey and from Elk River in Maryland, under Alexander Ross, crossed the Potomac into the Valley of Virginia and established Hopewell Meeting at Opequon about 1735. Hopewell Meeting was undoubtedly so called from Hopewell in Salem Co., N. J. That eminent minister among Friends—Thomas Chalkley, visited the Friends residing in the two settlements in 1738 and gave them some wholesome advice in relation to their encroachments upon the Indians' land west of the mountains.

Weeks, in his "Southern Quakers and Slavery," states that Friends from Salem, N. J., settled in the upper part of Prince Georges' county, Md., in 1723, and goes on to relate how the wave of emigration passed on down the Virginia valley to the Carolinas and farther south during the next succeeding few years.

When we come to analyse the "make up" of the Monocacy settlements one finds groups of family names identical with those peculiar to certain localities in New York and New Jersey, and appear as though they might have been transported bodily from one point to the other. Scattered through the "hundreds" of Prince Georges county, and in close proximity to each other are found the families of Morgan, Nevil, Hardin, Hedges, Johnsons, Bacon, Vance, Wright, Watson, Woods, Zanes, Rumsey, Evans, Lucas and Shepherd—all of which may be found at a prior date in Salem Co., N. J., particularly along the Cohansey river where there was a numerous colony including such names from 1690 to 1715.

From Monmouth county came the Foreman, Hodge, Crawford, Stockton and other families whose names became familiar in the vicinity of Winchester, Va., and farther down the valley. Benjamin Burden, the great proprietor of the Northern Neck went direct from Middlesex Co. to his vast possessions in the valley and Cornelius Wyncoop was a settler from Bergen Co., N. J.

Those living in Salem Co., N. J., migrating south had only to cross the Delaware river to be in New Castle Co., Pa. (now in the State of Delaware); moving onward over the narrow neck that separates the Delaware from the Chesapeake, to the head of Elk river, there, joined by the Wests, Swearingens and others, proceed down the bay, or overland to Western Maryland and the upper Potomac country.

We begin to get trace of Jerseymen in St. John's Parish, then comprising a vast territory lying beyond the Eastern Shore settlements. Among the twenty-seven persons who assembled at Rock Creek, 8th September, 1719, to select a site and erect a chapel for the parish, were L. Morgan, Walter and Philip Evans, Thomas Lucas, Isaac and John Hardin. This parish was divided in 1726 and the region beyond the eastern branch of the Potomac, including Rock Creek and Potomac Hundreds retained the old title, while all the territory co-extensive with Prince George's county and reaching to the western frontier was given the same name as the county. The Rev. George Murdock was chosen its first pastor, 29th December, 1726.

At a meeting of the Freeholders (an official term in use in South New Jersey to the present day) of the upper part of the parish, held in February 1728, a petition was prepared asking permission of the Governor and Council to fix a site for a new church. The petition was granted, and among the names of subscribers to a fund for building the new chapel in the western part of the county were those of Thomas and William Shepherd. After this date no further reference is found respecting Thomas Shepherd in that county, and the inference is, that he had been living in the upper part of the county and afterward crossed the Potomac at the mouth of the Antietam, into Virginia, where he established his Lares and Penates on the opposite shore, at Mecklenburg, now known as Shepherdstown which he subsequently organized. William Shepherd, his supposed brother, and William Shepherd, Jr., remained in Maryland, and were among other petitioners who about 1740 applied for a division of Prince Georges' Parish and the creation of a new one to be called All Saints Parish that was to extend northward from the Great Seneca creek, &c.

There appear to have been two distinct families of the Shepherds who located near each other in Western Maryland. Thomas and William Shepherd, whom I have mentioned, came, let us say: from 1720 to 1725, or, about the time Janney and Weeks fix upon as the date of the arrival of the first colonists from New Jersey. They located in the vicinity of Rock creek, perhaps nearer the Monocacy. Solomon Shepherd was the head of the other family that did not reach that part of Maryland till about 1779. He was the eldest son of William and Richmundy Shepherd, Irish Friends and members of Menallin Meeting in York Co., Pa. Solomon married Susanna Farquhar. They came down from York Co., and settled near Union Bridge, in Carroll county, where their descendants are now numerous. These two families were apparently in no way related to each other.

The trend of evidence points to the conclusion that Thomas and William Shepherd were the sons of a Thomas Shepherd of Salem, N. J., who died about 1721. He is known to have left at least one son whose name was Moses—a name that has been religiously perpetuated among the descendants of Thomas Shepherd of Virginia. Moses was born 1698, and being, perhaps, the eldest son, received at the death of his father the usual double portion and after his marriage to Mary Dennis in 1722 settled on the parental estate at Bacon's Neck, Salem Co., N. J. Notwithstanding there has been no record found of other children of this Thomas we may reasonably assume that there were such, and the sons, when they had received their patrimony, crossing over into Maryland with other colonists from those parts, that Janney speaks of,—hence we find them in St. John Parish, Prince George's Co., Md..

Thomas Shepherd, of Salem, was one of five emigrants of same surname who appear in Burlington Co., N. J., and are said to have come from Co. Tipperary, Ireland, in 1683. Of these: Thomas, David, John and James were brothers, the other, Moses, was supposed to be. Remaining but a short time at the seat of the Proprietary Government of West Jersey, they removed to Shrewsbury in the Province of East Jersey. The brothers stayed here but a short time; Moses remaining but afterward settling permanently at Woodbridge, in Middlesex Co. The four brothers meanwhile returned to West Jersey and bought contiguous tracts of land along the Cohansey river in Salem Co., about 1690, and named the locality Shrewsbury in remembrance of their first home in East Jersey.

In Ireland, these brothers were members of a Baptist Meeting at Clough-Keating, in Co. Tipperary. About the first thing that David did after getting settled on his Cohausey plantation was to organize a Baptist church and gave the ground for its first place of worship. Rev. Thomas Killingworth was called to minister over this congregation. Afterwards some of Davids' descendants were its pastors. Many of the Shepherds joined the Society of Friends who were quite numerous and influential in this neighborhood.

David Shepherd m. Eve (Abbott?). He died in 1695, leaving nine children. James Shepherd m. Ann (Chatfield?). He died in 1713, leaving two daughters: Rachael and Hester. John Shepherd died unmarried in 1715. Thomas Shepherd died about 1721. Thomas was an extensive owner of land along the Cohausey river, was a very active man of affairs in that community. Among his neighbors were James Nevil and John Hardin, both of whom paid quit rent on small properties in 1690. Richard Morgan was another paying quit rent in the same year, on 500 acres.

These were neighbors of Thomas Shepherd, the elder, in New Jersey; and of Thomas Shepherd in Maryland and Virginia at later periods. And it is a striking fact that in the list of Jost Hites' grantees for land in the valley of Virginia, appears the name of Richard Morgan for 500 acres, and of Thomas Shepherd for 220 acres, for tracts near each other, both grants being dated October 3rd, 1734.

ADDENDA AND CORRECTIONS.

The writer desires to correct some statements made on page 53 of the January number of this magazine, with reference to the Hite family.

It now appears that Jost Hite did not have a *son* named Thomas, nor a daughter named Susanna. The authorities upon which these statements were based being in error to that extent. And also: Jacob Hite did not marry Mary Van Metre. A valued correspondent writes me that Jacob Hite, the son of Jost Hite, married first: Cathrine O'Bannon, in Dublin, Ireland; second: Mrs. Frances (Madison) Beale, widow of Tavener Beale, sister of Col. James Madison, of Orange county, Virginia, and aunt of James Madison, sixth President of the U. S. She was a daughter of Ambrose and Francis (Taylor) Madison of Orange Co., Va.

Since the publication of the notes relating to the Van Meter family in the January number of this magazine, the writer discovers, that, in addition to the children of Joost Janse Van Meteren and Sarah du Bois named therein, that they had another son: Hendrix, who was baptized at Kingston, 1st Sept. 1695. The sponsors were: Abraham du Boys and Jan Hamel. A record has also been found, which states, that an inventory of the personal estate of John Jooster Van Metere (Dutch) was filed in Burlington, N. J., on 13 June, 1706, which fixes its value at £235,14.0 including: "6 negro slaves, a man, a woman and four children £145." This was sworn to by John Van Mater.

SAMUEL GORDON SMYTH.

West Conshohocken, Pa., March 14th, 1903.

MAJOR JOHN HANSFORD.

John Hansford was born in Orange county, Va., Feb. 16, 1765, and died in Kanawha county Oct. 6, 1850.

His father, William Hansford, married Mary Hyde in England, and came to Virginia and settled in Culpeper county, and they both there died with small pox. Some of the family went to the crab apple country in Kentucky, while John and his sister Sally came to the Kanawha Valley.

It is said that there was a Benjamin Hansford in Edinburg, and his name was cut in the stone door cap of house on High street.

MAJOR JOHN HANSFORD'S RESIDENCE—1798.

41

And the name figures in Virginia, during the days of Bacon's rebellion.

When John Hansford came to Kanawha is not exactly known— supposed to be in 1778. He married Jane Morris, a daughter of William Morris, and his wife Catherine Carroll Morris, and they— the Morris family—are said to have arrived in Kanawha in 1774. Jane Morris, was born Nov. 3, 1770, and she was brought by her father William Morris, with him when she was but four years old, and carried her in front of him on his horse. He was attacked on the road on Gauley mountain by an Indian, and he being ahead of the others of his family, jumped from his horse, placed little Jane behind a tree and prepared for war, and by some means made his enemy believe that he had reinforcements coming, and the Indian retreated and kept out of his way. We know not that the little girl ever went back to Greenbrier, but some say that she and John Hansford were married in the fort in Greenbrier, 15 Nov. 1787. We imagine it was in Kanawha at the mouth of Kellys Creek where she lived.

William Hansford, of Indiana, now in his eighty-fourth year, gives the following family tradition of early days: Walter Kelly, a refugee from Carolina, came from Donnally's Fort in Greenbrier county, to the Kanawha in 1773 and cleared a small patch of land at the mouth of a creek, which took his name and has ever since been known as Kelly's Creek, and in this patch he planted corn and pumpkins, and dug a tan-vat, in which he placed ten skins to tan for winter clothing, and then he returned to the fort in Greenbrier.

Next Year, or in the fall of 1773, he returned to the Kanawha and with him came a friend, with his servant, a negro man. Some say the friend was Col. Lewis, but Dr. Hale says it was Col. Field.

One day Kelly and his associates were removing the skins from the tan-vat, and the Colonel was down in the vat handing the skins to Kelly, who stood on the edge of the vat, when the Indians suddenly fired on them and Kelly and the negro were instantly killed.

The Colonel had taken off his clothing to get down in the vat, where it was wet and disagreeable, and had on only a tow linen shirt, and he sprang from the vat and made his escape from the Indians, and keeping in the woods, away from the trail, he succeeded in making his way back to Donnally's Fort, with his shirt almost gone, and his body torn by briars and bushes and covered with blood. Little Jane Morris told it that she was in the fort when he arrived, as near dead as alive. It is also told, that afterwards Sally Hansford, who was the wife of Samuel White, gathered up the bones of Waller Kelly in her apron and buried them.

This Samuel White was born in 1732, and he served through the Revolutionary war, and in 1784 married Sally Hansford, who was then sixteen years of age. Samuel lived to be near one hundred years of age and was buried close to the grave of John Jones, above Paint Creek, and a black flint stone marks his grave.

Tradition also gives the following incident of the early days of Kanawha:

Henry Morris had a cabin, and he was absent a short time from his home in the settlement, and on his return to his cabin he found his two daughters, about grown, both dead and scalped by Indians. Morris swore eternal vengeance on all Indians whenever or wherever found, and not long afterwards he heard of an Indian being seen, when he took his gun and started to find him, and he struck his trail going up Elk river and he followed the same for several days and he came up to the Indian when he had stopped for the night to camp and had built a fire. Morris crawled up as near as was safe and within gun shot and waited till day light and when it became light, he saw the Indian get up, and Morris stated that he was as fine a specimen of manhood as he ever saw. Morris cocked his rifle and the Indian heard the click and turned to look, when the bullet struck him and killed him instantly. Morris deliberately scalped the Indian and cut two strips of his skin on his back the length of his body, brought them home and kept them hanging in his cabin and used the same for razor strops. Mr. Lo was not the only savage that could kill and scalp and manifest his vengeance.

John and Jane lived near the home of Wm. Morris until they built in 1798 on opposite side of the river. His house that he first lived in was where J. G. W. Tompkins built his brick house, which is not far from the mouth of Kelley's Creek.

John Hansford built his house in 1798, below Paint Creek, on land said to have been given to him by his father in law, William Morris.

John Hansford had patent for 530 acres on Kanawha river, which he obtained in 1793, also for 400 acres on Paint Creek in 1800, and for 410 acres on Kanawha river in 1818, and for 197 acres on Paint Creek in 1822. His house was the best house, when built, that was in the Valley. It was a frame, two-story, six-rooms; the lumber was made by hand and the nails were hand made, and the bricks used are said to have been brought from England. The inside finish was of cherry and walnut and at that time was an unusually good house. It was a stopping place for travellers and persons stopping in the vicinity. Mrs. Martha Jane Hansford Smith says that he was a handsome, clean-shaven man, and dressed in blue broadcloth and silk hat and entertained most hospitably. That at the age of eighty years he could mount and dismount from his pony and would come in the house as gay as a boy.

He represented Kanawha county in the House of Delegates of Virginia at Richmond in 1811, 1812, 1813, 1814, 1815, 1817, 1818, and was in Richmond when the theatre was destroyed by fire in which so many lives lost. He rode to Richmond through the county on his own horse, on which he returned after the session was over. He had many very interesting matters to relate, of which he learned while in Richmond. He made purchases for his family, one of which was a dozen silver spoons with "J. H." engraved thereon, some of which are yet in the possession of his descendants. He was a magistrate of his county and was a captain in the militia of his State, the original of whose commission was shown us by J. E. Middleton.

John Hansford, commission signed bq Geo. W. Smith, Lieutenant Governor of Virginia, dated July 3, 1809, which appointed him captain in the 80th regiment in the 13th brigade in the 3rd division of the Virginia militia. He was a Whig, and a Baptist, a farmer and a salt-maker, and a man of affairs. He owned two salt furnaces, one of which he ran himself and the other he rented out. He had slaves of his own and was noted for his kindness to them and they always had to themselves each Saturday afternoon.

He was the principal instrument in the building of the Baptist church, which was erected near his residence. He was known in his later days as Major Hansford, but we have no date of his commission or appointment. While he was a captain, he drilled his company regularly on muster days, near his home, and it is said that after the muster was over, he provided his men with some of his own distilling, and that he then took leave and was no more to be found that day, and he said he wanted the boys to have their fun, and that consisted principally in drinking and fighting among themselves. Good soldiers are drilled to fight and there being no enemy convenient on which to practice, they cultivated bravery and other soldierly qualities among themselves, and there were no fines to be paid for that amusement, though on ordinary

HOME OF FELIX G. HANSFORD—1824.

occasions he was known to fine offenders for using profane language.

He died Oct. 6, 1850, and was buried at cemetery on hill near his home, where others of the family were also buried.

Jane Morris, his wife, was a woman of bright intellect and naturally of graceful manners, and it was her custom to gather her family and grand children around her, in later days, and tell them of the incidents of her early life, of the Indians and of the manner in which the settlers

45

had to live, and that often while she was milking her cows, her husband was standing guard with his rifle.

She was an invalid in her later life and for twenty years was confined to her house and the last seven years of her life she was confined to her bed.

She died Aug. 12, 1854, and was buried near the old homestead, beside her husband.

Their children were eleven boys and one girl.

(1) Herman, the eldest, was born ———— and he went west and was married.

(2) William Hansford was born June 6, 1790, went to Owensborough, Ky., and there married, lived and died.

(3) Sarah Hansford was born Jan. 19, 1792, she married William Morris, Jr., and had three children, Fenton, Joshua and John.

(4) Morris Hansford was born Jan. 18, 1794 and married Catherine Morris. He moved west and settled in Clarksville, Mo., but returned to Paint Creek. His children were William, Franklin, Monroe and Emeline. He died at age of 66.

(5) Felix Gilbert Hansford was born Dec. 12, 1795, married Sarah K. Frazier.

(6) John Hansford was born Jan. 1, 1798 and married a Miss Teays, a cousin, afterwards he married Maria Morris, a daughter of Carrol Morris. He was killed by a train on bridge at St. Albans, W. Va.

(7) Carrol Hansford was born Aug. 29, 1799 and he never married. He was a teacher.

(8) Charles Hansford was born Aug. 14, 1800. He went west when young, settled in Illinois, practiced medicine and was in the legislature of that State. His wife was a cousin, a daughter of John Morris.

(9) Alvah Hansford, born May 7, 1803, he never married. He went west but returned and he lived and died at St. Albans, 1886. "His Recollections" were gathered by Col. W. H. Edwards and were published in pamphlet and preserved by the W. Va. His. Soc.

(10) Marshall Hansford was born Jan. 2, 1807, unmarried. He died in 1891.

(11) Gallatin Hansford, born Dec. 17, 1808. He married Nancy Harriman.

(12) Milton Hansford, born June 22, 1811.

His first wife was Mary Parks, daughter of Major Andrew Parks, whose mother was Harriet Washington, a niece of General Washington's. Mary owned a locket with a picture of Geo. Washington, made when he was twenty-five years of age. His second wife was a widow Mrs. —— Brooks.

Of Felix Gilbert's family we have been able to learn more. He accumulated considerable real estate, and was possessed of the charm of a high tones Christian gentleman. He attended school at Lewisburg, and was a student under Rev. Dr. John McElhany, who was a Presbyterian minister and preached there for sixty years. While at the said school he met Miss Sarah Kennon Frazier, a young lady of cultivation and refinement. They were married July 19, 1821.

After their marriage they came to Kanawha and he built the two-story brick house just below Paint Creek in 1825. Their children were:

James Frazier Hansford, married Annie Noyes.

Martha Jane Hansford, married John Samuel Smith of south Carolina.

Sally Hansford, married Philip Doddridge.

Felix G. Hansford, Jr., married Luella Hamilton of Kentucky.

Bettie Hansford, married Jas. E. Middleton.

Delphia Hansford, married Wm. Hobson of Richmond, Va.

Paint Creek is said to have received its name from the fact that the Indians peeled off the bark from a number of large trees along this stream and painted them red to indicate their route through the country.

## THE HENDERSON FAMILY.

Among the earlier and more prominent settlers in the Great Kanawha Valley, opposite Point Pleasant, were the Hendersons. They came of a family of moderate fortune, but of gentle breeding and education.

According to Burke, the Henderson family of Scotland first came into notice in the fifteenth century. In 1494 James Henderson, first knight of Fordel, was appointed Lord Advocate of Scotland; in 1504, he was a member of the Scotch Parliament; and in 1507 Lord Justice Clerk—one of the second judges of the judiciary. Sept. 9th, 1513, he and his eldest son, John, fell in the battle of Floddenfield. From his younger son, George Henderson, descended the Hendersons of Fordel, and many of the other families of Hendersons in Scotland.

Omitting the intervening generations we will come to the springing off from the main family of the branch of interest here. Sir John Henderson, an officer in the army of King Charles I., married Margaret Monteith, about 1625, by whom he had five sons and five daughters. He was succeeded by his eldest son, John. The four younger sons married and left descendants in Fifeshire, Scotland, so that it is almost certain that one of them was the father of "John Henderson, Gent., of Fyfeshire, Scotland", with whom begins the records preserved by the family of Virginia Hendersons. This John Henderson married and had a son William, b. April 30, 1676; d. Aug. 1, 1737. According to the old records, Feb. 7, 1705, "William Henderson, Gent.," married Margaret Bruce, who was born Mar. 1, 1680, and d. Dec. 15, 1739. They had John, b. Feb. 9, 1706; d. 1766; *James*, b. Jan. 17, 1708; d. 1784; Bruce, b. May 1710; d. 1719; Samuel, b. Nov. 28, 1713; d. 1782; Jean, b. 1711; married a Stuart, and d. in Mar., 1730. About 1740, John, James, and Samuel came to America and settled in Augusta county, Virginia.

COL. JOHN HENDERSON AND WIFE.

John Henderson married Rose Finley, sister of John Finley, one of the first justices of Augusta county. They had a son William and two daughters unnamed in his will. Samuel Henderson left property to be divided among his wife, Jane, and children—James, Andrew, Alexander and Florence.

James Henderson, the second son of William and Margaret Bruce Henderson, married June 23, 1738, Martha, daughter of Audley and Elinor Hamilton. He was first an Ensign (2nd Lieutenant), and later a lieutenant in the Augusta Militia in the French and Indian War, for which service he received £2, 18s. in 1758. His sword was preserved by the descendants of his son John till it was stolen in the civil war.

By his will, James Henderson left two negroes and other personal property, and mentions his land in Kentucky, one tract of a hundred acres he had previously given his son Archibald, and other lands in Augusta county. He had the following children: David, *John*, James, William, Sarah—mar. Stuart—, Joseph, Jean—mar. Dickey—, Samuel, Archibald and Margaret. James, the third son had large grants of land in Greenbrier county, and during the Revolution was Colonel of the Greenbrier Militia.

John, the second son of James Henderson, Sr., was the father of the Mason county Hendersons. He was born cir. 1740, and died Mar. 24, 1787. In 1765 he married Anne Givens, who was born cir. 1740, and died May 28, 1819. She was the youngest sister of Mrs. Elizabeth Givens Lewis, wife of Gen. Andrew Lewis. About the time of his marriage John Henderson bought about three hundred acres of land where he settled on the Greenbrier river, not far from Lewisburg. In 1786, Gov. Randolph granted him three hundred and fifty acres more on the Greenbrier, and fourteen hundred acres of land lying south of the mouth of the Great Kanawha river, between the grants of Gen. George Washington and Gen. Hugh Mercer. About the same time he had a grant of forty-five acres in Montgomery county. The parchment grants for these tracts of land are still preserved by his descendants in Mason county.

After he settled on the Greenbrier, John Henderson became a member of the militia of that section, and October 10th, 1774, fought as a Lieutenant in the New River Company of Capt. Herbert at the famous battle of Point Pleasant. Later he was Captain of the Greenbrier Militia until Dec. 6, 1776, when he resigned and enlisted as a Corporal in Capt. Gregory's company in Gen. Daniel Morgan's Virginia Reg't., in which he served until April, 1779. In 1780 he was elected one of the Justices of Greenbrier county, and continued so until his death in 1787.

He left besides his land four negroes and £536 of personal property to the following children: Samuel, John, Margaret, James, Jean, and William. The two older sons received the Kanawha property, and the two younger sons the Greenbrier lands. The elder daughter, Margaret, b. Feb. 2, 1771; d. Sept. 8, 1853, married Wm. Vawter of Monroe county, and has many prominent descendants in that section of West Virginia and Virginia. Their oldest son, John Henderson Vawter was a civil engineer and located most of the Middle Tenn. R. R. He and four of his sons were all captains in the Confederate army. One of them, Capt. Charles Vawter is at present at the head of the Miller Manual Training School in Albemarle Co., Va. Elliot Vawter, the second son of Wm. & Margaret, was a surveyor and did a lot of work in Mercer, Raleigh, Wyoming and McDowell counties. During the war he was a Confederate Quartermaster. In 1872, he was elected, to the West Virginia Senate.

Jean Henderson married a Mr. Kirkpatrick, and died without heirs in 1805. James Henderson married in 1800, Elizabeth Maddy, of Monroe Co., and later removed to another state, where doubtless he left descendants. William Henderson, in an old letter written from Cabell county in 1828, mentions his wife Nancy, daughter Betsey, and tells of the marriage of his son, John to Elvira McComas, daughter of Gen. E. McComas, Feb. 21, 1828.

The two older sons of John and Anne Henderson, Samuel and John, settled on the Henderson grant at the mouth of the Kanawha in 1797.

Samuel built his log house on the bank of the Kanawha where that river flows into the Ohio; and in 1810 replaced it with a large two story brick house, now owned by his grand-daughter, Mrs. Ella Henderson Hutchinson. This is said to have been the second brick dwelling erected in Mason county. John Henderson built his log cabin about a quarter of a mile farther up the Kanawha, and a few years later replaced it with a more commodious two story frame house.

Samuel Henderson, b. Sept. 7, 1766; d. Dec. 24, 1836, married in 1794 Sally Donnally, daughter of Col. Andrew Donnally, who built

Donnally's Fort in 1771, and in 1790 was one of the first representatives from Kanawha county in the Virginia Assembly. Samuel and Sally Henderson were the parents of—John C., Andrew and Charles Henderson. The two younger sons were well known lawyers, practicing at the Mason County Bar from about 1825 till the time of their

SAMUEL HENDERSON HOUSE, 1811.

death. Neither one ever married. Some old letters and addresses written by Charles have been preserved, showing him to have been particularly clever and witty. Andrew was opposed to slavery and manumitted his three slaves in 1842. John Givens Henderson, the elder brother, was an officer in the county militia, a volunteer in the War of 1812, one of the early Justices of the county court, and deputy sheriff in 1822-3. Feb. 2, 1826, he married Sallie, daughter of Capt. John and Sallie Ogden Stephens, by whom he had three children—Samuel, Bruce, married Lydia George; Sallie A., married Jos. George; Mary Ella, married John L. Hutchinson.

John, second son of Capt. John and Anne Henderson, was more prominently connected with public affairs than any of his brothers. From an old order in May, 1795, we see that he was a Lieutenant in the Greenbrier Militia, and from old commissions, that he was Commissioner of Revenues for Greenbrier County in 1796 and 1797. After his removal to the mouth of Kanawha he was one of the nine justices who sat as the first court of Mason county, July 3, 1804. In 1809, 1810, 1813, 1814, 1817, 1818, 1819, 1820, 1822, and 1824, he was one of the representatives from Mason county in the Virginia Assembly. In 1814 he was Commissioner of Revenues, and Sept. 30, 1815, commissioned High Sheriff, which office he also held in 1816. After the organization of the county in 1804, he became one of the officers in the militia, and during the war of 1812 was promoted to the rank of Colonel, as shown by his old orders, still preserved. May 31, 1813, he was appointed by the Governor to take charge of the arms and military stores at Point Pleasant to be forwarded to the Army of the Northwest. Col. Henderson was born Aug. 30, 1768, and died Aug. 19, 1824. He has been described as "A quiet, courteous old gentleman, given to much reading and thinking, and shrinking from publicity;" even though he spent most of his life in the public service. From old tax receipts for 1813 and 1815, we see that he owned five hundred and fifty acres of land, twelve servants, and considerable other personalty.

In 1792, Col. Henderson was married to Elizabeth Stodghill, daughter of John and Elizabeth Stodghill, and to them were born the following children: Jane, Sarah, Rhoda, Angelina, Elizabeth, Nancy, Emily, and James Madison. Jane married Charles Hoy and died without heirs. Sarah became the second wife of John Miller, and from them are descended the Henderson Millers, Chancellors, Vaughts, Chas. E. McCulloch family and others of that section of West Virginia. Rhoda married Henry Hannan and left descendants—the Hannans of Swan creek, Ohio; and the Longs of South Side, West Virginia. Angelina married Wm. A. MacMullin and left descendants—the MacMullins, Judges, Barnes and others of Kentucky. One son, John Henderson MacMullin was Colonel of the 51st Va. Regt. in the Confederate army, and after the war closed served as a colonel under Gen. Loring for five years in Egypt. Elizabeth married Rev.

David Quinn Guthrie, and died without heirs. Nancy married Thos. J. Bronough and left descendants in Henry county, Missouri—the Bronoughs and Redfords. Emily married Dr. Jos. Shallcross, of Ohio, a descendant of the Shallcross and Cadwallader families of Philadelphia. Their descendants are the Shallcrosses, Newsomes, Hards and Kerrs, of Ohio. James Madison, the only son of Col. Henderson, died in 1828, unmarried.

References—Family records back to 1676, old family letters, commissions, land grants, and other papers, county records of Mason, Greenbrier, and Augusta, Burke Barowitage, Hanna's Scotch-Irish.

Dr. J. L. Miller.

Ashland, Kentucky.

# THE HENSHAW FAMILY.

BY MISS VALLEY VIRGINIA HENSHAW.

John Henshaw, of Boston, obtained from the Herald's College, London, in 1844, the lineage of the Henshaw family.

It is signed by G. W. Collin, Pursuivant at Arms of the Herald's College, London, and commences with Henry 3rd, King of England, whose son, Edward 1st, succeeded him on the throne, then Edward the 2nd; then Edward 3rd, whose fourth son, John of Gaunt, Duke of Lancaster, had a daughter who married the Earl of Westmoreland (Ralph Neville.)

Their son, Richard Neville, married the Countess of Salisbury, and he took her title. Their daughter, Eleanor Neville, sister of the great Earl of Warwick, the Kingmaker so called, married Sir Thomas Stanley afterwards created Earl of Derby. His second wife was Margaret of Lancaster, Duchess of Richmond, and mother of Henry VII, King of England.

Thomas Stanley's son George was held as hostage for the fidelity of his father, by Richard III.

Richard III was killed at the battle of Bosworth and Henry of Richmond was proclaimed on the battle field by his father-in-law, Sir Thomas Stanley, as Henry VII.

George Stanley died before his father. He left two sons, Thomas who succeeded his grandfather, as second Earl of Derby, and James, who was created a baronet and lives at Crosshall county, Lancaster, England. James had four sons, the three eldest died without issue, Henry the youngest succeeded and inherited the large estates of his father; he married Margaret, daughter of Peter Stanley, of Bickenstaff, another branch of the family.

Henry Stanley had several sons and daughters. His daughter Margaret Stanley married in 1595 Richard Houghton, of Wavertree Hall, near Liverpool, they had an only son and several daughters.

His son Evan Houghton, of Wavertree Hall, was his heir and married Ellen Parker, of Bridge Hall, county of Lancashire. They had a daughter, an only child named Catharine. She married William Henshaw, of Poxteth Park, near Liverpool, and they lived with her father at Wavertree Hall.

William Henshaw and his father-in-law, Evan Houghton, were killed on the 20th of June, 1644, at the storming of Liverpool, by Prince Rupert. They were fighting against King Charles I.

In 1651 the wife of William Henshaw died, leaving two sons, Joshua, age seven, and Daniel, about eighteen months younger. In 1653 the executor of the estate pretended to send those boys to London to attend school and reported afterwards that they both died there of the plague. In reality he sent them to New England and placed them in the family of Rev. Richard Mather, of Dorchester, near Boston, an eminent divine, who educated them with the money forwarded for that purpose. Their property to a large amount was appropriated by the executor to his own use or rather that part which came from the Houghton family. That part which came from Henry Stanley by marriage settlement upon his daughter Margaret probably went back into the family of the Stanleys. The executor of William Henshaw's estate was Peter Ambrose, a man much employed by the Parliamentary Sequestrating Committee in 1644 to 1650. He had charge of Knowlseley House, the seat of the Earl of Derby, for several years.

The youngest of the abducted boys died without issue. The eldest, Joshua, Married Elizabeth Sumner, of Dorchester, an ancestor of Governor Sumner of Massachusetts. Their children were:

William, (4) b. 1670.

Joshua, (4) b. 1672.

John, (4) b. 1680.

Elizabeth, (4) b. 1687.

Katharine, (4) 1689.

The arms of the family are described as being Argent, a chevron between three Moor-hens proper; quartering Houghton sable, three bars argent, crest, a falcon proper, billed or beaked and numbered sable, preying upon a bird argent.

ESSE QUAM VIDERI

Henshaw

Of his descendents we may especially note his son John (4) Henshaw, who married early in life.

He moved from Dorchester, Mass., to Philadelphia, where he lived a number of years, and not prospering as he wished, getting well up in years, and having a family for whom to provide, and hearing of the great fertility of the valley lying between the Blue Ridge and the Great North Mountain which was called by General Washington in a letter to General St. Clair in 1796, "The Garden of America."

John (4) Henshaw and his eldest son, Nicholas, consulted together and decided to move their families to that section.

John (4) Henshaw bought land from Lord Fairfax, the proprietor of that section. He also bought out some of the settlers, and located on Mill Creek, Frederick county, Virginia, about thirteen miles from Winchester.

I here give a copy of the parchment patent from Ford Fairfax:

THE RIGHT HONORABLE THOMAS LORD FAIRFAX, Baron of Cameron that part of Great Britain called Scotland; PROPRIE-TOR OF THE NORTHERN NECK OF VIRGINIA, To all to whom this present writing shall come sends GREETING.

Know ye that for good causes for and in consideration of the composition to me paid and for the annual rent hereinafter reserved I have given, granted and confirmed to John Henshaw of Frederick county, a certain Tract of Waste and ungranted Land on a Drain of the Opeckon in the said County and bounded as by a survey thereof made by William Baylis.

Beginning at a Red Oak and Hickory Corner to William Jolliffe, Thence leaving the said Jolliffe's Corner and running N. 41 E. One hundred and twenty poles to a Hickory on the brink of a Hill, Thence N. 49 W. One Hundred and forty Poles to a large Spanish Oak in a Valley. Thence S. 41 W. Two hundred and twenty Poles to a Spanish Oak on a level. Thence S. 49 E. Ninety Poles to a Locust stake near a marked Spanish Oak in William Jolliffe's line and thence with his Line N. 69 E. One hundred and twenty Poles to the Beginning containing One Hundred and Seventy Two acres of Land Together with all rights, members and appurtenances thereunto belonging Royal Mines excepted and a full third part of all lead Copper, tin Coals Iron mine and Iron ore that shall be found thereon To have and to hold the said One Hundred and seventy two acres of Land together with all rights Profits and Benefit to the same belonging or in any wise appertaining Except before Excepted. To him the said John Henshaw his Heirs and Assigns Forever. He the said John Henshaw his Heirs and Assigns therefore Yielding and Paying to me my Heirs and Assigns or to my certain Attorney or Attornies Agent or Agents o rto the certain Attorney or Attonies of my Heirs or Assigns Proprietors of the said Northern Neck yearly and every year on the Feast Day of St. Micheal the Archangel The Fee Rent of One Shilling Sterling money for every Fifty Acres of Land hereby Granted and so proportionally for a greater or lesser quantity Provided that if the said John Henshaw his Heirs and Assigns shall not pay the reserved annual Rent as aforesaid so that the same or any part thereof shall be behind and unpaid by the Space of two whole years after the same shall become due If Legally demanded that then it shall and may be lawful for me my Heirs or Assigns Proprietors as aforesaid my or their certain Attorney or Attornies Agent or Agents into the above granted Premises to re-enter and hold the same as if this grant had never Passed. Given at my office in the County of Frederick under my Hand & Seal, Dated the Tenth Day of September in the Sixth Year of His Majesty King George the

Third's Reign A. D. 1766. Registered In the Proprietor's office in Book N. Folio 204.

FAIRFAX.

HENSHAW HOME PLACE, BUILT 1776.

This place is near what is now (1903) called Bunker Hill, Berkeley county, West Virginia.

John Henshaw and his son Nicholas built two houses, one of which is now in ruins, the other, the picture of which is here given, was inherited by Edwin S. Henshaw, Esq., and is his home.

John Henshaw and his son Nicholas also built a log grist mill and a

HENSHAW MILL—1828.

saw mill. The settlement was a kind of center. The log mill was replaced in 1828 by a large stone mill by Levi Henshaw, Sr., a picture of one end of the mill is here given, which is now in ruins. The following is copied from the Gerardstown Times of 1900:

*"Old Stones in New Steps.*

"The stones of which the new entrance to the Presbyterian church was built were donated by E. S. Henshaw, whose timely and durable gift is highly appreciated. These stones formed part of the walls of the old 'Henshaw's Mill,' about three miles from this place, which was so well known throughout this section of the country for many years and was recently torn down by Mr. Henshaw.

"This mill was built by Mr. Levi Henshaw, a grand uncle of the present owner, and was erected about the year 1828. It took the place of a log mill, upon nearly the same site put up many years before by another ancestor of the family.

"As at the old mill for so many years flour was made to feed the body so over the old stones in the new steps may multitudes pass into the sanctuary of God and be fed with the bread of life for many years to come."

This was a large merchant mill in those times and the flour was hauled to Baltimore, Maryland about one hundred miles away, crossing the Potomac river at Harper's Ferry.

Nicholas (5) Henshaw, son of John (4) Henshaw, born about 1705, his will was probated in Berkeley county, Va. (Berkeley county was taken from Frederick county, Va. in 1772) August 19, 1777, it was made September 1, 1774.

The children of Nicholas (5) Henshaw and Rebecca, his wife, are:

1. John (6).
2. William (6) b. 1736, d. 1799.
3. Eleanor (6).

William (6) Henshaw married Agnes Anderson, she was more familiarly known as "Ann' and "Nancy," she was the daughter of William Anderson and Mary his wife and was the mother of:

1. Levi (7) b. 1769, d. Jan. 9, 1843.
2. Hiram (7) b. M. Mary McConnel.
3. Adam Stephens (7).
4. Jonathan Seman (7) M. Elizabeth Stafford, settled in Coshocton county, Ohio.
5. Washington (7) settled in Green county, Tenn. Widow Robinson was his third wife.
6. William Slaughter (7) M. Harriett Lyle. He was a captain of the 5th Infantry of the U. S. Army in 1808-1815, shown by old commissions in the family.
7. Uriah (7) M. Elizabeth McDonald, Sept. 29, 1807, daughter of John McDonald.

8. Nicholas (7)
9. Rachel (7) M. Joseph Lemmon.
10. Rebekah (7) M. Lewis Moore.
11. Rhumah (7) M. ——— Duncan, settled in Kentucky.

Captain William (6) Henshaw b. 1736, d. 1799, was one of the most active agents in having the county of Berkeley established in 1772, and among the most prominent actors in its early civil and judicial history.

He was a bondsman for General Adam Stephens, the first sheriff of

CAPT. WM. HENSHAW'S CAMP KETTLE.

the county. A copy of General Stephen's commission where he and his bondsment swear their allegiance to the King of Great Britain is in the court house in Martinsburg and is as follows:

### Stephens to the King.

Know all men by these presents, That we Adam Stephens, Samuel Oldham, Wm. Henshaw, George Cunningham, Archibald Shearer, George Stodgen, George Briscoe, Daniel Morgan and Henry Newkirk

62

are held and firmly bound and constituted to our Soverign Lord King George the Third in the full and just sum of One Thousand pounds, current money of Virginia to be paid to our said Lord the King his heirs and successors to the which payment well and truly to be made we bind ourselves our heirs, Executors and Administrators each and every one of them jointly and severally openly by these presents and sealed with our seal this 19th day of March, 1772.

The condition of the above obligation is such as whereas the above bond Adam Stephen is constituted and appointed sheriff of the county of Berkelcy, delivered by a commission from the governor under the seal of the colony dated the 18th day of April, 1772, therefore the said Adam Stephens shall well and truly collect and receive all

officer's fees and dues put into his hands to collect and truly account for the pay of the same to the officer to whom such fees are due respectively and at such times as are prescribed by law, and shall well and truly execute and due return and make of all presents precepts to him directed and pay and satify all sums of money and tobacco by him received by virtue of any such process to the person or persons to whom the same are due his or their executors, administrators or assigns and in all other things shall truly and faithfully perform the said office of sheriff during the time of his continuance therein then the above obligation to be void, otherwise to remain in full force and virtue.

ADAM STEPHENS, (Seal.)
SAM'L OLDHAM, (Seal.)
W. HENSHAW, (Seal.)
GEORGE CUNNINGHAM, (Seal.)
ARCH SHEARER, (Seal.)
GEO. STODGEN, (Seal.)
GEO. BRISCOE, (Seal.)
DANIEL MORGAN, (Seal.)
HENRY -|- NEWKIRK, (Seal.)
his mark.

Sealed and delivered in the presence of Will Drew.

At a court held for Berkeley county 19th day of May, 1772. This bond is acknowledged by the parties thereto and ordered to be recorder.

Test: WILL DREW,
*Clerk Court.*

In 1773 we find William (6) Henshaw at a court continued and held for Berkeley county the 18th day of November 1773.

Present:  John Neville.
Robert C. Willis,
Robert Stephen,
Godwin Swift,
William Patterson,

*Gentlemen Justices.*

The persons appointed to view the ground for a road to lead from Beeson Mill to Back Creek made their report, William Patterson came into court and objected to the establishment of the said road, alleging that as the said William Patterson had a mill upon his land it was necessary for him to have a road leading thereto and that the road now contended for would run parallel with that road three quarters of a mile and not above forty poles assunder. Thereupon it is ordered that William Slaughter, William Henshaw, James Strode and George Cunningham or any three of them being first sworn, do make a review of the same and report the convenience and inconvenience attending the same to the court. Ordered that that the court be adjourned till the Court in Course.

The minutes of these proceedings were signed by John Neville.

William Henshaw was in the battle of Point Pleasant, October 10, 1774, and was present at the signing of the treaty of peace with the Indians at Camp Charlotte near Chilicothe, Ohio. I copy extract from History:

"A biographical sketch of the life of the late Michael Cresap, by John J. Jacobs, Cincinnati, Ohio. Reprinted from the Cumberland Edition of 1826 with note and appendix for William Dodge, by John F. Uhlhorn, 58 West Third street, 1866. In the Appendix, page 136 of this work Capt. William Henshaw, of Berkeley county, Va., is referred to. At this place the deposition of Benjamin Tomlinson is introduced to show that Capt. Micheal Cresap had no hand in the murder of the relatives of Logan, the celebrated Indian.

"Tomlinson was asked, 'Who was present at the treaty by Lord Dunmore with the Indians near Chillicothe, at Camp Charlotte on the Scioto, in September or October, 1774.

"Question 8th. 'Do you recollect the name of any gentlemen who were present at the treaty?'

"Ans. 'Yes, I recollect the following persons, and believe they are still alive, and live at the following places, to wit: General Daniel Morgan, Berkeley county, Va.; Col. James Wood, now Governor of Virginia; Capt. Daniel Scott, Monongahela; Capt. John Wilson, Kentucky; Lieut. Gabriel Cox, Kentucky; Capt. Johnson, Youghiogheny; Capt. James Parsons, Moorefield; Gen. George R. Clark, Capt. William Herrod, Col. S. L. Barret, Lieut. Joseph Cresap and Capt. William Henshaw, Berkeley.' This deposition is quite lengthy, covering several pages and is dated Cumberland, April 17, 1797, and signed by Benjamin Tomlinson.' "

In June, 1775, under a resolution of Congress, Col. Hugh Stephenson raised a company of volunteers in Berkeley county, to serve one year in the Continental army.

William Henshaw, Geo. Scott and Thomas Hite were elected Lieutenants of this company. The company marched to Boston in 1775. On the 4th of October, 1776, this company arrived at Bergen Point, opposite New York, on the 12th of November they were engaged for three successive days in severe skirmishing at King's Bridge. See Aler's History of Martinsburg and Berkeley county, West Virginia, page 93. There is a family tradition that William Henshaw never collected any pay for his services in the Continental army.

At a court continued and held for Berkeley county, the 18th day of March, 1778,

Present: Robert Carter Willis,
William Patterson,
James McCalister,
Anthony Noble,
John Moran,
Thomas Hite,
*Gentlemen Justices.*

Upon the motion of William Henshaw, Elizabeth Tabb, William McConnel, William Cowen, Thomas Hite and George Cunningham, Jun., hath leave to inoculate their families for the small-pox in their own houses.

The minutes of these proceedings were signed by William Patterson.

In 1787 Middletown in the county of Berkeley, commonly called Gerardstown, was established. This town was laid off by the late Rev. David Gerard, and contained one hundred lots. William Henshaw, James Haw, John Gray, Gilbert McKewan and Robert Allen were appointed trustees.

At a court continued and held for Berkeley county the 27th day of February, 1798,

Present: Robert Stephens,
James Wilson,
William Henshaw,
David Hunter,
Henry Bedinger,
Edward Tiffin,
*Gentlemen Justices.*

66

Ordered that Robert Justin be appointed Captain of a Musquetry Company in the First Batallion in the 67th Regiment of Militia in the room of John Hunter, resigned.

Levi Henshaw a Captain of the Musquetry Company in the room of Adrias Davenport, resigned. Tebular Warner as. Lieutenant in the room of Henshaw. Paul Verdier, a Captain of Musquetry, in the room of Frederick Snyder, removed. Joseph Cromwell, Lieutenant and George Little, Ensign.

Capt. William Henshaw is buried in the old graveyard of Christ's church at Bunker Hill, and this is a copy of a quaint old receipt:

June, 1799.

Received of Levi Henshaw, for a sermon delivered at the burial services read at the funeral of William Henshaw, deceased, ten dollars.

Given under my hand this 14th day of April, 1800.

Winchester,                                        $10.00.

Frederick county.                          ALEX. BALMAIN.

CAPT. W. S. HENSHAW, U. S. A.        LEVI HENSHAW—1767-1843.

The Rev. Alexander Balmain, a chaplain in the Continental army during the war of the Revolution, and who was married to a relative of Mr. Madison, one of the Presidents of our country.

He lives in Winchester for more than thirty years and preached alternately there in a stone church and at the chapel and was the visitor for District No. 22, containing the parishes of Frederick, Norborne, Hampshire and Hardy.

Copied from the Right Rev. G. W. Peterkin's "History of the Church in West Virginia." Page 412.

DAVID HENSHAW

WILLIAM HENZHAW

1786 - 1799

Levi Henshaw, son of Capt. William Henshaw and Agnes Anderson, his wife, was born in 1769. The first account we have of him is in 1795, when he went to Kentucky to look after two thousand acres of land for his father. The land is described as follows:

THIS INDENTURE, Made this second day of January, one thousand seven hundred and ninety three, between James Frances Moore, of the State of Kentucky, and county of Jefferson, of the one part, and William Henshaw, of the State of Virginia and the county of Berkeley, of the other part; Witnesseth, that for and in consideration of the sum of five shillings in hand paid to the said J. F. Moore by the said William Henshaw aforesaid, a certain tract or parcel of land lying and being in the county of Shelby in the State aforesaid, granted to him, the said James, by patent issued from the Register's office of Virginia bearing date the tenth day of July, one thousand seven hundred and eighty six. Containing two thousand acres lying and being on the east fork of the Little Kentucky emptying into the main creek about fifteen miles from the mouth thereof, and about a mile below another east branch and bounded as followeth, to-wit: Beginning at two beaches and sugar tree corner to three thousand acres survey of Moores, thence west four hundred poles.

Which said land or parcel of land with all its appurtenances, ways, woods, waters, water courses, &c., &c., The said James Frances Moore for himself, his heirs, &c., and again all persons whereto claiming by, through or under him doth forever warrant and defend the same to the aforesaid to Wm. Henshaw and his heirs, &c., &c., forever, under the penal sum of five hundred pounds Virginia money; in witness whereof the said J. F. Moore hath hereunto set his hand and affixed his seal the day above mentioned.

JAMES F. MOORE.

Signed, sealed and delivered in the presence of
ABNER FIELD,
JOHN THURSTON,
JOHN HUGHES,
JONATHAN BOON,
LEVI HENSHAW.

Here are a copy of three letters he wrote to his brother while in Kentucky. This land was afterwards deeded by William Henshaw and wife to their two oldest sons Levi and Hiram Henshaw.

Washington, Oct. 20, 1795.

DEAR SIR:—
I have wrote several times since I have been in the county and am

69

surprised to receive no answer. My desire prompts me to embrace every opportunity, as I am not present to converse with you which would be my only pleasure at this time as there is frequent opportunity. In this way let me be able to hold a correspondence until I should see you, which I hope will be next spring at the furtherest, if I live so long. I am doing very well here, and have attended closely to my business. Property raises very fast here, lots which sold here three years ago at 4 pounds and 5 pounds are selling no wfrom eighty to two hundred pounds. I am about to buy some lots here and if you wish to have some lots, if you will send the moncy by Mr. Moore, I will make a purchase for you which may be advantageous in a little time. At the mouth of Kentucky there is a town laid off which will be very valuable in a few years as it is the object of the country in every trade. Take good care of my mare and colt. Give my compliments to my good friend N. D. and also my acquaintances.

I remain your loving brother, &c.,

LEVI HENSHAW.

Send my red jacket by Moore.
(Addressed to)
    Hiram Henshaw,
        Berkeley County, Va.
By Mr. Cooper.

Uniontown, Oct. 14th, 1796.

DEAR SIR:—

I've been at their court and general election and have seen the proceedings of their court and their election. Was determined very much to my wishes as you will be informed by the bearer.

Yesterday Jno. Springer was married to James McClair's daughter and it's with the approbation of both parties. I write from the infair, as I am one of the guests. Now my being detained here so long is injurious to me in my present affairs, but you will be particular to let Nancy Davidson know how I am whenever you receive any word from me At this time we have every prospects of rain. It is very cloudy and ·grown very warm. I am now in hopes to get off in a few days and if I do shall make my tower short. Cadeb Hountz is paying his addresses to Miss Bettie Stevens. Also be particular in sending the things on as soon as possible. Try to put them in some safe hands that will deliver them safe in Kentucky to Moore. You'll be particular to let me know when you hear from Mother Rust about the bond I left in your hands and let me know how Joseph Lamon's affairs stand with Capt. Thomas and the amount of his destruction. There has nothing particular happened since your departure that I can relate to you. Had I known the dry weather would have been at this time I should not have been here so long but should accomplished my errand there in a much better way. Be particular to give my kindest love to mamma. Read this letter to her, as no doubt she will wish to hear from one who considers her one among the most dearest and deserving of parents that now exist. Give my kind love to my brothers and sisters all.

I am with due esteem and respect your ever loving brother, &c.

LEVI HENSHAW.

(Addressed to)
   Mr. Hiram Henshaw,
      Mill Creek, Berkeley County, Va.

Delivered by Henshaw.

Uniontown, Nov. 8th, 1796.

DEAR SIR:—

I rec'd yours dated October 22d by Nicholas and no other, and I am sorry to hear of the dissatisfaction that prevails amongst you all. The matter is not so bad as was supposed. It appears that there is an instrument of writing between the contracting parties which says received a watch in part pay of a horse sold to James. He must pay the overplus sometime, which will amount to thirty or thirty-five dollars, at least. The horse got lame in the mountain and remains so, and will never do him much good, and as we know him we will always treat him according to his deserts.

Our parents have acquired a very handsome property by their industry and let us unanimously agree by our industry and care and respect and uncontroulable (disparation) to them to keep it together and add more to it. The salvation of children is to submit to their parents' will in all lawful things.

True it is we could live without their assistance now, but better with it, but for my part nature has bound me to render them every assistance to make them happy in their old days, and I wish you to be of the same opinion. I long to be on my way, but God only knows when that will be. I expected you would have wrote me how N. Davidson was, as I expect you have heard. You will let her know that I am well and will write when I arrive in Kentucky, or will see me in three weeks if the water does not raise in that time. There are a great many in our situation waiting for water.

Hiram do you prevail with our younger brothers to be careful of themselves in ever keeping bad company of either sex, as it is the bane of all evil and destruction of youthful minds.

I am with respect your loving brother,

LEVI HENSHAW.

P. S. I do expect my enemies will be very busy in blaming me for staying here so long, but my situation is bad. Was I to leave down there and the water should rise Moore would take every advantage of me and when we know we have our finger in a lion's mouth we must get out the best way we can and as I am entrusted I will not break my trust by any means whatever.

LEVI HENSHAW.

Addressed to
> Mr. Hiram Henshaw,
>> Mill Creek, Berkeley County, Va.

Del'd by Mr. Jones.

The following is a copy of an advertisement printed in Martinsburg in 1807. It offers for sale 600 acres in Berkeley county, and two tracts of 300 and 400 acres in the county of Monongalia, one of which is on Silwell's Creek, a branch of the Canawa.

It is a little bit disfigured but we give it the best we can.

## LAND FOR SALE

AGREEABLE to the last will and testament of William Henshaw, Esq. dec. will be sold a Farm, (called Springfield) containing about 600 acres of valuable lime-stone land, late the property of said Henshaw, dec. situate in Berkeley County, Virginia; more than 300 of which is cleared and under good fence, the residue well clothed with timber; about 12 acres in meadow, which can be watered, and much more can be made. The improvements are a large and convenient stone dwelling house; stone spring house, with good lime-stone water running through it, within 12 feet of the kitchen door; smoke house; barn; stables; with other necessary buildings for the convenience of a farm. About 120 yards across the creek stands the GRIST and MERCHANT MILL, with two pair of stones in her, one pair of burrs, and two water wheels, and near the mill is a house for the reception of a miller; Also, a large Stone Still House, with tubs, &c. and constant over head water. About half a mile below at a separate dam, are a Saw and Fulling Mill, with a log dwelling house; and two lime-stone springs breaking out of the side * * * These mills are built upon the * * * creek, for its constant * * * Mill-Creek, which runs through the above land. One fourth of a mile above the merchant mill is a double house, kitchen, barn, &c. and a never failing lime-stone spring within 40 yards of the door. Three other log buildings and a smith shop, suitable for tradesmen. There are four bearing apple orchards, containing about 600 trees of excellent fruit, and a sufficient number of other kinds of frnit It will be sold altogether, or in two or three tracts, as may best suit the purchaser or purchasers. This property is situated in a rich and fertile settlement, and not inferior to any in the county; about 12 miles from Winchester, 10 from Martinsburg, 1 from Maj. Stephenson's stone tavern, and 18 from Potomac, where the product may be carried to market to Georgetown, the city of Washington or Alexandria. We deem it unnecessary to give further description of the property. Any person wishing to purchase will please call upon the subscribers living on the premises, who will shew the property and make known the terms.

*Also, for sale by the subscribers*, three hundred acres of Land, lying in the county of Monongalia, adjoining lands of Anthony Sell, on Sillwell's Creek, a branch of the Canawa.

*Also*, four hundred acres of Land, lying on Salt Lick Creek in said county.

*LEVI HENSHAW and*
*HIRAM HENSHAW,*

*January 20, 1807.*                                                    *Admr's.*

*Martinsburg, Virginia: Printed by JOHN ALBURTIS.*

The good friend "Nancy D." to whom he referred was his first wife, Levi (7) Henshaw b. July 22, 1769; d. Sept. 9, 1843. His first wife, Nancy Davidson, b. March 30, 1770; d. Dec. 15, 1804, married Levi Henshaw May 18, 1797; they had children as follows:

1. Eleanor (8) b. Feb. 25, 1798; m. Hugh Lyle, 1821, settled in Kentucky.

2. Nancy (8) b. Jan. 1800; d. Sept. 3, 1807.

3. Rhuamah (8) b. Dec. 12, 1801; Nov. 1805.

4: William D. (8) b. 1803; m. Charlotte Cooper fall of 1825; settled in Kentucky.

Levi (7) Henshaw married his second wife, Ann McConnel, b. Sept. 18, 1778; d. Nov. 15, 1838; married Levi Henshaw May 1, 1806. They had children as follows:

5. Mary Ann (8) b. April 7, 1807; d. Feb. 14, 1836.

6. Washington (8)

and              twins, b. April 27, 1808.

7. James (8)

Washington (8) 1st wife Mary E. Delgarn m. April 12, 1838; 2nd Susan Kuykendall, m. Oct. 1841.

James (8) 1st wife Susan Heiskell, Mar. 19, 1833; 2nd Louise Beall, m. 1839; the two brothers and families went to California in 1849.

8. Isabella Jane (8) b. March 24, 1811; m. William B. Gorrell, April 17, 1834.

9. John (8) b. July 10, 1812; he was graduated from Kenyon College, Gambier, Ohio, about 1841, he was drowned in the Mississippi river a few years after his ordination as a minister in the Protestant Episcopal church.

10. Charles (8) b. Dec. 18, 1813; m. 1st wife, Ann Beall, 1840; 2nd wife, Susan Henning, Dec. 1856; settled in Missouri.

11. Levi (8) b. July 14, 1815; d. Feb. 21, 1896; m. Sarah Ann Snodgrass, Dec. 16, 1851.

12. Anderson (8) b. 1817; m. Jane Busey Oct., 1846.

13. Thornton (8) b. 1818; m. Susan Rawlings Snodgrass, Apr. 30, 1844.

14. George Warren b. 1828; m. Rebecca Montgomery, Nov. 19, 1850.

LEVI HENSHAW, JR.—1814-1896.

Levi (7) Henshaw, son of Capt. William Henshaw, was prominent in the affairs of the State and county. In 1810 he was a justice of the peace, he was a member of the county court of Berkeley. In 1821, 1822, 1830 and 1831 he was a member of of the House of Delegates of Virginia. In 1840 he was the sheriff of Berkeley county. He died Sept. 9, 1843, and was buried beside of his father, Capt. William Henshaw in the graveyard of the old Mill Creek Protestant Episcopal church. He was a member of the vestry of this church for many years. The church was about a mile down Mill Creek from the Henshaw place and is now (1903) known as Christ's Protestant Episcopal church, Bunker Hill, W. Va.

Howe, in his History of Virginia, on page 273, gives the following interesting history of this church: 'Morgan Morgan was a native of Wales, whence he emigrated in early life to the province of Pennsylvania. In the year 1726, he removed to what is now the county of Berkeley, in Virginia, and built the first cabin which was reared on the South side of the Potomac, between the Blue Ridge and the North Mountain. He was a man of exemplary piety, devoted to the church, and in the year 1740, associated with Dr. John Briscoe and Mr. Hite, he erected the first Episcopal church in the valley of Virginia. This memorial of his zeal, it is believed, is still standing, and forms that part of the parish of Winchester which is known as "Mill creek church."

Levi (8) Henshaw, Jr., son of Levi Henshaw and Ann McConnel, his wife, born in 1815 at the old Henshaw home place, married Sarah Ann Snodgrass, b. Nov. 1, 1827; d. May 21, 1899. Levi Henshaw and Sarah Ann Snodgrass were married at the home of her father, Col. Rabert Verdier Snodgrass at "Church Hill," by the Rev. J. H. Jennings, December 16, 1851.

They had children as follows:
1. Robert Levi (9) died in infancy.
2. Lily Snodgrass (9) m. Dr. M. S. Butler.
3. Annie Laurie (9) m. Dr. E. C. Williams.
4. Robert Levi (9) m. Mildred Shoemaker.
5. Edgar Craven (9) m. Sallie M. Lingamfelter.
6. Ella Snodgrass (9) died in infancy.
7. Valley Virginia (9).
8. Francis (9) died in infancy.

9. Mabel (9) m. Dr. I. H. Gardiner.
and            twins.
10. Frances Little (9).

Levi (8) Henshaw, Jr., was a man of sterling qualities, and he was loved and esteemed by every one who came in touch with him because "He had a heart that could feel for another's woe
With sympathies large enough to enfold all men as brothers."
He lived during the troublous times of the Civil War, 1861-1865.
In the early part of 1861 public opinion in Virginia was divided on the question of secession. On January the seventh, 1861, the Legislature met in extra session and provided for the assembling of a convention to determine what course should be adopted by the State.

The State Convention assembled in Richmond on Feb. 13, 1861, and was composed of 152 delegates, who had been elected on the fourth instant.

On April 17, 1861, this Convention passed an ordinance of secession by a vote of 88 yeas to 55 nays.

The people of the State had required that the action of the Convention should be submitted to the popular vote. The election for this purpose was held on the fourth Thursday of May, when the secession ordinance was ratified by a majority of 96,750 in a total vote of 161,018.

Levi Henshaw voted against the ratification of the ordinance of secession.

In taking this stand he but echoed the sad thought entertained by thousands of others, who through a lofty devotion to principle abandoned their homes and cut asunder the closest ties of kindred and friends to do what they believed to be right.

I here give copies of a few papers which show the loyalty of Levi Henshaw to the Union.

Office Provost Marshall,
Martinsburg, Va., Feb. 11, 1864.

This certifies that Levi Henshaw, of the county of Berkeley and the State of Virginia, has this day voluntarily taken the oath of allegiance to the Constitution and Government of the United States of America.

Description: age, 49; height, 5-10; complexion, dark; eyes, dark; hair, dark.

F. A. PALMES,
*Captain and Provost Marshall, Headquarters 3rd Brigade, Bank's Div.*

Bunker Hill, Va., March 10, 1862.

Mr. Levi Henshaw, of Springfield Mill, Va., states that he has eighteen head of cattle, seven horses, fifty-five hogs and forty-five sheep. That he has not to exceed five tons of hay, two tons of fodder, four tons of straw, one hundred bushels of corn and fifty bushels of oats. These being facts, he is hereby exempted from furnishing any more hay, fodder, straw, oats or corn, for the use of the troops of the United States.

By order of General Williams.

HENRY M. WHETTELSEY,
Capt. a Qu.

March 16, 1862.

GENERAL:—

I have been aided very much by Mr. Henshaw in buying grain at Bunker Hill. I should rely very much on his statements. I believe him to be a good Union man.

Yours,
HENRY M. WHETTELSEY,
Capt. 7 a Qu. 1 Brigade.

BRIG. GEN. A. S. WILLIAMS,
Commander 1 Brigade.

Levi Henshaw was an "Old Line Whig," and he voted for W. H. Harrison in 1840. Afterwards he was a Republican. He voted for Benjamin Harrison in 1888. He was a Mason, a member of the A. F. & A. M. Lodge at Shepherdstown, W. Va.

Levi Henshaw was a member of the vestry of Christ's Protestant Episcopal church of Bunker Hill until he moved to Hedgesville, Berkeley county, W. Va., in 1868, where he died at the good old age of eighty-one in 1896, and was buried in the graveyard at Mt. Zion Protestant Episcopal church at Hedgesville. The burial service was read by the Rev. W. T. Leavell, rector of the church

The name Henshaw in the old records is spelt variously by the clerks of the county courts: Handsheer, Hancher, Handshaw, Henchaw and Handshew. In one legal instrument it was spelt three different ways. The original signature was always *Henshaw*.

JAMES D. BUTLER,
The Youngest Member of the Henshaw Family.

# JOST HITE

PIONEER OF SHENANDOAH VALLEY

## 1732.

The first settlement of the Valley of Virginia, marks the first settlement of West Virginia, and in order to comprehend the situation of this attempt to settle the country west of the Blue Ridge, it will be eminently proper to give an account of the times and people, interested in or affected thereby.

The English made their settlement on the coast of Virginia in 1607. And their purpose, they avow, was to extend the commerce of Great Britain, to find homes for the residents of their overcrowded cities, and to spread the Gospel among the heathen of Virginia.

As the settlement grew, the settlers became Virginians and the heathen were known as "Salvages" or Indians.

At the end of one hundred years, the Virginians knew little or nothing of the country except along the coast and on the rivers where they could go in ships and boats. They found more territory east of the mountains than they could well care for and protect, and much more than they then had any use for, and they had not deemed it prudent to go to or to attempt to investigate the country beyond the High mountains, and it was proven by Col. Wm. Byrd that in 1709 it was not known that the Potomac passed through the said mountains. There was no attempt to extend their missionary work beyond the vicinity in which they lived, and no doubt they had all the work of that kind they could do, and the country and the people beyond the mountains were unknown to them.

In 1713 Governor Spottswood had found iron ore on the Rappahannock and afterwards established an iron furnace some where at a point which he called "Germania," because the men he imported to run the furnace and make the iron, were from Germany, brought over by Baron de Graffenreid in 1714.

In 1716, the Governor was moved to go on an expedition from his furnace town to the top of the mountain and see what was to be seen, and with quite a party he made the trip and even crossed the river he found on the west side, and was surprised to find it running north, and was lead to believe by the Indian reports that it emptied into the Great Lakes of the north.

This, with much else gathered from the report of the expedition, made by Fontaine, shows that they knew nothing whatever of the country on the west side of the mountain, and as far as is known, this is the first official report of any information on the subject.

In 1720, the Virginia Assembly stated in the preamble to an act establishing the County of Spottsylvania, that the frontiers towards the high mountains are exposed to danger from the Indians and the late settlements of the French to the westward of said mountains, and in the description of the boundary they speak of the river, but mention no name for it. This shows that they had no conception what ever of the country they were speaking of, and it will soon appear that as far as the country west of the mountains was concerned, they cared as little as they knew.

In 1722, there was an act of the Assembly passed—4 Hen. 103—entitled "An Act for enforcing and rendering more effectual the treaties already made and hereafter to be made with foreign Indians." This recites the treaty made at Albany with the five nations, by which it was agreed that the said Indians should not pass over the Potomac (which river was so called to the high mountains) nor should they come east of said mountains, and the tributary Indians were not to cross the Potomac to the north, nor go west of the said mountains—and all offenders were to be killed. This treaty shows that the entire country west of the Blue Ridge was abandoned to the foreign Indians, and tradition says that the Shenandoah Valley was inhabited by no Indians but was a hunting ground and battle field for the northern and southern tribes of wild red men of the forest. We have it also, that about 1725, there started from some point in the north, for an excursion, a band of Indian warriors to the south to capture and kill all other Indians and especially those from the south. It seems that there was with this military excursion, a white man from New York, who was a trader with Indians and on friendly relations with them. What his purpose was in attending this foray we have not yet ascertained, but they crossed the Potomac in the Valley and proceeded to the south, and they had not gone many days up the "Euphrates" before they met with the heathen that they were searching for—the result of this unexpected meeting was a terrific battle and the southern heathen destroyed the bloodthirsty foreign Indians from the north and Mr. Van Meter had the pleasure of making his way back unaccompanied and alone, and no doubt without any others to hasten his exit, as there were probably but few left and none what ever to disturb him.

John Van Meter had taken time, either in going or returning, to notice the lay of the land, and his report was that it was the finest landed country he had ever seen, and his account of the scenery seems to have been made known and he retained it in his memory— it impressed him.

In 1727, the town of Fredericksburg was laid out into streets and lots and offered for sale and this old town began its existence. In this year the Assembly passed an act to help out the Germania and other iron-works, by directing roads and bridges to be built and exempting all persons from taxes that did work on the roads to and from said furnaces.

The territory of Virginia, as inhabited, was designated as "Necks"—strips of land between streams—"The Northern Neck," was that part of Virginia claimed by Lord Fairfax, and was described as lying between the Rappahannock and the Potomac. Lord Fairfax had agents in Virginia attending to this great estate while he was in England, attending to other matters, &c.

In 1728, the Indians within thirty miles from Philadelphia were committing depredations to the extent that the citizens petitioned the Governor for protection.

Such was the condition of the country, and of the people and of the Indians. No settlement of any note on the Atlantic coast from Philadelphia to Williamsburg, Va., and the Indians roaming through the woods, searching for whom they might devour, and whose scalps they might carry away. The Shenandoah Valley, west of the Blue Ridge is a long distance from Philadelphia and from Williamsburg and for one to travel it on foot, through a wilderness of woods, it was a very long ways off, from civilization.

We do not intend to repeat any more than is necessary to make the situation plain, but on the 17th day of June, 1730, John and Isaac Van Meter visited Governor Gooch at Williamsburg and entered into a contract in relation to the settlement of that part of Virginia, beyond the mountains, on the Potomac and tributaries. The particulars of this contract are set forth in the April, 1902, number of this magazine, pages 16, 17, 18. The Van Meters were to locate forty families on the Shenandoah, and for so doing they were to have forty thousand acres of land, said location of said families to be made within two years. It appears that while these negotiations were before the Governor and his council, Robert Carter, Esq., agent for the proprietors of the Northern Neck, wished it entered of record that the land in consideration was that of Lord Fairfax, but the Governor and council proceeded to make the contract notwithstanding the proprietors claims.

Here is the first move to settle any part of the country west of the mountains. It has on its face a scheme for colonization, by the Dutch from New York and New Jersey on the one part, and to secure a large portion of the fairest land for themselves and their friends and relatives. And on the other part, it looks as if the Governor and council were anxious to secure between themselves and the foreign Indians and French, a living barrier of·men upon whom the said savages might amuse themselves when in a desperate way, and which said barrier might, the best it could, keep back the hated French and allies. It was no missionary enterprise on the part of either, it was a land speculation on the part of the Dutchmen, and it was a military move on the part of the Virginians, a move to secure some one else to keep back the marauding Indians.

Let us here pause in this part of the story, and go to New York, up on the Hudson, at Kingston, New Palaz, &c., where there were many people who had come from Holland and made a settlement many years before, where we will find the names of Van Meters, Dubois, Eltings and others. Turn to the January number, 1903, of this magazine and you will learn more of these people and their settlement. ·

*Hans Jost Heydt* was a German, and it is believed, was a Lutheran, but whether a Lutheran or German Reformed we cannot determine. He came from Strausburg, and landed in New York about 1710. He had a wife, whose maiden name was *Anna Maria DuBois*, and they brought with them their little girl, called Mary.

On their arrival in New York, they proceeded to the home of the friends of Mrs. Hite, and made their home in or near Kingston.

Anna Maria DuBois was a French woman, but evidently had been living in some part of the Netherlands and had acquired the Dutch language and customs and had become related to the people who had migrated to New York before she did. This assertion is based on the tradition of the family, that when Hans Jost Heydt, which being rendered into English, is John Joseph Hite, and Miss DuBois were first acquainted, they had some difficulty in making themselves understood; that his German and her Dutch were not at all alike—but it seems to have answered the purpose.

While Jost Hite (pronounced Yost Hite) as he was afterwards called, was in Kingston, there were born to him two other daughters, Elizabeth in 1711, and Magdalena in 1713.

In 1716 Hite and family were at Germantown, Penna., and in 1717 he was in the Perkeomen region on the Skuylkill. He seems to have bought and sold lands, established a mill at the mouth of the Perkeomen creek, which is just across the river from Valley Forge —and became a thrifty, enterprising busy manufacturer and farmer, and he was one of those that in 1728 signed a petition to the Governor of Penna. for protection against the marauding Indians.

He sold his holdings in this country in January, 1730, and the same now is owned by Gov. Pennypacker, of Penna. What Mr. Hite was doing from Jan. 1730, we do not know, but we do know that in June, 1730, the Van Meters went to Williamsburg, Va. and made the contract for 40,000 acres of land in the Shenandoah Valley.

It has been shown by Mr. S. Gordon Smyth, in the Jan. 1903,

number of this magazine, that the Van Meters, DuBois, Shepherds and Hite were related by marriage, &c., and perhaps there was communication between them.

At any rate on the 5th Aug., 1731, the Van Meters sold to Jost. Hite the contracts made with Governor Gooch of Va. No doubt that Hite was busy with the enterprise, as the Van Meter contract required him to locate his forty families in two years, and in all probability, after Hite knew of the Van Meter contract, he became interested and visited the land. In the meanwhile, he had secured the aid of one Robert McKoy, who was a friend, or Quaker, and on the 21st Oct. 1731, Hite and McKoy obtained an order of council for one hundred thousand acres on the west side of the mountains on the like conditions of settling one hundred families thereon within two years, the same kind of contract that Van Meter had made.

The time for making these settlements was extended until Christmas, 1735. The next we hear of the enterprise, we find Hite with sixteen families at Little York, Penna. early in the spring of 1732, and he, with his cavalcade, made their way through the wilderness to the Potomac, and crossed at the Ford, afterwards called the Pack Horse Ford, after Mecklenburg, and afterwards *Shepherdstown.*

Hite and his settlers seemed to have proceeded up the Valley and at first made a stop at a place called "Red-Bud," and afterwards Hite made his selection on the Opequon, called Springdale, and is now where the Valley pike crosses the Opequon, sometimes called Bartonsville.

These settlements were made early in 1732, and they were on the west side of the Shenandoah river, and hence were in no county of Virginia; the boundary of the county of Spottsylvania extended only to the said river, and the County of Orange, which it seems was contemplated, was not established until August 1734, but which did extend to the utmost limits of Virginia, towit: "from sea to sea"—when it was formed.

Hite and his associates went to work and prepared themselves houses and farms. Made surveys of land, and the county of Orange shows by its records, many deeds from Hite.

On the 12th June, 1734, an order of council was made, which stated that Jost Hite had made due proof that he had complied with the terms of the grants made to the two Van Meters and had set-

PACK HORSE FORD.

tled on those lands more than the requisite number of families, directed that patents should issue to him and his assignees, upon the surveys then returned into the Secretarys office.

In this year 1734, began the litigation between Lord Fairfax and Hite and others. Fairfax entered a *general caveat against* all orders of councils, deeds, patents, entries, &c., issuing from the crown office, for lands lying within his proprietary, until the dispute was settled.

By the 1st of January, 1736, Hite and McKoy had procured fifty-four families, on their 100,000 acres of land and had made some surveys, which were returned into the Secretary's office in due time, but the *caveat* was served before the patents were issued on the surveys.

In 1736, Lord Fairfax arrived with royal instructions and in that year and the succeeding year, a survey of the Northern Neck was made, by which it appeared that a large part of the contested lands lay in the bounds of the proprietary, which gave rise to certain petitions before the Governor and council, who confirmed the survey on the terms that Lord Fairfax should establish all the grants which had been made by the crown, and an order was made to that effect on Dec. 21, 1738. In consequence of which his lordship promised deeds to the grantees under the crown and particularly to Hite and his associates, who threatened, otherwise, to abandon their settlements and to remove to other parts of the country, which promise was to be performed as soon as his office for purposes of this kind should be opened, and thereupon Hite withdrew his 27 surveys and fees from the office of the Secretary, in order to lodge them with the proprietor for patents, and the surveys were so lodged and the claimants went on with their improvements on the lands.

After Lord Fairfax opened his land office he refused to make grants to Hite and his associates, and conveyed part of the lands to sundry persons. Hite and associates filed their bill against Lord Fairfax and those claiming under him, setting forth the above circumstances, praying that his lordship be decreed to make deeds to the plaintiffs for the surveyed lands, &c. The defendants filed their answers. On 13th Oct., 1769, the court made a decree that Hite and McKoy were entitled to the land surveyed before Christmas 1735 for which patents had not issued before 11th August,

1745, and that Lord Fairfax ought to issue deeds for said lands and appoint a commissioner to examine and state a memorial of all such surveys claimed by plaintiffs—that his lordship deliver to the said commissioners all the original surveys lodged in his office by Robert Green, gent. decd.

Thos. Marshall and others, comrs., reported twenty-seven surveys containing 37,834 acres and Fairfax produced a list of patents from the Secretarys office for 47,278 acres showing that the Van Meters orders were satisfied, with an excess.

In 1771 there was a final decree, which gave to Hite the 40,000 acres Van Meter land, and to Hite and McCoy 54,000 acres of the 100,000 acres mentioned in order of 21st Oct. 1731.

Lord Fairfax appealed to the King in council, but never prosecuted the same. Hite and others appealed from parts of the decree as confirmed grants made by Fairfax since the commencement of the suit, this went to the Court of Appeals of Va. In the meanwhile Fairfax died in 1781. Gabriel Jones was one of the Exrs. of Lord Fairfax. Randolph argued the case in Appellate Court for Hite et als. Baker for appellees. John Taylor for Hite et als. Marshall for tenants. The appellate court gave Hite all he claimed with rents of the lands from Jany. forty-nine-fifty, and costs. We have given more space to this controversy between the old pioneers and Thomas Lord Fairfax because of the characters of the parties, the character of the suits, and the circumstances of the case.

The Governor and council knew or should have known, whether they had title to the land they sold to the settlers, and if they did know it, they should have required the settlement to have been located on land the title to which was unquestioned.

Lord Fairfax who had more land than he know what to do with, should not have promised to make good the contract which had been made with Hite and McKoy, unless he intended to execute it, and the word of one so pretentious, should have been as good as his bond. Fairfax was a royal pet (see Jan. 1902 number of this magazine) and he was as much interested in having that part of the country settled as was the Governor and council, and it was almost as daring, on the part of Hite, to enter this suit against Fairfax, as it was to go into this wilderness to settle, for the influence of Lord Fairfax, with the Colonial Government and the King of England was probably as great as any other man or woman. Nevertheless the suit was commenced and fought to a finish, but the times had changed, and the influence of royal pets had ceased, and the courts became courts beyond royal favor. One other reason for giving the particulars of this cause is that for some cause, there seems to have been a want of information on the subject by the people, and an intimation that Fairfax had been wronged of his land, which is incorrect. For further particulars see Hite and others against Fairfax and others, 4 Call. Va. Reports 42-83.

There was besides Robert McKoy, interested in the one hundred thousand acre purchase, Robert Green and William Duff, but the extent of their interests we have not been able to ascertain or when and how they became interested.

### HITES FAMILY.

Kercheval says that Hite with his family and sixteen others, cut their way from Little York, Penna. in 1732.

Hite had with him, his wife Anna Maria, his three daughters, and their husbands, towit: Mary and George Bowman, Elizabeth and Paul Froman, and Magdalena and Jacob Chrisman. And there were also four sons, to-wit: John Hite, Jacob Hite, Isaac Hite, Abraham Hite and Joseph Hite.

The names of the other families that accompanied him, are not stated definitely by any authority we have seen. Robert McKoy and Peter Stephens were with them. Geo. Bowman was evidently a German, and he settled not far from where Hite settled, which latter place was known as Springdale, now known as Bartonsville and is about five miles above Winchester. Bowman built a substantial house and remained there all his life. He raised a large family, several of whom were soldiers of rank and importance; one was with Genl. G. R. Clarke in the Illinois campaign, one was Col. of the 8th Va. German Reg. in the Revolution, and there were others that lived to be men of high standing, some of whom settled in Kentucky. We cannot forbear to mention Mrs. Eleanor Bowman, who still lives near Strausburg, Va., who was a Miss Hite of Berkeley Co., Va., when she married Mr. Bowman. She is over ninety years of age, and her daughter married J. S. Davidson, who was a descendant of Isaac Hite.

The first white child born in the valley was John George Bowman whose birth day was Apl. 27, 1732, and the next was Sarah Froman, Nov. 16, 1732. If there were any previous to this, it is not known.

Paul Froman was a Friend, one of the Philadelphia Quakers, who had married Elizabeth Hite and went with Hite into the wilderness. He settled near Springdale, but subsequently removed to Kentucky and his sons became prominent in the establishment of this new commonwealth.

Jacob Chrisman was a German from Swabia, and he settled at Chrisman Spring near Springdale. He lived and died at his first home in the valley and his descendants were numerous, especially in the upper valley, not far from Harrisonburg, and a cemetery at New Erection Church, has many monuments to the family name, and the celebrated Massanutta Springs belonged to one of the descendants.

John Hite was the oldest son, he was educated to some extent, wrote an excellent hand, was a business man, became Colonel of the Frederick Militia, President of the Court Martial of that County, was a member of the County Court, was a vestry man of his parish, and took a great interest in the general welfare of the country and was prominent in all public affairs. He went to Maryland and married Sara Eltings, a daughter of Cornelius Eltings, a wealthy land owner who had come from Kingston, N. Y.

Col. John remained at Springdale, he built his barn in 1747, and his house which yet remains, in 1753. This place is where the valley pike crosses the Opequon, a mile or so north of Stephens City. He died about 1792. His oldest daughter, Rebecca, married Maj. Charles Smith, who afterwards owned the land where Berryville now stands and part of his farm was after his death in 1776, conveyed to Daniel Morgan. Another daughter of Col. John Hite, Margaret Isaac Brown, who is mentioned on page 59 of Jan. 1903 number of this magazine.

Another daughter, Elizabeth, married Maj. Hughes, who came with Braddock. After his death she again married Rev. Elijah Phelps, one of the first Methodist ministers of the valley, and they both are buried in the church yard at Stephens City, where the first Methodist church was erected in the valley and was built by Elizabeth Hughes and her brother, John Hite, Jr.

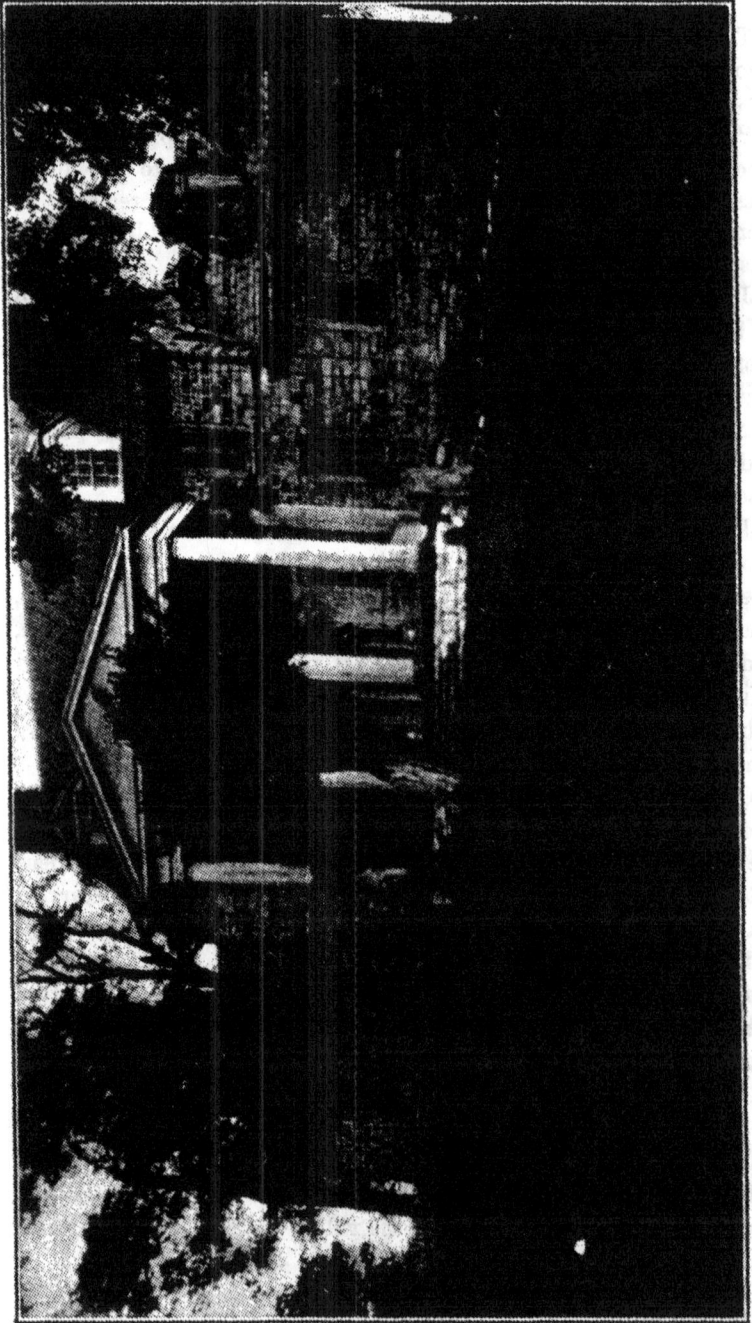

COL. JOHN HITE'S HOUSE—1753.

John Hite, Jr., was the only son of Col. John Hite. He built the largest and best mill that was in the valley at that day, 1788, and the same is yet running at Springdale. John, Jr., married Susanna Smith and afterwards married Cornelia Reagan, and moved to Rockingham county, near the Massanutta Spring. He had twenty children and a goodly heritage, and his descendants all went to the west as they grew up, some or whom settled on the Ohio river near Guyandotte.

Jacob Hite, the second son of Jost Hite, was an active, energetic impulsive man. He was engaged with his father in securing emi-

OLD MILL—1788.

grants to the valley and they had ships of their own, as will appear· by Jacobs will recorded in Berkely Co., and on one of his trips, while in Dublin, he married Cathrine O'Bannon, and after her death, he married Mrs. Francis Madison Beale the widow of Tavener Beale, *nee* Francis Madison.

Jacob lived at Hopewell, near Leetown; he sold to Genl. Chas. Lee,. and removed to South Carolina before the Revolution, taking with him a part of his family. While there, the Indians, who had been friendly to him, were instigated by the English, massacred him and his entire family, except one or two small children and a few colored servants. The servants were recovered but no news was ever heard of the chilldren.

Of his children that did not attend him to S. C. there were John Hite, Jr., who died in 1777. Thomas Hite who married Miss Beale; he was in the House of Burgesses and left a large family. Mary Hite, married Rev. Mr. Manning. Elizabeth Hite who married Col. Tavener Beale, Jr. George Hite, who was at William and Mary was in the cavalry service in Revolution, known as Capt. Hite, married Deborah Rutherford, was the first clerk of Jefferson Co., 1801, till his death in 1817, when he was succeeded by Maj. Robert G. Hite his son. Maj. Robert was a graduate of West Point, married Miss Briscoe, was clerk until his death in 1823. His sister, Sally,

MAJ. ISAAC HITE.

married R. B. Beckwith, the father of Judge Beckwith, and another sister, Susan, married T. R. Flagg, the father of Capt. Geo. Flagg, decd.

The descendants of Thos. Hite were numerous, and they did much for the good of the county in which they lived. The Misses Willis of Charlestown, and Miss Julia Grove of Shepherdstown are representatives of this branch.

Isaac Hite, the third son of Jost, was born 1723, in 1740 built his house at Long Meadows, and it is supposed his father lived with him. He married Eleanor Eltings in 1745 a sister of Mrs. John Hite, and they raised a large and interesting family, an account of which has been published. He died in 1795. Their only son Isaac, afterwards known as Maj. Isaac Hite, was in the Revolution and was present at the surrender at Yorktown. He built what was called "Belle Grove" and lived there in more than usual style and comfort, being quite wealthy and popular. His first wife was Nelly C. Madison, and his last wife, Ann T. Massey.

Abraham Hite, the fourth son, married Rebecca Van Meter, and lived on the South Branch of the Potomac, in the Van Meter vicinity, near Moorfield. His sons, Abraham and Isaac, were among the first settlers in Kentucky and the parents in their old age removed there also. Abraham Hite was a man of wealth and influence, was a member of the House of Burgesses and aided in the struggle for independence.

A TYPICAL HITE—MRS. A. C. HOLDERBY, GUYANDOTTE, W. VA.

Joseph Hite, the youngest son, married Elizabeth — and lived until 1757-8 and left Joseph, John, William and Ann. They also went west and settled in Kentucky.

It is not our purpose to attempt to write the Hite family, this we reserve for a book, where they can all appear and all the particulars which would be interesting only to the family.

Strange as it may appear, the Indians did not disturb Hite and his associates; they passed and repassed through the country but no settler was molested. Who can explain this? This peaceful attitude continued until 1753 when an emissary from the west came among the Indians in the valley and in the spring of 1754 there was not an Indian to be found, all had quietly departed to the west of the Alleghanies and joined the Indians on the Ohio and the French.

After the fall of Fort Necessity, the Indians became troublesome and on the retreat of Braddock's defeated army, the Indians followed with the settlements on the Potomac, and were soon afterwards hunting about, always ready to kill and burn, and their presence and disposition made the construction of Fort London, at Winchester, an immediate necessity.

There were many of the late settlers from Virginia that returned east of the mountains, but the early settlers stood by their guns, built houses that could not be burned and that could stand against bullets. Frequently the settlers had to fly for refuge to some such fort.

This continued, more or less, until about 1766-1767. Are not the chronicles of Withers border warfare full of it? and does not Kercheval relate enough of it?

### PRE-HISTORIC SETTLERS

There have been attempts made to create the impression that prior to 1732, there were settlers and settlements in the valley near the Potomac and we read of the mysterious German mechanics and others that came some time from some where and had a settlement which they called Mecklenburg; the names and dates can not be secured.

Dr. John P. Hale after his visit to this section gave to the Historical Society a report in which he stated all the arguments and reasons and supposition that he had heard or could secure to convince his readers that there must be something in the claim.

All of these were taken up, in the next years report to said Society, and Dr. Hale was compelled to admit that most of his arguments were not convincing, but he continued to hold on to one circumstance, which he believed in. This was the tomb stone found

CATARINA BEIERLIN.

in the Rosemons grave yard near Shepherdstown, which he claimed showed the death of a German woman, Catarina Biererland, in 1707. This stone he secured and had brought to the Historical Society rooms in Charleston, and the same is there now.

The stone does not say 1707, and the proposition is a wild one on its face. What the stone did say, we cannot now tell, but it was probably 1767. There were no people in this country known prior to 1732, and not one single word of evidence can be produced to show it. Had there been a German settlement on the Potomac at Mecklenburg, would not Hite and associates have known it, would not Washington have known it when he was surveying for Fairfax, would not there have been soldiers there to help out when soldiers were wanted, would there not have been some thing to show it?

We know that the land was obtained from Hite by Thomas Shepherd and others, and Thomas Shepherd was the founder of the town. There was nothing public known that Kercheval did not know and what he knew he wrote and he says Hite was the first.

### GROWTH OF THE COUNTRY.

Thomas Shepherd in 1734 took patents for lands on the Potomac. He had an eye for business, and knew a good thing when he saw it. He knew that at this point the inhabitants must come to cross the river, no matter which direction they might wish to go, and the trails for ages led to this point—the Ford. Yet the town did not grow rapidly, for it was in 1762 that it was made a town by land, and it was in that year that he began selling lots and placed on record his map of the place.

Winchester began about 1738, at least it has been said that in that year there were three houses there.

Stephens City, then called Newtown, was about the same age and probably had about the same growth, and was a rival for the county seat when it had to be determined and had the help of his lordship, Thomas Lord Fairfax, who was angered when the court determined in favor of Frederick Town, afterwards called Winchester.

Charlestown is supposed to have begun about 1760.

There was a church built in 1740 by Morgan Morgan. Dr. Briscoe and Jacob Hite on Mill Creek of the Opequon. Afterwards there was a church built on the Opequon above Winchester, known as the Opequon church, which was in a Presbyterian settlement.

There is the ruins of an old church near Charlestown of which no one can give the history, and there seems to be some mystery connected with it. It is called St. Georges Chapel.

Washington first came before the public by his arrival in this part of the country, as a surveyor. when he was but sixteen years of age in 1748.

Washington was born about the time that Hite was preparing to make his exit from Little York, and to start on his march to the promised land in the Shenandoah.

Washington was but a boy when he first came in 1748, and his record shows he made his headquarters with Capt. John Hite. In 1753 Washington again passed through on his way to the Ohio with his notice to serve on the French official, at the junction of the rivers, afterwards known as Fort du Quesne, now Pittsburg. Again in 1754, Washington went with an army, part of which he obtained in Frederick county, to dislodge the French, and was glad to give up Fort Necessity and get back alive. And in 1755 he went again with Genl. Braddock and afterwards was sent to Winchester to erect Fort London and to protect the people.

He was a candidate for the House of Burgess in this county in 1757, but was defeated. Then in 1758 he was elected. There is a record of the vote printed in the Jan 1901, page 58-60 number of this magazine and the names of the Hites are found recorded for Washington, and from many acts of kindness, he showed himself a friend of the family.

The growth of the country was rapid. One reason for this was that Hite had only a limited time to settle his one hundred and forty (140) families in the land in order to secure the title to the land. This made his efforts in this behalf energetic and successful, and this also advertised the country and there seems to have been a rush for good and cheap land on which to settle.

In 1758 there were 443 voters, the names of whom are given in the Jan. 1901 number of this magazine. There were 40 grantees of Hite lands in 1734. From 1736 to 1744 there were 45 deeds of said land recorded in Orange Co. From 1748 to 1750 there were 90 Fairfax surveys made. It looks as if there had been a real estate boom..

Jost Hite had seen the result of wars in Germany, had seen the French and Indian wars in his new home, he had seen the wilderness made to blossom as a rose, he had seen Frederick county organized and the courts established, business had grown and the county with it. He lost his wife in the year of 1739 or '40. His sons and daughters had married and had homes and families of their own. The vicinity in which he lived had many German families, and he had German associations in his old age. He has been called "the old German Baron," he had lived a long while, the exact age is not known, but must have been between seventy-five and eighty. In 1757-8 he made his will and in 1760 he died.

While in life he gave his sons-in-law lands in Frederick and in Augusta; by his will he gave his estate to his four sons and the children of his son Joseph. His personal estate was not large, but in the appraisers list, there are mentioned seventeen Dutch books.

He must have been a man of more than ordinary talent, with good judgment, decided character and great energy. He left a war-ruined, starving country and by observation and tact improved his opportunities with each move he made. What he brought with him, we know not, but when he entered the valley he was a man of means and his investment was a good one. He obtained 40,000 acres by the Van Meter contract, and he and others obtained 54,000 of the 100,000 acres which he and McKoy contracted for. He risked his all, he endured much, but with his judgment, his energy, and perseverance, he made a success of his colonization scheme; he became wealthy, his family independent and respected—and, he died.

There may not be much in any life, it is a record generally of "born, married and died." The struggles and worries of a life time may not be compensated by all that is acquired, and that life is not worth living with the more successful, but we have here given a sketch of one whose work was not a small one, and few would have undertaken it and few of those, would have succeeded so well.

The counties of Berkeley and Jefferson of West Virginia, and that of Frederick of Virginia, presents a choice spot on the earths surface, and the same has been called the garden of the world. To Jost Hite we are indebted for its settlement, for its arrest from "the heathen of Virginia"—for its occupancy by thrifty Germans and others he induced to come and help him hold it. Friends, Presbyterian Scotch-Irish, and Irish not Scotch, and English from every colony and country from which they could be secured—to all and to each, we are indebted for the invasion of 1732.

-----------

## THE HOUSTONS OF MONONGALIA.

### "OUR PIONEERS, WHENCE CAME THEY?"

The above is the title of an article published in the Trans-Allegheny Historical Magazine a few months ago. In reply to that query I submit a few items that may be of interest to some of your readers.

On page 488 of Wiley's History of Monongalia county, West Virginia, is a list of the names of Revolutionary officers and soldiers living in Monogalia in 1832, and, it is stated, "showing the nativity of those born outside of the State of Virginia." In the list is the name of Purnell Houston, but as there is no foot-note "showing his nativity" the impression it gives is that he was born in Virginia.

On page 348, it is stated that Waitman Willey Houston was born

May 9, 1858, and that "his father, William H. Houston, was a son of William Houston who married Abbie Baker and came from *New Jersey* to this country." This is incorrect. William Houston was born in the State of Delaware about 1782, moved to Virginia with his father when a small boy, and was married in Monongalia county.

Instead of being a native of Virginia, as above indicated, Purnell Houston was born in Somerset county, Maryland, on February 1. 1755, where his parents then resided. He was the second child and only son of Robert H. Houston and Mary (Purnell) Houston. Not long after his birth his mother died and his father moved to Sussex county, Delaware, where he married Miss Priscilla Laws, about 1757. The fruit of this marriage was thirteen children, one of them, John A. L. Houston, the father of the late Judge John Wallace Houston, who was a member of the 30th and 31st Congresses and for many years thereafter ont of the Judges of the Supreme Court of the State of Delaware.

Purnell Houston was a great-grandson of Robert R. Houston the immigrant, who came to this country from Scotland in the year 1664, and died in December, 1693.

Purnell Houston was married, probably in Sussex county, Delaware.

His name appears in the list of taxables for that county in the year 1787. He moved to Monongalia county, Virginia, in 1790. In the latter part of 1832 he made application for a pension as a Revolutionary soldier. He was then living near Prentiss, Monongalia county. In his application he declared:

"I served two months in the militia of Delaware but do not know when. The companies were authorized to be raised to guard the Delaware bay. I volunteered in one of the companies commanded by Capt. John Hazzard. About Nov. 1, 1776, I volunteered in Philadelphia in a company of Pennsylvania militia commanded by Captain Chambers, which was attached to Gen. Cadwalader's brigade. These troops were raised to guard against the enemy who were running over New Jersey. In the latter part of November or first of December we moved to and were encamped near Trenton, the enemy being in possession of Trenton. On Christmas we crossed over to Trenton when the American troops captured 900 Hessians. The next day we marched eight or ten miles into New Jersey and encamped at a place called Blackbird where we remained until the first week in January, 1777, when we marched back to Trenton. We were discharged in Market street, Philadelphia, ifter being in service five months. In April, 1777, I went out in Col. Bland's regiment of Virginia light horse to serve two months. I was mmediately sent to Morristown where I was employed in repairing saddles for the troopers. At the end of two months I was discharged )y Col. Bland. In July, 1777, I went from Philadelphia to Egg Harbor and boarded a *brig going round to Boston. Near Cape Cod we were captured by a British vessel, taken to Rhode Island and put on )oard a prison ship where we were kept eight or nine months when we were discharged. After the Revolution I resided in Kent and Sussex counties, Delaware, until I removed to the county of Monongalia, Virginia, aforesaid, forty-two years ago. The record of my age is taken from my father's Bible, in the possession of my sister Carlile in said Sussex county."

Witnesses,

Rev. John Shackleford,

John Evans.

Application sworn to before Thos. P. Ray, Clerk.

The inscription on his tombstone states that he was born February 1, 1755, and died March 9, 1835. His wife, Mary Houston, died January 31, 1830.

### THEIR CHILDREN WERE:

1. Susanna Houston, born, ———; married Wm. Hollefeld, Monongalia county, 1800.

2. James Houston, born, 1780; moved to Indiana.

3. William Houston, born, 1782; married Abigail Baker, near Morgantown, Va.

4. Purnell Houston, born, 1794; married Sarah McVicker, near Morgantown, Va.

5. Sarah Houston, born, 17—; married Joseph Hill, near Morgantown, Va.

6. Robert Houston, born, ———; married to Susanna Bear, near Morgantown, Va.

7. Elizabeth Houston, born, ———; married John Saunders, near Morgantown, Va.

8. Rhoda Houston, born, ———; married William Hill, near Morgantown, Va.

The original ancestor of the Houston family was Sir Hugh de Padvinan, a Frenchman who went to Scotland about 1160. He obtained a grant of land of the Barony of Kilpeter and erected his castle on it. In the course of time a number of houses were built around the castle, and the place was called Hugh's Town. Afterwards it was called Houstoun and the family was known as Houstoun of Houstoun.

R. R. SWEET.

Washington, D. C., Aug. 17, 1903.

*Privateer.

# THE PIONEER JOHN LEWIS AND HIS ILLUSTRIOUS FAMILY.

John Lewis, who settled Augusta county, and laid off Staunton, was of Scotch-Irish descent, born in France, 1673. His ancestors took refuge in Ireland, from the persecution that followed the assassination of Henry the Fourth. He was the son of Andrew Lewis and Mary Calhoun, of Donegal, Ireland. He had two brothers, Samuel and William. William's sons came to Virginia, and Meriweather Lewis was of this family. Samuel went to Portugal. John Lewis married Margaret Lynn, the daughter of the "Laird of Loch Lynn," in 1716. After his marriage in Scotland they went to Ireland. There he took up a "freehold lease of three lives" in the county of Donegal, known as "Campbell's Manor," which estate belonged to Sir Mingo Campbell, his father having died not long before. His great dissipation had caused him financial embarrassment and he determined to raise his rents on his tenantry. The visit of John Lewis to Sir Mingo Campbell's castle, where he went to remonstrate against his great injustice and found the lord and a number of his followers in a drunken carousel was very tragic. This visit has no effect upon the purpose of the "Lord of the Manor," but seemed only to kindle his wrath and indignation. When he came with an armed force to eject him from his castle he found John Lewis ready to resist him. He rushed out with his shelalah and in the encounter the lord and some of his men were killed, the others put to flight. This dreadful tragedy made it necessary for John Lewis to flee his country. This occurred in 1729. After much trouble he reached Portugal and being advised by his brother, set sail for America, his family to follow when possible. After reaching Philadelphia how anxiously he must have watched the arrival of every ship. What must have been the happiness of this family when they were once more reunited. They spent sometime during the years of 1731-1732, around Lancaster, Pa., but being afraid to remain longer so near a seaport (a price having been put on his head) he took his family and went down into Virginia, near Williamsburg, it is supposed. A weaver of that town, John Salling, had explored into the unknown wilderness farther than any one else at that time. He was taken prisoner by the Indians, and upon his escape, gave such graphic accounts of the country that it excited the interest of John Lewis and John Mackey, and they determined to find this "Garden of Eden." When John Lewis reached what is now known as Augusta county, he halted at a spring he named "Bellefonte," and there pitched his tent beside the beautiful little river, which has ever since borne his name. In course of time, assisted by his sons he built himself a stone house, afterwards known as "Fort Lewis," and is said to have resisted an attack of the Indians in 1754. This house was east of the city of Staunton. John Lewis and Margaret Lynn were educated and refined and William J. Lewis in his narrative speaks of "their industry, piety, and stern integrity." John Lewis was great, in that he acknowledged his need of God, and one of his first acts was to make provision for a place of worship. There has been much discussion about the number of John Lewis' children, Samuel being omitted by some historians, but J. Lewis Peyton, in his "History of Augusta County," speaks of Samuel being the eldest, born in 1716, that he served with distinction in the war between the English and French Colonists, and was in Braddock's defeat; was also conspicuous in the defence of Greenbrier county, against the Indians, and that he died unmarried. The sons of John Lewis were all noted for their courage and bravery. The Indians regarded the red clover introduced into the country by John Lewis as the white dyed with their blood.

A "diary" said to have been written by Margaret Lynn Lewis, and published in the magazine, "Land We Love," in 1869 by Fanny Fielding, of Norfolk, Virginia, has excited much interest among the Lewis descendents, but to historians generally it is nothing more than a piece of fiction cleverly written. The diary does not agree entirely with historical dates. In speaking of her American born boy she says: There is a grave by Great Kanawha's side which tells where Charles Lewis, my blue-eyed American boy fell, bravely fighting, honored and beloved, in the fierce affray at Point Pleasant. God rest him! The gentle at home are the best in war." She then closes her diary with: "I say to one who standeth hand in hand with me on this heighth, who hath been a helpmeet every step of the way, only a little longer John Lewis and the Lord of the mountain will open to us and we will enter the door together.

The tombstone of John Lewis, two miles east of Staunton, bears this inscription:

JOHN LEWIS MONUMENT.

"Here lies the remains of
JOHN LEWIS
who slew the Irish Lord, settled Augusta county, located the town of Staunton and furnished five sons to fight the battles of the
AMERICAN REVOLUTION.

He was the son of Andrew Lewis and Mary Calhoun, and was born in Donegal county, Ireland in 1678, and died Feb'y 1st, 1762, aged 84 years. He was a brave man, a true patriot and a friend of liberty throughout the world.

*Mortalitate relicta vivit immortalitate inductus."*

John Lewis was buried at Bellefonte and an enormous lime stone slab, rude and uncut was placed over his grave, where it still lies half buried.  In 1850 this was replaced by a marble slab bearing the inscription above.

John Lewis died thirty years after coming to Augusta county, in his eighty-fourth year.  He was a man of superior ability and virtuous principles, prudent in concerting his plans and perseveringly vigorous in executing them.

The last thirty years of his life were devoted to advancing the interests of the little community he founded.  His mind was improved by a liberal education, and few possessed greater knowledge of every thing capable of forming and qualifying a man for public employment.  Tall, vigorous and commanding in figure, he was distinguished for the manly beauty of his person; the cordial frankness of his address; the charms of his conversation and the desperate character of his courage.

John Lewis was made colonel of militia of Augusta county in 1743, presiding justice in 1745, and sheriff in 1748.  In the year 1751 he assisted his son Andrew, for the "Loyal Co." to explore and survey the Greenbrier river; he was then 73 years old.  The banks of the river was covered with a greenbrier, (still to be found there) and they named the stream "Greenbrier."  John Lewis amassed a large fortune while his companions in the wilderness, John Mackey, died in almost poverty.  John Lewis' children were: Samuel, born in 1716; Thomas, in 1718; Andrew, 1720; William, 1724; Margaret, 1726; Anne, 1728; Charles, (born in America) 1736.  The most famous of these children were Andrew and Charles.  Thomas was very nearsighted, and was not conspicuous in Indian warfare.  He was a man of fine ability, and had the most extensive library in Virginia at that day.  He married Jane, daughter of William Strother, of Stafford county, Virginia.  He was a fine surveyor.  He died in Augusta, Jan. 31, 1790.  William married Anne Montgomery.  He was called the "Civilizer of the Border."  He died near the Sweet Springs in the old brick house in 1811; his wife 1808.  They left eight children.  The two daughters of John Lewis, Margaret and Anne died unmarried.  Andrew Lewis married Elizabeth Givens, of Augusta county, and at his death left five sons and one daughter.  His will was probated on the 23 day of Jan. 1780; he left 30,000 acres of land, the children all named and the amount to each one.  John, the eldest son, married Patsy Love, of Alexandria, Virginia, made his home in Bath count.  Thomas settled on the land given to him by his father in Mason county. Samuel died unmarried. Andrew, U. S. A., married Eliza, daughter of John Madison, by whom there were five children; his second wife was Miss Bryant, they had one daughter, Catherine, who married Joseph King. Catherine Lewis King was born during Washington's lifetime, and knew the Republic in its infancy. She died July 12, 1879. Her descendents still live in the historic old home, "Longwood," and it is said to be the most beautiful place on the mountain. Col. Andrew Lewis resembled his father, Andrew Lewis, so strongly that his portrait, a small medallion, was used by Rogers in his equestrian statue of General Lewis at Richmond. This portrait is owned by a descendent, Mrs. G. W. Powell, of Bent Mountain. It was on exhibition at the "Philadelphia Centennial." Bent Mountain is a spur of the Blue Ridge 2900 feet above the level of the sea; eighteen miles from Roanoke. Here was entertained John Randolph, Light Horse Harry Lee, Louis Phillippe, with his brother, Count De Montpensier, and many other notables of that day. As the mountain was full of game, large and small, some of them very fierce, we can imagine what an invitation to that hospitable home meant. The first duel in Virginia with rifles at close quarters (30 paces) took place on this mountain between the distinguished lawyer and son of Col. Andrew Lewis, Thomas Lewis, and Mr. McHenry. Both were killed in the encounted, Lewis instantly. Both were experts with a rifle. Col. Lewis' favorite horse was named "Slouch," and one day, jumping a log, fell, injuring Col. Lewis so badly that he died. The progeny of this mare is still preserved by the family. In the last clause of General Lewis' will he made provision for a "mourning ring to be made for each one of his children. Col. Andrew Lewis' ring is in the possession of his family on Bent Mountain, and is one of the many priceless relics to be seen at "Longwood."

Anne, the only daughter, married Roland Madison, of Kentucky. William married Lucy Madison, his second wife, Nancy McClenahan, they left nine children. General Andrew Lewis was spoken of as a "king among men;" he was six feet four inches tall and finely proportioned. The Governor of New York, at the treaty of "Fort Stanning," in 1768 spoke of him as being so commanding in person "that the earth seemed to tremble as he walked." General Andrew Lewis' military career was a successful one, but his greatest achievement was the battle of Point Pleasant. It has been conceded to be, by historians next to Saratoga, in advantages gained to our government, securing the great northwest and preventing the Ohio river from being the boundary of the British possessions. General Washington acknowledged the ability of General Lewis and urged his appointment as Commander-in-Chief of the Continental army. Washington was ever a staunch friend of the hero of Point Pleasant. His son, Col. Andrew Lewis, of Bent Mountain, was supposed to have been with his father in his march to the Ohio river, through the wilderness. He wrote of the treachery of Lord Dunmore, and of the indignation of the Virginia troops on account of this, that it was with great difficulty they could be restrained from killing him at Camp Charlotte at the time of the "treaty." General Lewis had the great satisfaction afterwards of driving him from Gwynn's Island in 1776. He resigned his commission in 1781 from ill health and on his way home was taken sick at his friends, Captain Talbots, of Bedford county, and then died, over twenty miles from his own home "Birchfield." He was buried on his own estate, which reached up into Bedford, among his friends; present was Col. Wm. Preston and Col. Eliza McClenahan. In a letter to a friend Col. Preston wrote: "On last Thursday, Sept. 20, 1781, General Lewis, remains were decently interred beside those of his youngest son Charles, on his own estate in the presence of his family and a number of friends. He was taken up by the wish of his descendents and buried in the center of a circle in the middle of "East Hill" cemetery, near Salem, on an eminence overlooking the Roanoke Valley. A strip of walnut, a part of his coffin, was found perfectly preserved with the letter "L" formed on it with brass tacks. The Margaret Lynn Chapter Daughters of the American Revolution, of Roanoke, in 1902 shortly after this reinterment, placed a monument over his grave with imposing ceremonies.

This written order of General Andrew Lewis is the only writing of the General's known to exist by his many descendents. It was kindly furnished me by Mrs. Thomas Lewis of Roanoke.

### WILL OF GENERAL ANDREW LEWIS.

In the name of God, amen. I, Andrew Lewis, of the county and parish of Botetourt, make this my last will and testament. I resign my soul to its Creator, in all humble hopes of its future happiness, as in the disposal of a being infinitely good. As to my body, I leave it to be buried at the discretion of my executor, hereinafter named. And

Octr ye 3: 1765

Sir

fullness and straitness of Capt Jones Men makes that Company useless. Therefore you are appointed Capt over that Company is in his Room. This you are to make it then agreeable with. and with Capt Company to obey such orders as I shall from time to time send you. you are to show this to Somerset Lander that he may have no further instructions of Company

I am your servant

Andw Lewis

To Captn George Wilson

as to my worldly estate, I dispose of it in the following manner and form: First, I leave to my beloved wife two negro men, and two negro women for her life time, with a right to work one third part of the farm I live on, called and known by the name of "Birchfield." Also such part of the stock not exceeding the sixth part, as she may find it necessary for her support for life.

To my son John I give the tract of land on which he lives, containing 470 acres, also a tract of land on both sides of Greenbrier river, at the mouth of Ewing's Creek, containing 480 acres. Also 1000 acres in Sinking Creek, in the Kentucky county, part of my 5,000 tract, and that he take 1,000 acres in a body at either end of this tract as may best please him.

To my son Samuel I give all my land near Staunton, in Augusta county, there being three distinct tracts, to-wit: the stone House tract, containing 740 acres, and a tract joining the lower end thereof, on which I lived, containing 680 acres, and the third joining the southeast side of the two above named tracts, containing 185 acres, deeded to me by Bobert Beverly, also a tract of land in Greenbrier county on the Sinkhole lands, containing 1,200 acres. I also give him my gold watch. To my son Thomas, I give the tract of land joining the upper end of the tract I live on, known by the name of Burks or Old Place, containing 283 acres, and on the north side of Roanoke river; also a tract of land on the north side of Greenbrier river, near to Weaver's Nob and known by the name of Richland, containing 1,170 acres; also a tract in Greenbrier county on which John Cook lives, containing 500 acres and known by the name of Falling Springs tract; also a tract containing 200 acres joining the southwest end of the Warm Spring tract, and on both sides of the Warm Spring branch.

To my son Andrew I give the following tracts of land, to wit: the mill tract, on which he lives, containing 269 acres, formerly Thomas Lash's; also a tract of land joining the lower end of the above, containing 100 acres, and known as Burk's Spring; also two tracts adjoining the southeast side of the above tract, one containing 116 acres, the other 63 acres; also a tract of land in Greenbrier county, on south side of Greenbrier river opposite to the mouth of Muddy creek, containing 780 acres; also a tract of land in the same county, on the branches of Indian creek, known by the name of Fork Survey, containing 400 acres.

To my son William I give the following tracts of land, to-wit: the tract on which I live, called "Birchfield," containing 112 acres and a tract joining the north side thereof, containing 625 acres; also the Red Spring Meadow tract, containing 800 acres or there abouts; also a tract containing 400 acres on the head of Back Creek, a branch of Dunlap's Creek, and about five miles from Sweet Springs.

To my daughter Ann, I give to be sold for her use, the following tracts of land, to-wit: 250 acres on Wolf Creek, a branch of Roanoke, and on the north side of the river, and a tract of land on the head branches of Peter's Creek, containing 190 acres; also a tract of land adjoining the northeast end thereof, about 100 or 106 acres, patented in the name of Robert Breckenridge, and by his will Col. Preston is to make me a title; also my part of the land surveyed in partnership between Breckenridge, Preston and myself and patented as the last mentioned ract, and the title made in the same manner by Col. Preston to the lands lying between Peters Evans' and Tinker's Creek; also 280 acres between Warm and Hot Springs, on which Jeremiah Edwards lives; also all my rights held by my brother Thomas and myself in two small surveys containing the Hot Springs; also a tract of land on the Hot Springs branch called Cedar Run and joining the end of Thomas Fitzpatrick's containing 175 acres.

To my three grandsons, Andrew, Samuel and Charles, sons of John Lewis, I give all my part of the Pocotaled tract (intended for Pocotalico no doubt, but incorrectly spelled in transcribing) of land which part I think is 2,100 acres, and the whole patented in the name of John Fry, Adam Stephen, Archer Lewis, Peter Hogg, John Savage, Thos. Butler, —— Wright, and John Daniel Wilper; all the residue of my lands, to-wit: 1,000 acres, part of the 2,000 acres on Sinking Creek in Kentucky county and the 3,000 tract on Elkhorn and the 9,000 acres in the forks of the rivers Ohio and Great Kanawha, and a 100 acre tract on Pocahontas Creek, near the 9,000 tract together with 750 entered by warrants, on the Cole river and Kanawha be equally divided, having respect to the situation and quality of the land, between my sons, Thomas, Andrew and William. Any money, negroes, and stock I may die possessed of, after my wife has set apart what is devised her, and even that part after her decease, and after my daughter Ann has made choice of a negro wench, or girl and man, to be equally divided between my sons, Samuel, Thomas, and Andrew, and William and my daughter Ann.

My wearing apparel I give to my son Andrew, and after Samuel, Thomas and Ann has each taken a bed and furnature, all the remainder of the house and kitchen furnature be considered the property of William, his mother having a right to retain the use of such of them as may be absolutely necessary whilst she lives. In case any of my sons and daughter die before her, or without lawful issue, the part of the estate willed to such deceased be equally divided between the survivors above mentioned. It's my besire that my brother Thomas, Col. William Preston, and my three sons, Samuel, Thomas, and Andrew, and I hereby appoint them executors of this, my last will and testament, and that each of them, with my brother William and sister Margaret as well as my other children, wear a mourning ring to be purchased at the expense of the estate before a division.

I hereby revoke all former wills by me made, ratifying and confirming this, and no other to be my last will and testament. In witness whereof I have hereunto set my hand and affixed my seal, this 23d day of Jan'y, 1780. Signed, sealed, and delivered by the testator in the presence of us as his last will and testament and on the day and year above mentioned.

ANDREW LEWIS, (L. S.)

JAMES NEILY,
WILLIAM ARMSTRONG,
WILLIAM NEILY.

Proved and admitted to probate on the 14th day of February, 1782, by the County Court of Botetourt.

W. H. ALLEN, *D. C.*

Col. Charles Lewis, the youngest son of John Lewis, and brother of General Andrew Lewis, lies buried with those who fell in the battle of Point Pleasant , Oct. 10, 1774, on the point between the two rivers, Ohio and Kanawha. He married Sarah Murry, half sister of Col. Cameron, of Bath county, Virginia. They had four sons, three daughters. Elizabeth was born 1762, died unmarried; Margaret, born in 1765, married Major Prior; John, born 1766, married Rachel Miller, of Augusta county, Mary, born 1768; Thomas born 1771; Andrew, born 1772, married Margaret Stuart, daughter of Col. John Stuart, and Agatha Lewis. Here is a statement made by Agness Lewis Sehon, their eldest daughter:

"My father, Col. Andrew Lewis, came to Mason county in 1801, was the son of Col. Charles Lewis, who fell at the battle of Point Pleasant with the Indians.

"My father married Margaret Lynn Stuart, daughter of Col. John Stuart, who was also in the battle of Point Pleasant, and married the widow of McFrog, who was killed in the same battle; her maiden name was Agnes Lewis (she was the daughter of Thomas Lewis, son of John Lewis, and Margaret Lynn) Col. John Stuart my grandfather, had four children. My mother, Margaret Lynn Lewis, Jane Crocket,

MRS. AGNES LEWIS SEHON, OF MASON CO.

Charles Stuart, (grandfather of Jennie Sehon) and Lewis Stuart, father of Jane Price, wife of Governor Price. My father had two brothers, John Lewis, who lived in Bath county, grandfather of Jane Price, and Charles Cameron Lewis, father of John D. Lewis, and Charles Cameron Lewis, and grandfather of Peter Lewis. His two sisters were Margaret Lynn Lewis, who married Major Pryor, and Elizabeth Lewis, who never married. My father, Col. Andrew Lewis,

113

had nine children, six lived to years of maturity: Charles Cameron Lewis, Agnes Stuart Lewis, Sarah, Francis Lewis, and Elizabeth Lewis. I, the oldest daughter, married John Leicester Sehon, son of Major John Leicester Sehon, who married Fanny Wagoner, daughter of Mary Wagoner, of Berkley county, Va. I have had nine children, seven now living—was married in my seventeenth year; am now in my seventy-fourth year, Sept. 19, 1878. My grandmother Stuart was 84 when she died, and her husband, Col. John Stuart, (my grandfather) 85. Written by request of my youngest son, Edmund Sehon. (Signed) Agnes Lewis Sehon.

Col. Charles Lewis married Sarah Murry, a half sister of Col. Cameron, of Bath county, Virginia." This statement was distributed around among the descendents of this branch of the Lewis family of Mason county. Col. Andrew Lewis died 1833.

This Col. Andrew Lewis, who came to Mason county in 1801, son of Col. Charles Lewis, bought some of the grant land of Andrew Lewis. He named his place "Violet Lawn." The only daughter now living is Mrs. Benjamin Thompson, of Huntington. His son John Stuart Lewis, after his father's death, lived at the old home. In 1837 he married Mary T. Stribling, of Staunton, Virginia. She died the 22nd April, 1887, and her husband, April 13, 1902. They left three daughters, Francis, who married Judge John English, Agnes, the wife of Columbus Sehon, and Sarah, unmarried. Margaret Lynn died young. Charles Lewis, son of Col. Charles Lewis, came to Mason county in 1800. He served as Lieutenant in the Wayne expedition. In 1798 he married Jane Dickenson, supposed to be the daughter of Captain Dickenson who fought in the battle of Point Pleasant. His son John D., was born June, 1800, and came to the county with his mother on horseback. He afterwards became the wealthy coal operator of the Kanawha Valley. He married four times, women of prominent families, and left at his death six children, four of whom reside in Charleston and Mrs. J. M. H. Beale, of Point Pleasant. The other son, after his father's death, which occurred in 1804, took charge of the farm named "Beechwood.' The widow married in course of time W. Wilson, of Kanawha county, and she went with her husband there. This son, named for his father, Charles Cameron, married Eliza Steinbergen, daughter of P. H. Steinbergen (one of the early settlers of Mason county, father of J. W. Steinbergen) in 1826. He died August 18, 1841. His wife June 2, 1896. Only two of their five children are now living, Sallie Lewis, wife of J. D. McCulloch, and P. S. Lewis, who owns "Beechwood." Thomas Lewis, son of General Andrew Lewis, came to Mason county earlier than the other two. His father in his will left him a large tract of land in the forks of the rivers Ohio and Great Kanawha. He must have come somewhere near 1789, and settled at the mouth of "Old Town Creek,"

JOHN S. LEWIS, OF MASON CO.

where once stood an Indian village. His name appears as "Trustee" when Point Pleasant was laid off, and the forty acres laid out in the town Dec. 9, 1791, belonged to him. He was sent to the Legislature at Richmond from Kanawha county along with George Clendenin, in 1795, again in 1795 with David Ruffner. He was member of the first court of Kanawha county, held at "Clendenin Fort," and being the

115

oldest member, was made Sheriff. He made John Lewis, a descendent of Thomas Lewis, son of John Lewis the, "founder," his deputy. Thomas Lewis established the ferries across both rivers at Point Pleasant Dec. 9, 1791. History makes him an important man in Kanawha and Mason counties. He was killed in the public road, near his home by the falling of a tree (in Mason county). His wife was Miss Evans, of Mason county. Across the creek from "Beechwood" on a beautiful rise is the old burying ground. Many sad hearts have gone in and out its gate, for here lies the Lewis family of more than a century, "sleeping their long sleep." The first log house of Charles Cameron Lewis of 1800 was built on the river bottom, afterwards moved to this rise, near the graveyard, and then finally to the site which is now occupied by a handsome residence, built by P. S. Lewis not a great number of years ago. It would be a herculean task to attempt to name the Lewis descendents of the Kanawha Valley, the genealogy of the family being a very confusing one from the same names being so frequently used in the different branches of the families.

DELIA AGNES McCULLOCH.

# SAMUEL LEWIS AND JOHN D. LEWIS AND GENEALOGY OF LEWIS FAMILY.

## By W. S. Laidley.

Before giving the genealogy of this family we would call attention to some difficulties that appear in our way. A majority of the early writers seem to agree that John Lewis, the founder of the Lewis family of the Valley of Virginia was born in Ireland in the year 1678, and that his ancestors were compelled to leave France in consequence of the revocation of the Edict of Nantz, but as the revocation was not until 1685, how is this to be acounted for?

Was it not most probable that he was born in 1688?

This would make his age 74, for he died in 1762. His marriage was in 1716, at which time he would have been 28 if born in 1688, which is more probable.

## Samuel Lewis.

There is a question whether John Lewis had a son Samuel?

Peyton writes that he had seven children, and that Samuel was his eldest son, born in 1716, and that Samuel served in Braddock's war, and afterwards was engaged in the defence of Greenbrier county, and that he died unmarried.

Waddell says it is a question what number of sons John Lewis had and that various writers mention Samuel as one.

Ex-Governor Gilmore, of Georgia, a great grandson of John Lewis, in his book giving an account of the family, makes no mention of Samuel; this was printed in 1854.

Howe says that John Lewis had six sons and all of them were in Braddock's war, and that Samuel, the eldest, was a captain of a company. Yet Howe in another place speaks of Thomas being the eldest son.

Campbell speaks of Thomas as the eldest son and Charles, the fifth son, as the youngest.

Gen. Samuel H. Lewis speaks of his grandfather Thomas, as being the oldest son of John Lewis.

Col. Wm. I. Lewis, son of Wm. Lewis, of the Sweet Springs, has Samuel, Thomas, Andrew and William, when they left Ireland.

Chas. H. Lewis, minister to Portugal said that John Lewis had four sons, viz: Thomas, Andrew, William and Charles.

John Lewis's will, written November 28, 1761, mentions Thomas, Andrew, William and Charles, and says nothing of Samuel.

Dr. J. P. Hale says that the record of Kanawha county in 1789 mentions Col. Samuel Lewis and Daniel Boone as lieutenants of militia.

Withers says that Col. Samuel Lewis and Capt. Stuart with 66 men marched to the relief of Donnollys Fort in 1778.

We here have evidence that there was a Samuel Lewis and at the same time we find members of the family and others who fail to mention his name.

It is not proof that there was no Samuel because some parties never heard of him. Neither is the evidence that there was a Samuel, contradicted by other evidence that some writers did not know of him or that others that ought to have known him, if he existed, and did not mention him in a will or otherwise. He may have departed this life before his father wrote his will and not having left children, there was not necessity of mentioning him. He may have been alive in 1755 and not alive in 1761.

John Lewis had a brother Samuel who was killed at the time that John Lewis resisted the Irish landlord, and he would probably named his son after his brother.

There was unquestionably a Samuel Lewis in 1778 in Greenbrier, and in Kanawha in 1789, but this was probably not the son of John

Lewis. If.there was not a son Samuel, who was the Samuel Lewis hat commanded the Augusta company in the Braddock's war?

JOHN D. LEWIS, OF KANAWHA..

We are satisfied that there was a son, the eldest son of John Lewis, lamed Samuel, and that he died unmarried, and that the grand sons had not seen his name mentioned, hence they did not mention his name.

### John D. Lewis.

We here give a sketch of the life of John D. Lewis, of Kanawha county, written by his son, Chas. C. Lewis, which, with the photos, gives a very correct idea of this worthy man.

John Dickinson Lewis, was a son of Charles Lewis, who married Miss Dickinson, of Bath county, Va. She was a daughter of Col. John Dickinson, who was also at Point Pleasant. Charles Lewis was the youngest son of Col. Charles Lewis, who fell at the battle of Point Pleasant, who was the youngest son of John Lewis.

John D. Lewis, spent the most of his life in Kanawha county, and lived near Malden in the vicinity of the salt works, and he was engaged in the manufacture of salt and other enterprises and became a large land owner.

He was what is called an upright and a merciful man, and one of his peculiarities or characteristics was that he was a very positive, decided man and who relied on his own judgment. And he did not hesitate to give expression to that opinion. But the following letter tells it all as it was known:

### John D. Lewis.

The subject of this sketch, John Dickinson Lewis, was born in Bath county, Virginia, June 6th, 1800, on the old farm on the Cow Pasture river, his grandfather, Colonel Charles Lewis, who was killed at the battle of Point Pleasant October 10th, 1774, was born in Augusta county, Virginia in 1736, in 1760 he married Sarah Murray and left seven children, viz: Elizabeth, Margaret, John, Mary, Thomas, Andrew and Charles, the father of the subject of this sketch, who was born in Augusta county, Virginia in 1774, probably September 11th,, as Colonel Charles Lewis in his will dated August 10th, 1774, just before starting on his march to Point Pleasant provides for the unborn child of his wife, Sarah. This unborn child was Charles Lewis, who served with distinction under General Anthony Wayne, in 1795 in his Indian campaign in the west; as a lieutenant, as attested by his commission dated August 7th, 1795, and signed by General Washington, and now in possession of his descendent, P. S. Lewis, of Mason county, West Virginia. After Wayne's campaign he resigned from the army and returned to Bath county, where, in 1799, he married Jane Dickinson, a daughter of Colonel John Dickinson, who commanded a company in Colonel Charles Lewis' regiment, and was wounded in the battle of Point Pleasant. Lieutenant Charles Lewis died September, 1803, aged twenty-nine years, and was buried in the family graveyard on the farm now owned by P. S. Lewis in Mason county, West Virginia, leaving two children, John D. Lewis, the subject of this sketch, and Charles Cameron Lewis, who was born in Mason county, April 27th, 1802, married Eliza Steenbergen, and died August 15th, 1841; two children survive them, P. S. Lewis and Sallie, the wife of Daniel McCullock, both at this date residents of Mason county. John D. Lewis' mother was Jane Dickinson, the youngest daughter of Colonel John Dickinson, who served as captain in Colonel Charles Lewis' regiment and was wounded in the battle of Point Pleasant in 1774.

John D. Lewis was brought an infant in his mother's arms to Mason county, Virginia, now West Virginia, where he remained until his mother's second marriage with Captain James Wilson, in 1805, when he was brought to Charleston. At the proper age he was placed in school with Mr. Crutchfield, where he received his early education, afterwards taking a course in latin and the higher branches of mathematics under General Lewis Ruffner. After leaving school he returned to Mason county on the farm owned by his brother Charles and himself. At about the age of twenty-two he sold his half interest in the farm to his brother and returned to Kanawha county, and for a short time was employed by Dickinson and Shrewsbury as salt maker. He then engaged in the manufacture of salt for himself, and remained in the busines until 1856, and then for a period of five years he was engaged in clearing and improving his lands on Campbell's Creek. When the Civil War broke out and the price of salt advanced, he again engaged in the manufacture of salt until 1866, when he returned to his farming in Kanawha and Nicholas counties. My father was one of the first to use coal in the manufacture of salt, hauling the coal for two and one-half miles in wagons, afterwards using first a wooden tramway and then the iron rail; he was also the second or third to use natural gas to manufacture salt. The greater portion of his life was spent at the old homestead five miles above Charleston on the bank of the Kanawha river, just above the mouth of Campbell's Creek, on the 502

121

acre tract of land patented to John Dickinson in 1785 and by him sold to Joseph Ruffner in 1793 and by his heirs sold in part to my father. This John Dickinson was Colonel John Dickinson, before spoken of as the father of Jane Dickinson. On this 502 acre tract was the celebrated Salt Spring located near the edge of the river about 1,000 feet below a point opposite the Thoroughfare Gap. My father once told me that when he was quite young the old settlers told him that when they first came to Kanawha the elk and deer came down Campbell's Creek to this spring to get salt, and that they could go there and see hundreds of them waiting their time to get to the spring. And to this day the path made by the elk, deer and Buffalo in places is distinctly traceable for several miles up this creek. My father was a member of the Episcopal church and worshiped with the church of his choice so long as there was a church of that denomination in the town of Malden (one mile above his residence) ; after that time he regularly worshiped and communed with the Presbyterians, Rev. J. C. Brown, pastor, to whom he was devotedly attached. So far as I am informed, he never made but one public speech, that one was in the town of Malden in the spring of 1861 against the ordinance of secession before a threatening and angry mob. In politics he was a Whig and in his younger days he took an active part in all presidential campaigns. He had no aspirations for office. He served for many years as magistrate by appointment, in those days when magistrates served without compensation, and rarely had an appeal from their decisions, to cost the county hundreds of dollars, as now. My father rarely had to make a decision, generally, after talking to the contestants and mking up his mind which of the two ws right, he either convinced the other of his error or induced them to compromise, both parties usually left satisfied and often good friends. My father, like most of the Scotch-Irish, was a man of more than ordinary determination and will power. I remember well when I was a boy he used to tell me when I complained that I could not do something that he had told me to do "that there ought not to be such a word as 'can't' in our language; that we could do most anything if we would go at it in the right way and with the right determination." As an illustration of this fact I will mention one instance that occurred when he was nearly eighty years of age, one evening I received a letter from my stepmother asking me to come up at once. I drove up and asked what she wanted, she said my father had been confined to his bed for ten days and that he had that day requested her to put the

122

necessary clothing in his saddle pockets, that he was going to his farm in Nicholas county, (a distance of 75 miles) on Monday morning, this was Friday. I said to her if he had made up his mind to go he would go, and it was useless for me to speak to him. The next day she sent for the family physician, Dr. Ewing. When the doctor arrived she asked him to go and pursuade Mr. Lewis not to attempt the trip. When the doctor went to his room and said to him that he was too weak to make the trip, and if he attempted it, it would be at the risk of his life. My father looked up and asked the doctor if that was all he came for, he said yes, then said my father you can go back. I am going to Nicholas on Monday next. On Monday morning he arose, dressed himself, ordered his horse, had two men to help him down the steps and on to his horse, rode 'fifty miles the same day and the next day by noon the other twenty-five miles, and wrote back to his wife that he felt pretty well and that if he had had seventy-five miles further to ride he would have been entirely well. My father was married four times, first to Sally, a daughter of Mr. Joel Shrewsbury, who died a year or two after her marriage, leaving one son, Joel S. Lewis, now deceased. His second wife was Ann, a daughter of Colonel William Dickinson, who left three children, Sally, Charles and Mary. His third wife was Betty, a daughter of Mr. Jacob Darneal, who left two children, Julia and William. His fourth wife was Mrs. Sally Spears, now living with her daughter, by her first husband, in Wilmington, N. C.

My father died December 26th, 1882, aged 82 1-2 years, generally lamented, and especially by the poor, to whom he was always a warm friend and helper.

CHAS. C. LEWIS.

March 24th, 1904.

---

## GENEALOGY OF THE LEWIS FAMILY.

The Lewises were originally Hugenots and consisted of three brothers, William, Samuel and Andrew, who were compelled to quit France and bought a home in Wales; whilst there, they obtained a grant from the king of Great Britain of land in Colerain, near Londonderry, Ireland, where they lived for several years, but the prejudices of the

Catholics were such that they were forced either to move or change their name; the latter they chose, by substituting the letters ew for ou, making the name Lewis, instead of Louis. Andrew, one of the brothers, married Miss Calhoun in Ireland, by whom he had two sons; 1st. Col. John Lewis, of Augusta county, Virginia, and Samuel Lewis, who was killed by Sir Mungo Campbell. Col. John Lewis killed that nobleman the very day upon which his brother Samuel was murdered; he married Margaret Lynn, of Lock Lynn. He was born February 1st, 1678, and died near Staunton, Virginia, in 1762. His wife was born July 3rd, 1693 and died near Staunton in 1773. They left six children as follows:

## I.

Thomas Lewis, born in Ireland April 27th, 1718, who married Jane Strother, daughter of William, of Stafford, Va., January 26th, 1749, and left thirteen children, as follows:

1. John Lewis, born Nov. 1, 1749.
2. Margaret Anne, born July 5, 1751.
3. Agatha Lewis, born May 18, 1753.
4. Jane Lewis, born Aug. 8, 1755.
5. Andrew Lewis, born Oct. 16, 1757.
6. Thomas Lewis, born Jan. 26, 1760.
7. Mary Lewis, born Aug. 5, 1762.
8. Elizabeth Lewis, born Jan. 24, 1765.
9. Anne Lewis, born Oct. 8, 1767.
10. Frances Lewis, born May 17, 1769.
11. Charles Lewis, born Nov. 8, 1772.
12. Sophia Lewis, born Oct. 18, 1775.
13. Wm. Benpamin, born Aug. 8, 1778; died, 1822.

(1). John married and left four children: 1st: Thomas; 2nd: John; 3rd: Charles; 4th: Elizabeth, who married Col. John Francisco of Kentucky.

(2) Margaret married ———— McClanahan, of Staunton, and had but one child, John McClanahan. Her husband died and she married Col. Wm. Bowyer, and had five children: 1st: Wm. C. Bowyer; 2nd: Strother; 3rd: Luke; 4th: Peter; 5th: Malinda.

(3) Agatha married Col. Jno. Stuart, of Greenbrier, and had four children: 1st: Chas. A. Stuart; 2nd: Lewis; 3rd: Margaret; 4th:

Jane. C. A. Stuart married Miss Robertson of Augusta. Lewis married Miss Lewis, of the Cowpasture; Margaret married Col. Andrew Lewis, of Point Pleasant; Jane married Crockett, of Wythe.

(4)  Jane Lewis married Thomas Hughes.

(5)  Andrew died single.

(6)  Thomas died single.

(7)  Mary married Major John McElhany.

(8)  Elizabeth married Thomas Gilmer, of Georgia, and is the mother of Governor Gilmer.

(9)  Ann married Wm. Douthat, became a widow and married ——— French, of Kentucky.

(10)  Frances married Seyton Yancy, of Rockingham.

(11)  Charles married Miss Yancey, and left five children: 1st: Thomas; 2nd: General Samuel H. Lewis; 3rd: Charles; 4th: Mary; who married Dr. M. Chambers, of Ohio; 5th: Margaret Strother Lewis, who married Rev. Chas. Triplett, of Maryland.

(12)  Sophia married John Carthrae, of Rockingham.

(13)  Wm. Benjamin Lewis married Margaret Hite, of Rockingham, and left four children: 1st: William, 1803-1856; 2nd: General J. W. Lewis, 1805-1856; Louise S. Major, 1808-1904; Mary Jane, 1810-1891.

## II.

General Andrew Lewis, who so greatly distinguished himself before the Revolutionary War and who was the bosom friend of Washington, was born in Ireland, June, 1720, and emigrated to this country with his mother, about 1730. He married Miss Givens, of Augusta county, Va., and had six children. He died in his 61st year, 1781, at Buford's Jap in Bedford and was buried in Roanoke county. His children were:

(1)  John Lewis, who married Miss Patsy Love of Alexandria, by whom he had four children: 1st, Andrew, who married Jane McClanahan, of Botetourt, Va., and left seven children, as follows:

1. John, who married first Miss Donnaly, of Kanawha county;

2. William, who married Miss Tosh, of Botetourt county;

3. Samuel, who married Miss Montague, of Montgomery county;

4. Emeline, who married Mr. Ingles of Montgomery county;

5. Eliza, who married Mr. Pitzer, of Botetourt county;

6. Sallie, who married Mr. Wood, of Botetourt county, and Patsy and Jane, who died young.

(2) Samuel Lewis, who married Miss White, of Kentucky.

(3) Charles Lewis, who married Miss Trigg, of Montgomery.

(4) Elizabeth (the last child of John Lewis), who married Mr. Luke, of Alexandria.

(2nd) Thomas Lewis, son of Gen. Lewis, was killed by a fall from his horse. He lived in Kanawha and then in Mason county.

(3rd) Col. Saml. Lewis, of Greenbrier, died a bachelor, born 1757.

(4th) Col. Andrew Lewis, of Bent Mountain, married Eliza Madison, of Montgomery county, Va., and had children as follows:

1. Charles, who never married.

2. Thomas, who was a lawyer of great promise and killed by McHenry in a duel.

3rd and 4th died young.

5. Agatha Strother Lewis married Col. Elijah McClanahan, of Roanoke county, Va.

(5) Ann Lewis married Rowland Madison, of Kentucky.

(6) William Lewis, youngest son of Gen. Lewis, was born in 1764 and married Lucy Madison and had eleven children:

1. Andrew, died young.

2. Agnes married Mr. Adams and whose son, George Adams is now Federal Judge in Mississippi.

Lucy Lewis dying, he married Miss McClanahan, by whom he had nine children, making the eleven:

3. Mrs. Fleming, of Huntsville, Alabama.

4. Mrs. Beale; who left a daughter, Mrs. Norvell, of Huntsville.

5. Mrs. Lucy Bowyer.

6. Wm. Lewis, died young.

7. Gen. John Lewis, of Texas.

8. Charles Lewis, who was killed in a street fight in Mobile.

9. Ann Lewis, lives in the City of Mexico.

10. Mary Jane Lewis, died young.

11. Mrs. Christian lives in Tuscumbia.

### III.

Col. Wm. Lewis, of the Sweet Springs, was the third son of John Lewis and Margaret Lynn, and born in Ireland on the 17th day of November, 1724, and married Ann Montgomery, of the "Castle of

Montgomery," April 18th, 1754. She was born September 1st, 1737. He died at Sweet Springs, November, 1811; she died same place, July, 1808. They left eight children, as follows;

1st. Margaret Lewis, born October 14, 1754.

2nd. John Lewis, born August 24, 1758.

3rd. Thomas Lewis, born November 6, 1761.

4th. Alexander Lewis, born October, 1763.

5th. William Lewis, born July 3, 1766.

6th. Agatha Lewis, born April 13, 1774.

7th. Elizabeth Lewis, born March 2, 1777.

8th. Charles W. Lewis, born February 22, 1780.

1. Margaret married Mr. McFarland and had eleven children.

2. John married Jane Sophomisba Thomson of South Carolina, July 24, 1788 and had two children:

1. Eugenia, who married W. S. Thomson, of South Carolina.

2. Sophia, who died young.

His wife dying, he afterwards married Mary Preston, of Montgomery county, Va., by whom he had nine children:

1. Susannah Preston Lewis, who married Henry Massie, by whom she had six children, as follows:

1st, Sarah Cooke Massie; 2nd, Mary Preston; 3rd, Henry; 4th, Eugenia; 5th, Thomas; 6th, Susan Lewis Massie.

2. Mary Sophia, married James L. Woodville, and left one son, Dr. James Lewis Woodville.

3. William Lynn Lewis married Ann E. Stuart, of South Carolina, and had four children, as follows: 1st, Mary Ellen; 2nd, Ann Tabbs; 3rd, James Stuart; 4th, Clara.

His wife dying, he married Miss Thomson, of South Carolina, who left no children.

He then married Lettie Floyd, of Wythe, and had four children: 1st, Susan; 2nd, Letitia; 3rd, William Lynn; 4th, John Floyd.

4. Ann Montgomery Lewis married John Howe Peyton and has ten children: 1st, Susan; 2nd, John Lewis; 3rd, Ann; 4th, Mary; 5th, Lucy; 6th, Elizabeth; 7th, Margaret; 8th, Yelverton; 9th, Virginia; 10th, Cornelia.

5. Sarah Elizabeth married Col. Jno. Lewis, of Coal River, Kanawha, and had no children. (His second wife.)

6. Margaret Lynn married Jno. Cochran and have ten children: 1st, John Lewis; 2nd, James; 3rd, Henry; 4th, Howe Peyton; 5th,

George; 6th, William Lynn; 7th, Mary Preston; 8th, George Moffett; 9th, Magdalen; 10th, Preston McDowell.

7. John B. Lewis married Carolina S. Smith in South Carolina and have six children, as follows: 1st, Eugenia; 2nd, John; 3rd, Ann Stuart; 4th, William Thomson; 5th, Chas. Montgomery; 6th, Mary Lewis.

8. Thomas Preston Lewis, single.

9. Pollydora Eugenia Lewis, married John W. Goss, of Albemarle, Va., and have six children: 1st, Mary Preston; 2nd, Jane W.; 3rd, William; 4th, Lynn Lewis; 5th, John; 6th, infant.

3. Major Thomas Lewis, third child of William and Ann, died a bachelor.

4. Alexander Lewis died a bachelor.

5. William J. Lewis married Miss Cabell, of Campbell county, Va.

6. Agatha married Oliver Towles and had eight children, as follows:

1. Ann Maria, who married Dr. L. Rives;

2. Oliver;

3. Elizabeth, who married Jno. Blair Dabney;

4. William B., who married Miss Johnson;

5. Margaret Caroline, who married Wm. Sims;

6. Thomas Henry, who died single;

7. John Alexander, who died single;

8. Alfred Lewis, who married Jane Vaughn, of Missouri.

7. Elizabeth Montgomery Lewis married John Trent and left three children, as follows:

1. Eliza, who married Washington Swoope;

2. Ann, who married Judge John Robertson;

3. Dr. John Trent.

8. Dr. Charles W. Lewis married Miss Irwine of Philadelphia, and left seven children, as follows:

1, William J; 2, Thomas; 3, Ann; 4, Elizabeth; 5, Mary B. T.; 6, Armstrong, and 1, Callendar.

## IV.

Colonel Charles Lewis, who fell at the battle of Point Pleasant, was the last son of Col. Jno. Lewis and Margaret Lynn, and was born in Augusta county, on the 1th day of March, 1736, and married Sarah Maury, who was born on the 1st day of August, 1743. They had seven children:

1. Elizabeth Lewis, born October 17, 1762.
2. Margaret Lewis, born March 29, 1765.
3. John Lewis, born November 4, 1766.
4. Mary Lewis, born November 10, 1768.
5. Thomas Lewis, born February 25, 1771.
6. Andrew Lewis, born September 27, 1772.
7. Charles Lewis, born September 11, 1774.

It is not known who the first five married; the sixth, Andrew Lewis, married his cousin, Margaret Stewart, and left ten children:

1, Charles Cameron; 2, Agnes; 3, John; 4, Elizabeth; 5, Mary Jane; 6, John Stewart; 7, Margaret Lewis; 8, Sarah Frances; 9, ——————; 10, Andrew.

Charles died in 1836; Agnes married I. L. Sehon and had nine children:

1, Fanny; 2, Margaret Lynn; 3, Andrew; 4, John; 5, Sarah; 6, Stuart; 7, Columbus; 8, Edmund; 9, Agnes Lewis.

Margaret Sehon married Valentine Horton, Esq., and has one child, Virginia Lewis; the third and fourth children died young; the fifth married Charles Baldwin, Esq., and died next year; the sixth married Miss Stribling, of Staunton, Va., and have four children, to-wit:

1st, Fanny; 2nd, Sarah; 3rd, Matilda; 4th, Agnes.

The seventh died young; the eighth, Sarah F., single; ninth, Elizabeth Thomson; tenth, the last child of Andrew and Margaret, died young.

The seventh and last child of Charles Lewis, wha fell at Point Pleasant, was Charles Lewis, who married Miss Dickinson, of Bath county and left two sons, as follows:

1. John D. Lewis, born June 6th, 1800 (see sketch).
2. Charles C., born April 27, 1802, and died in 1841.

Charles married Miss Steenberger and left five children:

1st, Maria I.; 2nd, Caroline; 3rd, Peter; 4th, Sarah A.; 5th, Charles C. Lewis.

I have thus, Madam, given you a copy of my geneological table, which is the only one I have furnished any of my relations with, and which is imperfect, and·I doubt not, incorrect, in many of the junior members of the family, and therefore, not fit for distribution; but your advanced age and the interest you have so promptly taken to aid me, together with my great admiration of your own character, induces me to comply with your request and my promise, however imperfect it it. Whatever error you detect, if you will point it out, I will correct in my memoranda before it is printed.

Wishing you every earthly blessing and that your joint lives may be prolonged many years, I am, dear madam, your kinsman,

JOHN B. LEWIS,

*Orange C. H.*, Aug. 1848.

To Mrs. AGATHA McCLANAHAN,
Roanoke County.

---

## COL. JOSEPH LOVELL.

Joseph Lovell was born in London, January 10, 1793. His father, whose first name we have never learned, married Lady Mary Chapton. He died young, leaving his widow and several children. His mother then married James Bream, a London Merchant, of some considerable estate, but being only a merchant, her friends became offended and Mr. Bream sold out and took ship for Virginia and settled in Richmond.

Joseph was but five years old when he reached Richmond and there he was reared, educated and trained for the practice of law. We know little of him as a student, but from what we know of him when he became of age, when he came to the Kanawha Valley; he must have been a vigilant student, and one of more than ordinary energy and application. He came early in 1814 to Kanawha county, under his license to practice law and was well informed in all matters of public importance, with more than ordinary literary attainments and his speeches were of the character that bespoke high cultivation, both in oratory and logic. He was a young man of fine address and soon became and ever continued to be a popular favorite with the people of all classes.

An incident is told of him which shows something of his style of man. The Salt works was the business center of the Valley and on his arrival stopped at the public tavern, where the people called to see each other and discuss business and politics. The place has been known by various names, "the Licks," "Salines," "Terra Salta," and as now, Malden. While at the said tavern there were among the many persons present, two or more engaged in a discussion concern-

Col. Joseph Lovell.

ing a tract of land in this county, and he, as all others, could not help but hear them. It became interesting to him and he listened to the points of difference and the claims made, and before bed time he was engaged as counsel of one of the parties. This was his first case in this county and probably the first he ever had, and he afterwards had the pleasure of securing for his client all for which he had contended.

131

It was his purpose when he left Richmond to go west and to make investments in real estate for his stepfather, Mr. James Bream, and it was not even that day regarded as part of the country known as "out west," so far as making purchases of real estate as an investment. It was very much "out west" in many other respects.

Mr. Lovell remained here. He saw the thriving town, the manufacture of salt, the facility for transportation by the Kanawha, Ohio, and Mississippi rivers, and he saw all the demands of growth and thrift, and he knew a good thing when he saw it. He located and became one of the lawyers and also engaged in the manufacture of salt, which required him also to be a merchant, and it brought him in contact with most all the people in the vicinity of Charleston, and the merchants in the towns on the Ohio river.

He evidently had command of more funds than many of his associates, and he made purchases of real estate in localities in which he thought there would be an outcome and future developement and consequently great growth in value.

Not only did he purchase but he sold and the records show that he did a "Land office business" not only in buying and selling, but also in making loans and taking mortgages on real estate.

In May, 1815 the County Court recommended him and the Governor appointed him an Ensign in the Virginia militia.

In June, 1815, he was made a Lieutenant in the First Battalion of the Eighth Regiment of the Thirteenth Brigade of the First Division of the Virginia militia.

In July, 1815, he was recommended by said county for appointment of Coroner of this county. He continued in the line of promotion until he was made a Colonel, and he was ever afterwards known as Colonel Lovell.

In view of the fact that there were many other older men that had seen some service, that he also a young Englishman, he must have in a very short time gained the confidence and respect of the Court of his County.

In 1816 he had so conducted himself and his business affairs, that he induced James Bream to dispose of his business in Richmond and remove to Kanawha County. He had contracted for all the land on the north side of the Kanawha river from the mouth of Elk river down to Two mile creek, and when Mr. Bream came and saw the land and the prospect of the country, he concluded the contract and became the owner of this land, and also land in the Salines where he engaged in the manufacture of salt.

In the year 1719, Col. Lovell, with Claudius Bruster, were elected to the House of Delegates of the Virginia Legislature, and he continued to represent his County for years afterwards. In 1820, he with N. W. Thompson. In 1821 he with Lewis Ruffner. In 1824 he with John Welch, and he could have continued being elected, but he declined to become a candidate for re-election.

BETTY W. LOVELL.

In the year 1818, on the 19th day of February, he was married to Miss Bettie Washington Lewis, a daughter of Howell Lewis, of Mason County, Va. The officiating minister was Rev. Henry Ruffner.

The children of Joseph and Bettie W. Lovell were:

Alfred Lovell, born December 27, 1818, who died unmarried September 6, 1842.

Richard Chauning Moore Lovell, born March 3, 1822, who married Miss Mary Patrick.

133

Howard Lewis Lovell, born July 9, 1824, who married Miss E. A. Beuhring, of Cabell County.

Joseph Lovell, Jr., born March 31, 1827, died March 22, 1865; his wife was Sarah S. Nye, of Marietta, Ohio.

Fayette A. Lovell, was born July 2, 1830, who married Miss Sally Shrewsbury.

### Betty Washington Lewis.

Col. Fielding Lewis married Betty Washington, a sister of the General. Their children were:

George Lewis, Capt. of Washington Life Guard.

Lawrence Lewis, Aid to General Morgan.

Robert Lewis, Secretary to George Washington.

Howell Lewis, who also was secretary to Washington, was surveyor of land for United States and came to Mason County, Va., in 1791.

In 1836 he removed to Henry County, Missouri, and died in 1843. His wife was Ellen Hackley Pollard, and Betty Washington Lewis was one of their daughters.

Betty W. Lewis was born in Richmond, Va., October 14, 1796, and lived as a child at Mt. Vernon, while her father was secretary of the General. She was a favorite with her grand father, the child of the General's only sister.

She was an Episcopalian, and wherever she was, she was engaged in the work of her Master and His Church. This was the case while she lived in Charleston, and equally so while she lived in Marietta Ohio, to which place she removed after her husbands death and where she remained until her death, July 2, 1866.

The history of the churches in both of these places, mention her as one of the liberal contributors and most faithful workers.

Col. Joseph Lovell first lived on the Kanawha river at the mouth of the Wilson Hollow Branch in a double log, one story house, that has since been removed.

He afterwards removed to Charleston and built a brick residence on the cottage order, with his brick office near his residence.

He was engaged in the merchandise and general store business and he afterwards disposed of this business to James A. Lewis. This business house still stands on the river bank on the lower side of Capitol street.

He was now a busy and successful man in all his enterprises. As a lawyer and politician he came to the front. As a speaker there were few that were his equal and none his superior, and he was called upon for his services in all campaigns and on all public occasions, and the crowd was always enthusiastic when he addressed them. He was also engaged largely with Mr. Bream in the salt business, and he had business engagements with the barrel maker, the boat maker, and the farmer, of whom he bought farm produce for his customers at the salt works. His commercial and political and legal business brought him in close contact with the people of his county. Kanawha had been a Democratic County, but the question of tariff and especially tariff on salt was a question that affected a large number of the people and the voters of this County.

The manufacturers wanted protection and it was but a short time before Kanawha was enrolled among the Whig counties of Virginia, and it never unrolled therefrom until it rolled into the republican hands where it has most of the time remained. Col. Lovell was the originator of the trust. He organized all the salt manufacturers into one company, the purpose of which was to reduce expenses, but principally to control the market. No one could obtain Kanawha salt except through the company, which like companies are now denominated trusts. Their salt company became opulent, and with their aid and the aid of the barrel makers, and boat builders and farmers whose market was in the salt works, they controlled Kanawha politics.

The fame of the County went out far and wide, and it delighted Henry Clay as he passed through the Valley, to stop over and consult with his Whig brothers. He frequently made addresses while here, and after he had .concluded, nothing would satisfy the people until Col. Lovell had been heard, and who did not fear to follow the celebrated Kentuckian, on the stump, although they advocated the same political views, yet none but able men and eloquent ones would speak upon such occasions. Col. Lovell continued as the leader of all these many enterprises, and his professional engagements became more burdensome, and his attempt to conduct them all, together with the duties attending to his growing family, was more than his strength could bear. He however, continued in the harness for many years, but finally his strength gave way, and he died November 25, 1835. He was buried in the Bream cemetery, but was in after

135

years removed to the Spring Hill cemetery, under the control of the authorities of the city of Charleston, where his monument may now be seen.

Few men accomplished more in so short a time or did so much for their country than did Col. Joseph Lovell. He will ever be remembered as the active, brilliant, popular business man of his day and the eloquent leader of his political party.

*More Concerning the Children of Col. Lovell.*

Alfred Lovell, born December 27, 1818, died September 6, 1842. He was much like his father in his social qualities and was very popular with the people, with whom he liked to mingle and enjoy their sociability. He never married.

R. C. M. Lovell, born March 3, 1822, and he inherited from his father his busy, active habits of life, and has in his long life done more than two ordinary men would do. He lives in Covington, Ky., and has retired from active business.

Howell Lewis Lovell, born July 9, 1824; married Emma A. Beuhring August 26, 1856; died May 22, 1900. In many respects he was unlike his brothers, in that he was quiet and retiring and avoided the public. In his early manhood he engaged in business in Charleston, and after his marriage went to California, where he remained for many years, when he returned and settled in Covington, Ky. He engaged in business in Cincinnati and in Covington, and by his strict integrity and business methods he accumulated a handsome fortune. He was a consciencious and a most liberal man. His wife and daughters survived him.

Joseph Lovell, Jr., lived and died in Marietta, O., in March 22, 1865.

Fayette A. Lovell was born in Charleston, July 2, 1830. He attended school at Lexington, Va.; married Sally T. Shrewsbery at Malden, April 29, 1861; practiced law in Kanawha until his death. Resided in Charleston and died in Malden, March 8, 1869.

He was a man of most courteous manners, both in and out of Court; was kind and obliging to all, and was greatly esteemed by all who ever met him. He also went to California and returned by Panama.

The will of Col. Lovell was recorded in Kanawha in December, 1835, by which he gave one-third of all his estate to his wife, and the residue to his children, and appointed his wife his executrix.

By the will of James Bream, recorded in 1842, Mrs. Lovell was remembered like one of his own children, although the bulk of his estate was given to his wife, Mrs. Mary Bream, the mother of Joseph Lovell.

By the will of Mrs. Mary Bream, recorded in July, 1845, she gave to Mrs. Betty W. Lovell in the same way that she did her own children, and her estate was not a small one.

Lovell street, in the city of Charleston, was named for Col. Joseph Lovell, who owned much of the property in the vicinity thereof.

---

# HENRY McWHORTER AND DESCENDANTS—COL. JOHN McWHORTER.

### By L. V. McWhorter.

In the article on Henry McWhorter, published in No. 3, (July, 1901), of this Magazine, are a few errors that should be corrected.

First, the writer is his great grand son, instead of *great great*, as was stated.

Second, the foot note on page 65 is badly jumbled—a mistake of the printer.

It should read:

Photographed by Prof. G. F. Queen, for the writer in 1894, with Mr. Ned J. Jackson, a noted 49-er, who then owned it, sitting in the door. The cut is taken from "An Historical Account of the Scotch Highland Settlements in America." By J. P. MacLean, Ph. D., 1900.

His son Thomas, who died Dec. 28th, 1815, was the first buried in the McWhorter cemetery, and no other interment took place until 1822.

Henry died Feb. 4th, 1848, as stated.

Since the article was written, an old family record has been found which shows that it was about 1787 when he came to Hackers Creek, instead of 1784.

This places the building of the house three years later (1790), which still entitles it to the claim of being the oldest residence in that part of the State.

There is a fine hickory grove between the house and the pike on the west, grown from the nuts, planted by Mr. Ned J. Jackson, in the first week in October, 1857. The house as photographed, fronts the creek, on the north.

Henry was bound to a mill wright when a lad, and mastered the trade at sixteen years of age; then enlisted in the New York troops, patriotic army, and participated in the Battle of White Plains.

His military record at Washington shows that he was born in New Jersey, and was only a *resident* of Orange county, New York, at time of enlistment.

The place of his birth, as given in previous article, (also in "Border Warfare") was data taken from his grave stone, which is erroneous.

In 1783 he was married to Miss Mary Fields, a noble woman, to whom he owed much for his success in life. She was born 1761, died 1834.

It is due the memory of these old pioneers that brief mention be made of their descendants.

They had but three children—John, Thomas and Walter.

John *, the eldest, was born April 28th, 1784, and from early childhood was noted for his eccentricity and absent-mindedness.

Many are the amusing incidents related of him in this respect, one or two of which are here given.

Like most pioneer lads, he was fond of the rifle, and one morning was busy preparing to go deer hunting, when his mother requested that he first bring a pail of water from the spring near the forest surrounding their cabin home.

Hastily snatching a bucket he strode to the spring, oblivious to everything but his expectant hunt, passed directly by the spring and was soon buried in the deep unbroken woods of the hillside.

Cautiously wending his way through thicket and glen, soon discovered a buck standing partly concealed by intervening

—————
*In after years familiarly known as "Colonel," "Judge" McWhorter.

brush, and while seeking a point more advantageous for a rifle shot, the irrepressible *bucket* pending from his arm, came noisily in contact with a log over which he was stepping, bringing him back to the realities of life with startling effect —*he had no gun.*

We could give other stories of like nature—of how, starting with bridle one morning to bring a horse from the pasture, mysteriously lost the bridle, spent hours in fruitless search for it, when at noon, his mother going to the spring house found it lying beside a crock of milk, where he had been down on his knees *licking the rich cream.*

Of his "bachelor day" efforts at tailoring, how after fifteen minutes spent in diligently sewing a button to his coat, let go the button only to see it fall to the floor.

Nor did this trait of character diminish, but rather grew with years and the cares of public life, as the following incident will illustrate:

By the road side near his home stood a large gum tree, whose branches hanging low over the highway, was in autumn, laden with dark rich looking berries (of such nauseating bitterness that, in comparison, gall is as honey to the taste), in appearance not unlike the sweet palatable fruit of the black haw, of which the Colonel was extremely fond.

One day riding under this tree with mind deeply engrossed with some case in law, the clustering berries so temptingly within reach arrested his eye, and without slacking his pace, hastily snatched a handful as he passed, emptied his mouth of a "quid" of tobacco and filled it with the supposed haws.

The effect can be better imagined than described, and unlike the traditional Christian, he invoked his God *after* the feast.

Early in life he studied law, and soon became a noted barrister of extraordinary ability. As a pleader his logic was hardly surpassed, and his judgment on contested points unerring. Not through his long career at the bar was he ever known to champion the cause of wrong, while his respect and reverence for Christianity even in his wildest moods was proverbial, and he has been known while engaged in a game of cards, to throw down his cards, push back from the table in disgust and in scathing words of indignation rebuke a boon companion for irreverent remarks and reflections on religion.

He was notorious for his bad penmanship, irritable temper, * generosity and kindness of heart, and was ever ready with loosened purse strings to relieve the needy and distressed.

With a naturally wild and reckless nature to contend against, and without the advantages of an education, his genius and force of ability soon brought him into prominence and places of public trust.

When the war of 1812 broke out, with the spirit of liberty that prompted his father to take up arms against oppression in 1776; he raised a company of volunteers, offered his service to his government, was accepted and on the 16th of November, 1812, commissioned captain in Col. John Connell's Regiment, Virginia.

With his band of patriots he footed it from Weston, or Clarksburg (his residence) to Parkersburg, from thence to Point Pleasant by flat boat, where they were armed and equipped, then proceeded on foot to the Maumee river, where they campaigned or did garrison duty.

They were in the service until April 13th, 1813, at which time their term of enlistment expired.

The company returned home by the same conveyance that took them to the field of action. On the return trip one of the men, becoming exhausted, the Captain relieved him of his knapsack and camp baggage, adding it to his own burden.

Resuming his law practice ,he remained at his office in Clarksburg until the 17th of March, 1814, when he again enlisted as Captain under Colonel Wm. King, 3rd Regiment, United States Rifles.

He was afterwards made Colonel of Militia. (On May 2th, 1871, aged 87, he applied for and was granted a pension for entire time of his enlistment.).

He represented Harrison county in both Houses of the Vir-

---

*An amusing incident is related of him in this respect. While Prosecuting Attorney of Lewis county, he one day presented to the Court an indictment drawn up in his own hand writing, so intricate and unintelligible to the Clerk did it appear, that that dignitary's most scholarly efforts failed in deciphering its meaning, and the Colonel was called upon to "translate" it. Solemnly scanning the document for a moment, a puzzled expression came over his face which deepened, as, utterly unable to read a word of it, he was about to lay it down, when becoming irritated at the suppressed tittering of the entire Court, burst forth with: "Now, who in H—l wrote that. Why, the D——l could not read it." Upon being informed that it was his own production, he bravely declared that "anybody could read it," and proceeded to do so without further trouble. Members of the bar ofttimes amused themselves and disturbed the dignity of the Court by stealing the Colonel's papers when deeply absorbed in an interesting case; "just to hear him rave," and seldom, if ever, were they disappointed.

ginia Legislature, and with his colleague, Dr. Jackson, originated the bill that created the new county of Lewis, (named for General Lewis, of Point Pleasant fame), stricken from Harrison.

He was for many years Prosecuting Attorney of Lewis and Braxton counties, and after retiring from the bar served as Judge of the Lewis County Court for several years.

When old age compelled his retirement from public life, he was ordained a local minister in the M. E. Church, in which capacity he served until his death, April 14th, 1880, in his 96th year; was buried on Rush Run, Lewis county.

He was never married.

Thomas, the second son, was a prosperous farmer, and a man of sterling worth to his community.

His only son, Henry, was killed in the Civil War, Union Army, in the fight in Pocahontas county, W. Va., Jan. 23, 1863. Early in the fight he fell badly wounded, and congratulated himself that it was his privilege to die as a true soldier in defense of his country. A few moments later he was shot through the heart, dying with a whispered prayer on his lips.

(Two of his sons were in the same company and saw their father killed. One of them, Fields, was made prisoner, and received injuries from which he died soon after the close of the war. The other son, John S., escaped, but was injured for life.)

One grand-son, line of Thomas, is a minister and doctor. Two other grand-sons, or great-grand-sons, are doctors.

The third and last son, Walter, was also a farmer, and under the old military law, Major of his regiment, (militia). Was a noted athlete, and never met his equal in wrestling or foot racing. Lithe and active, fond of daring sport, he would capture and toy with a living rattlesnake, dodging or avoiding its deadly and lightning-like blows, with all the ease and grace of an East Indian snake charmer.

No church in the community, his home, (the old homestead on McKenzie's Run), was for years, as with his father, the recognized place of public worship, and the free home of the itinerant minister and traveler.

His wife, Miss Margaret Herst, ever bore this additional hardship added to the burden of caring for a large family of children, without murmur or complaint.

Of his grand-sons, line of Walter, three were ministers and

141

orators of ability, two doctors, including one of the ministers, two of whom are still living.

Of his great-grand-sons, some live; one was a commissioned captain in Union army, civil war, who had a brother killed in same service.

Two brothers (including the captain) served in the West Virginia Legislature, one in both Houses, and was Speaker of the Senate, both have been, and are still, acting Judges, one in Circuit Court, the other on the Supreme Bench of the State.

Three others, two great, and one great-great-grand-son, same line, are lawyers of ability.

Several daughters of both Thomas and Walter lived to maturity and raised families of whom some have filled places of honor and public trust.

---

## THE MILLERS AND THEIR KIN.

### By Dr. Joseph Lyon Miller.

September 15th, 1749, there landed on the banks of the Delaware five hundred and fifty foreigners from several of the German states and cities, having sailed from Rotterdam, Holland, over a month before in the ship Phoenix, John Mason captain.

Most of them settled in Pennsylvania, but some moved on and joined their countrymen already settled in Virginia. It was of this class of pioneers that John Esten Cooke, one of Virginia's leading historians, says: "These Germans or Palatines were excellent people, and remarkable for their true piety. Like the Huguenots, they infused an admirable element into Virginia society—a brave and sturdy element which lingers in their descendants; among whom is a hardy soldier and ex-governor of Virginia, General Kemper."

Another writer says that though plain people they could nearly all read and write, which was more than could be said of any other class of settlers taken as a whole.

142

Among those who came in the Phoenix were, Jacob, Christian, Philip, and Peter Mueller, sons of Ulrich Mueller, a Burgher of Zweibrucken one of the chief towns of the Palatines. A burgher, I am told, belonged to a class in the German society of that day corresponding to that of the country squire in England.

The Muellers stopped for a season in the town of Yorke, Pennsylvania; then two settled permanently in that colony, one went to Maryland, and the fourth, Jacob Mueller, with his wife Bar-

CHRISTIAN MILLER.

bara and six children, crossed into Virginia by way of the old Packhorse Ford just east of Shepherdstown, Maryland, and settled in the Shenandoah Valley early in 1752.

From an old patent in my possession, I notice that Lord Fairfax, April 2, 1752, granted him 400 acres of land on Narrow Passage river near the border line between Frederick and Augusta counties. March 31, and April 1, 1755, he purchased from Joseph Helm two tracts of land of two hundred acres each for one hundred pounds and five shillings, and "the rent of one year of Indian corn on the Feast of Saint Michail if the same shall be lawfully demanded." In the next four years he bought about four hundred acres more from various parties; and on the 1st and 2d of January, 1766, Lord Fairfax made him two more grants, together containing 740 acres, thus making him owner of about 1,950 acres of land in one of the finest parts of the valley. According to Henning of March 1761 he laid out 1,200 acres of this land into a town, ninety-six acres being divided into half acre lots and the remainder into streets and outlets of five acres each. At first the town was called Muellerstadt, as can be learned from Kercheval, who says, "This town seems to have been originally laid out upon a larger scale than any of our ancient villages." In 1761 when the place was "erected into a town" its name was changed to Woodstock by George Washington, who was the Burgess at that time from Frederick county. The main street was called King street, and the parallel streets on either side were known as Duke William and Queen, while two of the cross streets were named Fairfax and Martin. These names were all changed after the revolution. The lots were not sold but leased by Jacob Miller, the consideration varying from twenty shillings to twenty pounds; and each lease contained a curious provision binding the owner to build a house with either "a stone or brick chimney."

Jacob Miller was born about 1698 and died in May 1766. He was a man of some education for he signed all his leases and will, and his inventory mentions "to all the Books English and Dutch £2, 5s." This same inventory calls for personal property worth five hundred and twenty-seven pounds, three shillings, and one penny, showing him to have been one of the wealthiest men of his day in that section. His will and inventory mentions besides his wife, Barbara, his children, Ulrich, Jacob, Barbara (mar. Brubaker), Christian, Susannah, Mary, and Martin named for Lord Fairfax's nephew; with "George Decon servant man" and "Elizabeth Smith servant maid."

———————

Christian Miller, 3rd son of Jacob and Barbara Miller was born in Zweibrucken in 1744 and died in Woodstock, Virginia, April 28th, 1836. A newspaper account of that date states that he was the last of the soldiers of the revolution in Shenandoah county and that his funeral was the largest ever seen in that town. From August 1780 to May 1781 he was a Sergeant in Captain Jacob Rinker's Virginia company of Continental soldiers. Kercheval, the historian, refers to him several times regarding some of the old Germans customs and the Indian raids around Woodstock. He has been described as being "Rather tall and portly with brown eyes and clean shaven face, his hair in a queue. He wore a cocked hat, long blue coat a frilled shirt and stock, yellow waistcoat, grayish homespun breeches and low shoes with silver buckles." He was comfortably well off.

In 1771 he married Catharine Wiseman, born in 1746, and died in May 1837, who bore him ten children, eight of whom grew to maturity and married, leaving descendants that are now scattered in sixteen southern and western states. In all branches of the family there are many who have held offices of public trust and honor, from the lowest county offices to those of the State Assembly and Auditor; one sat in Congress for several years and another was a personal friend of President Cleveland and his Commissioner of Internal Revenue. They have done their duty on the battlefield also. Two sons and a grandson as private, corporal and ensign in the war of 1812; grandson and great grandson as private and captain both gave up their life in the Mexican war; nineteen grandsons and great grandsons did their duty in the Confederate army, there being ten privates, one musician, one sergeant, two lieutenants, three captains, and two majors; and lastly four gt., gt., grandsons and one gt., gt., gt., grand son served their country as two privates, one corporal, a captain, and a major in the war with Spain. As to occupation they are farmers, merchants, lawyers, doctors, civil engineers, etc. Their names are to be found on the roll books of most of the leading colleges of their native states, as for example in Virginia we notice them on the rolls of: The University (since 1830), Va. Military Inst., Randolph Macon, Hampden Sidney, Univ. College of Medicine, Hollins, Fairfax Hall, Episcopal School at Staunton, and Weslyn Female Institute at the same place.

And so it may be said of Christian Miller that:

"The lad that sported years ago
  In Shenandoah fields,
Hath made his life as bountiful
  And as blessed as their yields;

As tender as the skies that stretch
  Above old Woodstock town
And as pure as are the winds that blow
  From bleak Mount Jackson down."

I have collected the necessary data for an extensive genealogical history of nearly all of the descendants of Christian Miller, but the remainder of this sketch will be devoted to the family of his son, John Miller who settled in the Kanawha Valley. To save space I shall omit many of the dates of birth, etc., of the generations now living, and also some other matter of minor importance.

———

John Miller, third son of Christian and Catharine Miller, was born at Woodstock, May 31, 1781. Being of an adventurous spirit he went "west" to the Great Kanawha Valley in 1795 to make his own fortune. His father gave him forty pounds in money and the advice never to go security for any man, as he had done to his sorrow, and "always act fairly and squarely in everything." He stopped for a time at Fort Clendenin, where he met the girl who became his first wife ten years later. Later he settled in Gallipolis, an old French town four miles below the mouth of the Kanawha, where he found but two other persons who could speak English—a Colonel Safford and a Mr. Murry—so he had to learn French which made him conversant with three languages, French, German and English. Here he followed the business of a hatter until 1810 when he abandoned it for farming which was more to his taste.

January 26, 1806, he was married to Sophia Clendenin, daughter of Maj. William Clendenin, and his wife Margaret Handley. Wm. Clendenin, the second son of Charles Clendenin, was born May 23, 1758, and died in 1828. His wife was a daughter of John Handley, born May 10, 1762, and died in 1835. William Clendenin was a private in the battle of Point Pleasant in 1774.

146

and later was commissioned Major in the Kanawha militia of which his brother George was Colonel and Daniel Boone Lt. Colonel. He represented Kanawha county in the Virginia Assembly in 1796, 1801, and 1803; and was her Collector of Levies in 1792, 1793, and 1794. Was also a Justice of the Peace and member of the first court in the county held at his house in 1789. About 1790 Major Clendenin settled on the Ohio river nearly opposite Gallipolis. In 1804 he carried the petition to the Assembly asking for the organization of Mason county, whose first representative he became in 1805. His daughter Anne, born July 31, 1799, married in 1815 Henry Miller (brother of John), a Corporal in the war of 1812.

In 1810 John Miller moved his family across the Ohio to the Virginia side where he had purchased a part of the farm now known as "Elwell," home of Judge C. P. T. Moore. Here he built in the valley between the river and hill a brick house one and a half stories high with big rooms and a wide hall on the first floor. This old house stood until a few years ago, and is said to have been the first brick residence in Mason county (Sketch of C. C. Miller in the History of the Kanawha Valley). The second brick house is that opposite Point Pleasant owned by Mrs. Ella Henderson Hutchinson, and built by her grandfather Samuel Henderson in 1811. The Elwell place was given to John Miller's eldest son, Christopher, who sold it to Judge Moore. In 1819 John Miller moved again, this time to Teay's Valley where he bought a thousand acres on the Richmond and Lexington turnpike, to which he later added several hundred more and continued farming. Here the family were often called upon to entertain strangers travelling that thoroughfare connecting Virginia with Kentucky; for as Miss Emily Mason, in speaking of her first visit to Virginia from Lexington with her father and his family in 1820 and of subsequent journeys across the mountains, says: "In all the distance from Leesburg, Virginia, to Lexington, Kentucky, there did not exist an inn or a tavern, only in cities could such a demoralizing institution be found. In the morning, we would leave our lodgings, with every expression of good will,—no word being hinted of payment, which would have been an insult. My father would go in advance, as evening approached, to look for the most available house. There we

147

would be received with a cordial and cheery welcome; the best was set before us; and the yawning feather beds soon closed above our weary heads. I remember hearing one of our kind entertainers say of a family living near, 'oh, they are very fine; the daughters wear calico every day.' That was in the day when all wore homespun, and we wove our own blankets and our linen sheets.'' I have heard my father say that several times Henry Clay, Marshall and other great Kentuckians were the honored guests of his father in Teay's Valley.

It was here in the valley that John Miller's wife died April 17, 1823, (having been born March 27, 1783). October 23rd of the same year the widower married Sallie Henderson, daughter of Col. John and Elizabeth Stodghill Henderson, of ''Henderson,'' at the mouth of Kanawha. Col. Henderson came from one of the oldest families of Fifeshire, Scotland, and was connected with the families of Bruce, Hamilton, Harrison, Stuart and others. His grandfather was Lieut. James Henderson, of the French and Indian war; his father, John Henderson, was a lieutenant at the battle of Point Pleasant in the army of his brother-in-law Gen. Andrew Lewis, and later served through the revolution in Gen. Daniel Morgan's Virginia Regiment. Col. Henderson himself was first a lieutenant in the 79th Va. Regt. in 1795, then 1st Major of the 106th Regt. according to an old muster roll of 1812, and in 1815 commissioned Colonel of the same regiment. He was Mason county's representative in the Virginia Assembly for eight years between 1809 and 1820 inclusive; in 1804 he was a member of her first court and in other years between that and 1820 he was her Collector of Levies and High Sheriff. He was born August 30, 1768, and died August 19, 1824. In 1792 he married Elizabeth Stodghill, daughter of John and Elizabeth Harvey Stodghill. She was born August 3, 1776, and died February 20, 1846. One of her sisters married Hugh Caperton, and another John Arbuckle.

Sallie Henderson Miller was born January 6th, 1797, and died January 26th, 1872. In 1831 the Miller family removed for the last time, this time settling in the Kanawha Valley about four miles from Point Pleasant; here John Miller purchased a farm known as Locust Hill, and another about five miles farther up the river known as Beech Hill, the two together contain about nine hundred acres and are still owned by his descendants. Originally they were a part of the George Washington grant in 1772. Besides his land John Miller owned about twenty-five negroes and other personal property in proportion. June 12th, 1838, he divided his lands, negroes, and other property among the children of his first wife, excepting the Kanawha land, nine negroes and other property which he retained for the children by his second wife; the children of the first binding themselves not to claim any of this reserved property at his death. For over forty years he was a Master Mason and was one of the charter members of Morning Dawn Lodge, at Gallipolis. John Miller died of quinsy, March 19th, 1846. In appearance he was tall and muscular, clean shaven, and had black hair and eyes; and it has been said was very fine looking. He had a fair education, was very shrewd, fond of a jest and of ''good living.''

The four sons and one daughter by his first wife, and the six daughters and one son by his last, who grew to maturity and married, will be taken up with their descendants in regular order.

————

CHILDREN OF JOHN AND SOPHIE CLENDENIN MILLER.

Christopher Miller, born December 6th, 1806, and still living in 1900. In 1830 he married Letitia Hamilton, of Richmond, a neice of Major John Cantrell. Before the war he was Sheriff of Mason county for two years. Being of a roving disposition he has travelled and lived in nearly every Western State, but principally in Missouri, where his children live in Union county.

————

William Clendenin Miller, born January 26th, 1809, died July 27th, 1886. For over half a century he was one of Cabell county's most prominent business men, as a farmer and merchant. His home at Barboursville was one of the most elegant and hospitable in the county. The house and ''office,'' built of brick, contain fourteen rooms and four halls, and before the war were always filled with a crowd of gay young people. March 6th, 1838, he married Eliza Gardner, of Greenup, Kentucky. Her family history is both interesting and romantic. A few years before the French Revolution her grandfather, the Marquis

149

Maison De la Geneste, left France and settled in the Island of St. Domingo. Here he purchased three sugar plantations and several hundred negroes—nine hundred I was told by his great grandson, the late Judge H. J. Samuels, of Cabell county. He had but one child, a daughter named Marie Terese Sophie Clotilde Rason De la Geneste, who at the age of fourteen became the wife of Mr. Gardner, a merchant trader sailing out of Boston. Her father opposed this marriage very much on account of the difference in family rank. But Mr. Gardner sold his ships and settled down on the plantation in St. Domingo. In 1796 came the Insurrection of the Slaves. By means of a faithful slave they escaped to a United States vessel and later landed at Philadelphia, with only their clothing, two servants, who chose to come with them and some costly jewels that Madame had concealed from the mob. Here they sold a pair of solitaire diamond earrings for two thousand dollars, with which they decided to go to the French, in Louisiana. They went to Pittsburg by stage coach and there took passage on a flat boat loaded for New Orleans. The water was low in the Ohio and near Greenup, Ky., the boat ran aground. Being tired of the slow journey already Mr. and Mrs. Gardiner decided to stop here instead of going on to Louisiana. So they rented the largest house in the village and opened an inn, which became a famous hostelry in that part of Kentucky in the first half of the nineteenth century. Several pieces of costly jewelry were handed down to their descendants, among them a pair of diamond cuff buttons to Judge Samuels. Later they received a partial indemnity from the French Government. From an old letter written at Paris in 1854 I see that the "fifteenth annuity of the St. Domingo Indemnity due the heirs of the late Mq. Maison Dela Geneste" was due in 1852. William and Eliza Miller were the parents of six children: Charles, the first son, is a large timber land owner in the back counties on the Guyandotte.

George F., second son, was a captain on the staff of General John S. Williams, C. S. A. After the war he entered the Clerk's office at Indianapolis, Indiana. Here he married a daughter of Colonel Alexander Davidson, and granddaughter of Noah Noble, Governor of Indiana in 1831 to 1837.

William, third son, owns a beautiful farm and home on the Guyan river. His wife was Annie Curtis, of Kentucky.

Joseph S., fourth son, is a prominent lawyer and for eight years was Commissioner of Internal Revenue under President Cleveland. He was Auditor of West Virginia from 1877 to 1885; and is a writer of dialect verses and short stories for the New York Sun. His wife was Florence Trice, of Maryland.

Eugenia, the eldest daughter, married Prof. B. H. Thackston, of Marshall College, West Virginia.

Florence Gardner married George F. Miller, president of the Huntington First National Bank.

————

Charles Clendenin Miller, born February 23d, 1811, died March 13, 1898, took a prominent part in the affairs of Mason county as a merchant, farmer and banker. From 1834 to 1846 he was High Sheriff of the county, and later State Senator from that district. In 1843 he became the first president of the Point Pleasant Merchants' and Mechanics' National Bank, and continued so till 1879, when he retired to "Spring Hill," his country home, about a mile from Point Pleasant. This is considered one of the handsomest places on Kanawha and contained at that time about three thousand acres. The house built of brick and set in a grove of trees that cover several acres, is a fine example of the big, roomy antebellum Virginia home. In 1831 Charles C. Miller was married to Eleanor, only daughter of John Cantrell, who was a major in the war of 1812, and for several years a member of the Virginia Assembly. There was but one son, John Cantrell Miller, who grew to maturity. He was a merchant, and married first Amanda Handley, daughter of John Handley, of Mason county. His second wife was Maria Bowyer, daughter of Hon. John Bowyer, of Putnam county. There were four daughters born to Charles and Eleanor Miller. Sophia married General George Bowyer, of Winfield. Eleanor B. married Captain Robert Buffington, whose first wife was her aunt, Eliza Miller. After Captain Buffington's death she married Frank Dashner. Margaret married John Dashner, a farmer in Carroll county, Mo. Anna married E. S. Bright, a Mason county merchant.

In 1856 Charles C. Miller married again. This time to Virginia

Middlecoff, daughter of Jacob and Sarah Wilson Middlecoff. Her grandmother was Sarah Christian, a sister of Colonel William Christian, of the battle of Point Pleasant and the Revolution. The Christians are one of the oldest and best families in the Isle of Man. There were two children born to this marriage: Blanche Cantrell, married Rankin Wiley, a Point Pleasant lawyer, and one time president of the West Virginia Senate (1892). And Edith Clendennin, who married Ben Stephens, a Mason county farmer and stockman.

––––

Henry Harrison Miller, born December, 1813, and now living in Covington, Kentucky. Before the war he carried on a large mercantile business in Guyandotte, but owing to his Southern sympathies his home and other property, with that of other sympathizers, was burned by the "Home Guards," of Proctorsville, Ohio. After the war he moved to Covington and became a Cincinnati commission merchant. In 1837 he married Eliza Chapman, of one of the best families of Cabell county. Of their children, who grew up, Edgar, the only son, is a wholesale fruit merchant in Cincinnati. His wife was Matilda Bond, of Louisville. Frances married Fred Beuhring, of Cabell county. Leonora married Collins Thornburg, of the same county. Arabella married Colbert Cecil, a Catlettsburg, Ky., merchant, grandson of Kinzy Berry Cecil, one of the early Kentucky pioneers from a good old English family. Cora married John Metcalf, of Cincinnati.

––––

Margaret Miller, born November 25th, 1818, died August 19th, 1859. December 12th, 1837, she married Hon. Thomas Thornburg, a Cabell county farmer and merchant. He was a member of the Virginia Assembly beginning in 1857 and in 1872 a member of the West Virginia Constitutional Convention. He was a Master Mason and for forty-six consecutive years secretary of the Cabell County Lodge No. 13. Their eldest son, John Thornburg, was a first lieutenant in the command of General A. J. Jenkins, C. S. A. He married Mary Long, of Mason county, where he now lives, doing business as a banker and Kanawha farmer, making a specialty of thoroughbred Hereford cattle. George, the second son, is a merchant at Barboursville, also owning and managing several large farms in Cabell county. His wife was Nannie Wilson, of that county. Bayley, the third son, was also a farmer and merchant. His wife was Nettie Samuels, daughter of Judge Samuels, one time member of the West Virginia Legislature. Elizabeth Thornburg married Dr. A. B. McGuinnis, of Guyandotte. Ellen married Captain Will Hovey, U. S. A. Mary and Margaret are yet single.

––––

CHILDREN OF JOHN MILLER AND HIS SECOND WIFE, SALLIE HENDERSON.

Nancy Miller, born October 1st, 1827. Married, September 16th, 1852, Rev. Stephen Kisling Vaught, of Kentucky. He was one of the leading ministers of the Southern Methodist Church in the West Virginia Conference from 1842 till 1879. They had two sons who grew to maturity. First, Dr. Robert Lee Vaught, who graduated second in a large class at Vanderbilt University in 1886, besides receiving several other honors, including a place as Interne at the Nashville City Hospital. Later he removed to Chattanooga, where he built up a large practice and became professor of anatomy in the Chattanooga Medical College. August 28th, 1895, he was drowned while bathing in the Kanawha river. Second, William Henderson Vaught, who now owns Locust Hill, the old Miller home. He is considered one of the best farmers in the valley, and makes a specialty of thoroughbred Black Pole cattle. In 1895 he married the only daughter of Walter Hardin Hogg, of Mason county. He is a descendant of Major Peter Hogg, the famous Augusta county lawyer. Major Hogg was an intimate friend of Washington and of Lord Fairfax, as well as one of the latter's executors. In 1754 he was commissioned a captain in Washington's regiment in the French and Indian war. In 1772 he was granted some eight thousand acres of land in Mason county.

James Henderson Miller, the only son of John Miller by his second wife, was born June 6th, 1829, and died at Beech Hill February 19th, 1898. He was educated by private teachers and at Marshall Academy, where all the boys of that section of Virginia before the war were sent to school. He was there in 1845 and 1846, about seven years after the founding of the academy. In 1849 he moved on the Beech Hill place, part of which he in-

herited and part purchased from his sister. He was an old-time
Southern Democrat, and in 1860 voted the Breckinridge and
Lane ticket, though he took no active part in the war or in politics, except as a commissioner or judge of the County Court for
four years. I have a copy of this old ticket that he perserved,
which, besides pictures of the candidates, tells also the principles
they represented—"The Constitution. The Sovereignty and
Equality of the States; The Repeal of the Missouri Restriction;
The People of the Territories in forming State Governments to
adopt their own Institutions; Equal Protection to Citizens Native and Naturalized, and to every species of property." Below
is given a list of the electors, and I notice that the Fourteenth
District was represented by John G. Newman, of Kanawha.

March 27, 1851, Henderson Miller was married to Harriet E.
Craig, daughter of James Kennerly Craig, one of the leading
planters of the Kanawha Valley. His old chum at Marshall, Albert J. Jenkins, who later was one of the generals of the Confederate Army, was the groomsman on this occasion. James K.
Craig was a grandson of Rev. John Craig, one of the first Presbyterian ministers in the Valley of Virginia. He was born in
New Dunager, County Antrim, Ireland, August 7th, 1709; received the degree of M. A. from the University of Edinburgh in
1733; and arrived in America August 17th, 1734. There are
many interesting stories related of this old gentleman, but I have
not room for but one. In selecting the site of the "Tinkling
Spring" Church the congregation disregarded his wishes and he
declared that "none of that water should ever tinkle down his
throat," and for forty years he kept his word, even in the summer days, when he preached from ten in the morning until sunset
with only an hour of intermission. One of his sermons yet ex-
tant, is divided into *fifty-five* heads. Mrs. Miller's mother was
Catharine, daughter of Captain William and Catharine Madison
Arbuckle. Captain Arbuckle was a well known Indian fighter,
and his wife, the widow of another one—Lieutenant John Mc-
Clannahan. Her father was John Madison, the first clerk of
Augusta county, and for several years her representative in the
House of Burgesses. His relationship to President Madison's
father has never been positively settled—whether he was uncle
or cousin—but they both sprang from the same ancestor. This

154

was Captain John Madison, who settled in Gloucester county in 1652-3, between which date and 1662 he was granted 2080 acres of land. One of Catharine Madison Arbuckle's brothers was Bishop James Madison, the first American born Episcopal Bishop; another was a general in the Revolution; and the others held high positions in Virginia and Kentucky.

Henderson and Harriet Craig Miller were the parents of six children, who grew to maturity. First, Willie Anna, married Henry Hannan Eastham, a grandson of George Eastham, of Farquier county, one of the soldiers in the battle of Point Pleasant. Second, John David, who married Elizabeth Downing Wilhoite, of one of the oldest families of Woodford county, Kentucky. Third, Minnie J., married V. B. Bishop, a large retail and wholesale merchant in Highland county, Virginia. He is a descendant of the Bishop and Peale families of Rockingham. Fourth, George Kennerly, married Anna Moore, of Ohio. Fifth, James Henderson, Jr., married Beatrice Brockmeyer, of Huntington. Sixth, Sarah Vaught, married Samuel Couch, son of the late Hon. James H. Couch, of "Holmwood," Mason county, and grandson of Dr. Daniel Couch, of Williamsburgh. Mrs. Miller died February 2d, 1872, and September 29th, 1874, J. H. Miller married Finetta Lyon, daughter of Joseph Lyon, of Woodford county, Kentucky. The Lyon family were among the early settlers in Central Kentucky from Virginia. The family came to Maryland from Perthshire, Scotland, about the middle of the eighteenth century. Stephen Lyon, the emigrant, was killed in the French and Indian war, October, 1754. Mrs. Miller's maternal line, also early settlers in Central Kentucky, goes back through the Jelfs, Davises, Criglers, Aylors, Fieldings and others to the early years of Virginia. The first of the Davis family in Virginia was John Davis, son of John and Johanna Hewlinge Davis, of Gloucestershire, England, who settled on Queene's Creek, York county, in 1623; his inventory was recorded here September 14th, 1646. After Bacon's Rebellion John Davis' grandson, John Davis, settled in Westmoreland county, where he married in 1691 Susannah Day, widow of Solomon Day, as shown by an old deed in my possession, in which they convey to George Brent 200 acres of land. Their son, Thomas Davis, who owned a large plantation in Stafford county, married Sarah

155

Fielding, daughter of Edward Fielding, one of the wealthiest planters in Northumberland county. Their son William married Catharine Carter, daughter of James Carter, November 17th, 1755. Thomas and Sarah Fielding Davis were the great-great-great-grandparents of Finnetta Lyon Miller. Space forbids me from mentioning the generations that come between. The name Fielding has been used as a given name in all the generations of the Davis family since 1720. There were two sons born to the second marriage of Henderson Miller. First, Dr. Joseph Lyon, the author of this sketch. I spent all my early life on the farm in the Kanawha Valley, except the years spent at college. I was educated at the Methodist School in Cabell county, now known as the Maurice Harvey College, had two years at the University of Nashville, and received my medical training in Richmond at the University College of Medicine, in charge of the celebrated surgeon, Dr. Hunter McGuire. Inheriting a love for Virginia history, I have made considerable research into her early history, and have embodied some of it in several newspaper and magazine articles. In 1900 I accepted the position of assistant physician to the Davis Coal and Coke Company's employes at Thomas, Tucker county. The second son is Stephen Kisling Miller, who now owns the old home at Beech Hill, on the Kanawha, that has been in the Miller family since it passed from the hands of the Washingtons. He is considered one of the brightest business men that have gone out from Mason county; and being a fine machinist is employed by the Deering Harvester Company to travel over West Virginia and part of Virginia setting up and starting their machines.

Anne Eliza Miller, born November 8, 1831, died of cholera at St. Louis July 16th, 1854. November 13th, 1850, she married Captain James Robert Buffington, of Mobile, Alabama. He was a native Virginian and was from one of the oldest families of Cabell county. They had one son, Llannes Buffington, who now lives in Fort Worth, Texas.

Mary Caroline Miller, born February 20th, 1834, died December, 1899. May 24th, 1859, she married Absalom P. Chapman, a merchant at Guyandotte, and member of an old Sandy Valley family. They had one daughter, who grew to maturity. This is Emma Evelyn, now the wife of Charles E. McCulloch, who owns one of the largest Kanawha Valley places in Mason county. He is a son of John and Mary Bryan McCulloch. The McCullochs were originally from Maryland, where they settled prior to the Revolution. Mrs. McCulloch was a granddaughter of George Clendenin, founder of Charleston, colonel of Kanawha militia, first representative of Kanawha county in the Assembly, &c.; her mother, Parthenia Clendenin, was first married to Governor Jonathon Meigs, of Ohio, and was mother of Return Jonathon Meigs, also Governor of Ohio.

Rhoda James Miller, born October 13th, 1836, married July 25th, 1855, Edmund Pendleton, Chancellor of Wood county. Most of his life was spent as captain of one of the large Ohio river passenger steamers, and under President Cleveland he was United States Inspector of Steam Vessels for the Ohio river and its tributaries. He is descended from a fine English family dating back to one of the law officers of William, the Conqueror. In 1682 Captain Richard Chancellor, a soldier of Charles II., was implicated in Monmouth's Rebellion and fled to Virginia, where he settled in Westmoreland county. His sword and other relics were handed down in the family until destroyed in the burning of Chancellorsville, the home of Rev. Melzi Chancellor, in the civil war. Here Captain Chancellor married Catharine, daughter of William and Catharine Fitzgerald Cooper, and granddaughter of Richard Cooper, one of the charter members of the Virginia Company, who settled in Virginia in 1634. Edmund Pendleton Chancellor's grandfather, Thomas Chancellor, was a private in the Virginia line in the Revolution: his wife was Judith Gaines, neice of Edmund Pendleton. Edmund and Rhoda Miller Chancellor are the parents of four children: Edmund Pendleton, Jr., married Belle Carnahan. Eugenia married Castella Rathbone. Rose Carroll and Nan Preston still single.

Sarah Emily Miller, born November 20th, 1839, married September 18th, 1870, Hunter Ben Jenkins, of St. Louis. He is general agent of one of the large Mississippi river packet companies. He is of Virginia descent and is connected with the Leggets, Yosts, Kyles and other families of the Valley of Virginia. They have two sons, William and George.

# THE WILLIAM MORRIS FAMILY.

## PIONEERS OF KANAWHA VALLEY.

### By W. S. Laidley.

It has been conceded by all persons that pretend to know anything of the history of this Valley that William Morris and his family were the first white people that made a permanent settlement in the Kanawha Valley, and that they arrived here in the spring of 1774, or the fall of 1773, the exact date not now being known. He came from Culpepper county, Virginia, but whether he came directly or stopped on the route, is uncertain.

Before the arrival of William Morris, there had been an attempt made by one Walter Kelly to make a settlement on the Kanawha river, at the mouth of Kelly's creek, and some small improvement made, but Kelly was killed by the Indians, and when William Morris arrived, there was no white man in the valley and no settlement whatever.

We append hereto a diagram of the river, showing the streams from the junction of the New and Gauley rivers, along the Kanawha river, down to the mouth of Elk river. These streams have since acquired their names and are given, as they are now known.

KANAWHA AND NEW RIVER, WITH TRIBUUTARIES.

William Morris, when a boy about twelve years old, was about the Scotch-yards in London, which place was a police headquarters, and near the Thames, and out of curiosity he went aboard of a vessel, and while the boy was aboard and looking about, the ship left her mooring and he found himself on the way to America. After he arrived at Philadelphia, he found that the vessel would not return to England for some months, and the owner of the vessel took the boy to his own home and there he was cared for and given an opportunity to show the spirit that was in him. The merchant was so pleased with young William Morris, that he wrote to the boy's father for permission to retain him, and William remained until he was grown and afterwards. He then went to Virginia.

. He married Miss Elizabeth Stips, in Orange County. Whether he lived in Orange, and after the organization of Culpepper, found himself in the new county or whether he made a removal, we know not.

When William Morris reached the Kanawha Valley, he made his settlement at the mouth of Kellys creek, on the spot where Walter Kelly had attempted to make his home.

The family of William Morris was of such number and strength that an ordinary Indian party was not willing to make an attack

159

upon them, and the Morrises made arrangements to remain and if necessary to fight it out on these lines.

They were on the ground when General Andrew Lewis with his little army marched from Lewisburg to the mouth of the Kanawha, or from Camp Union to Point Pleasant, which was in the fall of 1774. The sons of William Morris, John and Henry, went into this army, and were at the battle of Point Pleasant.

Afterwards, as the children of Walter Kelly became of age, William Morris presented each with a horse, saddle and bridle, although said heirs had no title to the land and had no claim against Morris, but to satisfy them that he did not want to take from them any claim they might have had, without compensation, as Kelly had cleared a small patch and had tried to raise a crop and made some improvements thereon, he paid this compensation.

It seems that William Morris and family went to work immediately upon his arrival in this new country, and with his family made rapid progress in opening farms and building houses, and making preparations of defense against marauding parties of Indians, which for many years afterwards, were constantly prowling through the country.

Shadrach Harriman was the last white man killed in this part of the country, which was in 1794. This Morris settlement was in a wilderness. It was one hundred miles west of Lewisburg in the then county of Botetourt, afterwards Greenbrier, and about the same distance to the Ohio river, on which there were no settlements below Wheeling or Pittsburg.

In this wild wilderness of woods there were all sorts of animals: in the river there were fish, and plenty of wild fruits and nuts in the woods. There was no danger of starvation, and in one season they would have their corn and gardens to rely upon.

But for the great drawback, the savage Indians, the enterprise of making the settlement would have been made a pic-nic, but with this eternal danger, it was anything else but a frolic.

Imagine this small settlement, in the upper part of the valley, with no market, they had to depend upon themselves for everything.

They brought their guns and ammunition, their plows, hoes, axes, mattocks and all other tools they had. There were no markets and no transportation, no stores nor mills nor factories. They must manufacture their own goods or wear buckskin, and it was a long ways east to go for powder, and nothing to the west could be had.

There were not many other settlers that came until in 1788 when the Clendenins came and made their settlement at the mouth of Elk river. And when the county of Kanawha was organized in 1789, it was said there were but thirteen voters in the county, but there were 118 residents of said county, in the year 1792.

William Morris was now an old man, and in 1792 he made his will and in January, 1793, it was admitted to probate, which was the first will recorded in the new county and it will be found in deed book A, page 30.

His age is not known, but from the best information we have, he was at least seventy years old and probably older.

The will of William Morris disposed of his real estate and mentions the names of his ten children. He evidently had fears that his wife might wish "to engage herself in the bonds of wedlock" and he provided that in such event, that the property he had given to her should revert to his estate. She was not satisfied with the provision that he had made for her by his will, for the record of the Court shows that "she came into Court and broke the said will." She preferred to take her dower provided by law, rather than accept the provisions of the will made for her.

She afterwards married a young Irishman by the name of Thompson, but she did not long survive her first husband.

Leonard and John, the sons of William Morris, were the executors of said will, and the witnesses thereto were Jacob Skiles, John Cammel, William Morris, Jr., John Jones and Franky Jones.

John Jones and Levi Morris were on the bond of the executors, in the penalty of one thousand pounds. Jacob Casdorph, John Moss, and John Cammel appraised his personal estate, which was three hundred and sixty pounds. There were Dudley, Jim, Deriah, Sally and a girl, slaves of deceased.

From 1774 to 1792-3, William Morris resided in the Kanawha Valley with his family. He had a wife and ten children when he arrived, eight sons and two daughters, probably each of his sons had a wife with some children, and they came with some horses and other stock through a wilderness where there was no road, and settled down to hew out of the woods a home for themselves and their posterity.

They were English and they were Baptists, and they had a little church near the mouth of Kellys creek, close to the spot where the little brick Methodist church now stands, and we hear that the records of this church are with some of the descendants to this day.

They were all moral men and many of them religious men. They lived for years surrounded by dangers that might at any hour destroy their lives. They saw a civil government established, and a town spring up near to their homes.

He lived through the Indian wars, through the war for Independence, saw the government of the United States inaugurated as well as that of the county of Kanawha and the town of Charlestown. Then the old Patriarch William, the Pioneer of this Valley, found that he must go to another world, and he made his last will and he died and was buried, somewhere, no one knows where.

In the history of Kanawha county by Gov. G. W. Atkinson, he did not attempt to give the genealogy of this family and said it could not be done, and still insists it can not be done, owing to the great number of them, the repetition of the names and their inter-marriages, the want of family records, and the absence of monuments, &c.

We shall not raise any issue on this allegation, but will give such as we can, in the best way that we can, and we know of no one that can contradict the same.

The children of William Morris, the Pioneer, are as follows:

A. William Morris, Jr., known as "Major Billy".
B. Henry Morris.
C. Leonard Morris.
D. Joshua Morris.
E. John Morris.
F. Carlos or Carrol Morris.
G. Levi Morris.
H. Benjamin Morris.
I. Elizabeth Morris.
J. Franky Morris.

These are given by the will of the old pioneer, to which we have referred.

## MAJOR WILLIAM MORRIS.

This was the eldest son of the old Pioneer. He was born December 17, 1746. Whether in Orange or Culpepper or some other county, is not definitely known.

Catherine Carroll was born March 15, 1751, somewhere in Maryland, and they were married May 10, 1768.

When and how this family learned of the Kanawha valley and caught the western fever of emigration, has not been learned. In 1769 the western limit of civilization was in the country now called Greenbrier, and the inhabitants were not numerous. There may have been some hunters or explorers that had visited this part of the world, but there are no particulars of their reports.

This son came with his father, and with his own wife and children, He seems to have made his home at the mouth of Kellys creek, and it is supposed that when his father became old, this son took the care of the farm from his father.

He seems to have been engaged in making his home and farm comfortable, and especially engaged in searching out the country for good tracts of land, and he became possessed of many large tracts of choice lands.

When the new county of Kanawha was formed, he was one of its Justices, and he was also one of the trustees appointed for the town of Charlestown and Point Pleasant, when said town was afterwards established.

There was no more important person in the settlement than he, who was known in later life, as Major William Morris, to distinguish him from the many bearing the same name.

He was in the Legislature from this county in 1792, 1793, 1794, 1796, 1797, 1798, 1800.

He was sheriff in 1801.

In an old family Bible, in which is written "The property of Will Morris, June 2, 1796," we find the following:

"Aug. 19, 1794, William Morris and Catherine Morris, his wife, "were taken in the Baptist church and on the 20th she was bap- "tized."

This book became the property of John Morris, says: "John Mor-"ris, this his book, Apl 2, 1816." Afterwards we find the endorsement, "Catherine Morris, the owner of this book, died Sept. 3, 1823. Signed, "John Hansford, Sr., 1824."

This book was also the property of John Hansford, Sr., and in 1854 it belonged to Felix G. Hansford, and now is in the hands of Bradford Noyes Hansford. The book was printed in 1791, by Isaiah Thomas in Mass.

It also appears in this Bible that William Morris was born December 17, 1746, and Catherine Morris was born March 15, 1751, and that Catherine died September 3, 1823.

The children of Major William and Catherine Morris were:

1. Jane—born Nov. 3, 1770; mar. Maj. John Hansford.
2. Gabriel—born Dec. 27, 1772.
3. William—born Dec. 16, 1775, mar. Polly Barnes.
4. Catherine—born Jan. 13, 1778; mar. Chas. Venable.
5. Carroll—born Nov. 2, 1779.
6. John—born Aug. 24, 1783.
7. Cynthia—born Jan. 5, 1792; mar. Isaac Noyes.

OF CATHERINE CARROLL.

In our Oct., 1904, Mag., it is said that Stephen Teays married Mary Carroll, and that she came to the Kanawha on a visit to her aunt, Mrs. Catherine Morris. And it is tradition that the Carrolls, whose ancestors were Catherines, owned land where the city of Washington was afterwards located. If this is correct then they were descendants of Daniel Carroll of Maryland, who owned a farm where Washington now is.

Mrs. Morris was a woman of more than ordinary attainments, and was highly respected by all who knew her. She outlived her husband about twenty years, and by her will she left her estate to her daughters Mrs. Jane Hansford, Mrs. Catherin Venable, and Mrs. Cynthia Noyes.

• The Morris family secured a large estate in land and there were patents issued to them in Botetourt, Greenbrier and Kanawha, and other counties; and Major William was the owner of most of these lands.

In the early days, the accumulation of a large personal estate was unusual if not an impossibility. There was not much money, and tobacco was made a legal tender. This was neither a safe nor a convenient investment for pioneers, so far from market.

The will of Major William Morris was recorded in April, 1803, and he left a large estate in land and six negroes

We will close our remarks on this member of the Morris family by publishing an account of him and of the valley, which we find in the Southern Literary Messenger of 1856, written by Dr. Henry Ruffner, who had lived in this county and knew the people thereof.

### BILLY MORRIS.

There was a Presbyterian minister who made a visit at an early day to the Kanawha Valley, who was known as "Little Bobby Willson," and who passed safely through the wilderness of Sewall and Gauley mountains, and on a Saturday evening arrived at the first inn that he found in the Kanawha Valley, old Billy Morris's.

Old Billy Morris, as everybody called him, because he had a son called young Billy, was one of the seven brothers who were among the first settlers in the country. They were a family of large, brave and worthy men and all, except old Billy, hunters, while hunting was the deep occupation of the country, but quiet and industrous farmers, after they had farms large enough to yield them substance.

Old Billy differed from his brothers both in body and in mind. They were tall and spare made; he was less tall and corpulent. They were not, but he was remarkable for energy and strength of character. He was born to command, as much so as Nopoleon Bonaparte, though in an humble sphere.

All the poor men and the ordinary men around him for miles, fell naturally, so it seems, under his authority. He ordered and they obeyed. He reprimanded, often severely, and they submitted, nearly always humbly. He made them fear him, though he had no power over them but the moral power of a strong mind. He made them love him also with a sort of filial affection, though neither they nor any one else could tell why, for he was often gruff in speech, overbearing in manner, and when he exercised kindness towards his neighbor, he did it often more as a master than as a friend. But then, when he chose he had a masterly way of showing kindness, making the recipient feel more grateful than if they had secured the same favor from another man. In truth, he had a strong heart with an imperious will, and loved and hated with a power which was always felt by those around him. To his children he was very kind and to his neighbors, who did not oppose him, or offend his prejudices, he was a good neighbor, a remarkably good neighbor.

He had sagacity in matters of business, while others hunted bears, he acquired choice lands, and improved his farm, erected mills, and built flat boats for families emigrating to Kentucky, by which means he became the wealthiest man among the primitive settlers in the Kanawha valley.

Yet the man was not on educated man.

But he gave his children, especially his sons, a liberal education. It may be supposed that such a man was bigoted in his opinions and full of prejudices. Strong minded, self-relying men, not liberalized by education, always are. As he was not disposed to tolerate opposition to his will, neither would he regard those with favor who differed from him in religion or politics.

He was a Baptist, wholly and exclusively. He knew little of other religious denominations, and had imbibed unfavorable opinions of them. He seems to have some how gotten a particular dislike to the Presbyterians, which was rather unfortunate at first for our Little Bobby Wilson, though in the end, it was not.

It being Saturday evening when he arrived, Mr. Wilson was properly concerned to discern how he might spend the next day in a Christian manner, and whether providentially a way might be opened for him to do a little good among these heathenish, whiskey-drinking, bear hunting barbarians of Kanawha, for such was the character he had heard of them. When Little Bobby saw what a corpulent backwoodsman he had for his host, how loudly and authoritatively he spoke to those around him, how rough were his manners and how dogmatical his conversation, he was almost afraid to say a word to him about religious worship. But in the course of the evening he found that Morris was himself a member of the Baptist church, and that his rudeness of manner proceeded not from ungodliness but from early associations with rude and ignorant backwoodsmen. Therefore, he ventured before going to bed to inquire if there was to be any preaching in the neighborhood to-morrow. "No," said his host, "None nearer than Elk." "How far is that, Mr. Morris?" "Eighteen miles." Mr. Wilson then said, "Well, Mr. Morris, as I am a preacher of the Gospel, and do not wish to travel or to be idle on the Sabbath day, would it be convenient and agreeable to have preaching appointed for me in this neighborhood? I suppose that a small congregation could be collected?"

"What profession are you of?"

"I am a Presbyterian."

"A Presbyterian are you! then you can't preach about here. We are "all Baptists, and have not much opinion about your sort o' peo- "ple."

This settled the question. Mr. Wilson left early next morning, and went to the little village of Charleston, just above Elk ferry, where he found a Mr. Johnson, a Baptist, preaching out under the trees, and Mr. Wilson was pressed by Mr. Johnson to preach, which he did to the great satisfaction of his rural congregation, and the next day he preached again in the Court House.

Mr. William Morris and George Alderson, were the first delegates from Kanawha county to the General Assembly of Virginia. Both were able men in their way, but rather uncouth legislators by reason of their ignorance of public affairs, and of the usages of polite society. They both attracted notice by their backwood garb and manners, and Alderson, also by his stammering tongue, which had often to make three or four trials at a word.

*Jane Morris* (A—1) was born Nov. 3, 1770, and became the wife of Maj. John Hansford in 1787, and it has been said they were married in Lewisburg.

She was the oldest child of Major William Morris, and a sketch of the Hansford family was published in our Jan., 1904, magazine.

She came with her father when she was but four years old and rode in front of him on the horse and before she reached the end of her journey they were attacked by an Indian.

She lived near her father until in 1798, when her husband built on the opposite side of the river below Paint creek. Major Hansford was in the House of Delegates from Kanawha from 1811 to 1818, both inclusive.

She was an invalid for many of her last days, and she died on August 12, 1854.

She had twelve children, one of whom was a girl, and she, Sarah Hansford, born in 1792, married a William Morris, whose children were Fenton, Joshua and John.

Her sons were Herman, William, Morris, Felix G., John, Carroll, Charles, Alva, Gallatin and Melton.

For further particulars of the Hansfords, see said January, 1904, magazine.

Of Gabriel Morris (A—2) we can give no information.

*William Morris* (A—3) the third of the name, was born Dec. 16, 1775, and his wife was Polly Barns, who was the daughter of Joseph Barns of Shepherdstown, and her mother was the sister of James Ramsey, the inventor of the steamboat. See our magazine for July, 1903, for the family of Ramseys.

After the death of her husband she married Edward Hughes—see July, 1904, magazine.

This Billy Morris invented the "Slips or Jars," a simple tool which made deep well boring possible, and that the great utility of the invention entitled him to be ranked among the inventors, and as a great public benefactor.

The children of this family were:

1. Joseph Barns Morris; mar. Sally Hughes.
2. Catherine Morris; mar. Morris Hansford.
3. Roxie Morris; mar. Joel Alexander.
4. Janette Morris; never married.
5. Cynthia Morris; mar. Wm. White.
6. William, the IV; mar. Julia Mitchell.
7. Maria Morris; mar. Norborn Thomas.
8. Thomas Morris.

Catherine Morris, who married Morris Hansford had four children: William, Franklin, Monroe, and Emeline.

Roxie Morris, who married Joel Alexander, had a large family, whose names are unknown.

Janette Morris never married, and lived with her sister, Catherine Hansford. She lived to be 80 years of age, and danced with the children and never grew old.

*Catherine Morris,* (A—4), born January 13, 1778, and married Charles Venable in 1800. He was one of the first to emancipate his slaves. They left no children, but their home was one where the young people delighted to assemble and where they were always found.

We have by tradition an incident of her that gives some insight to her character, while she was a young lady, and at home, there was an entertainment of some kind to be given, and to which she was invited, to take place at the house of a relative on the opposite side of the river, and it so happened that at the house there were none of the family that were going, neither were there any one who was known to her to be going; neither was a boat on her side of the river known to her, and it looked as if she would have to remain at home. She did not like this situation and she wanted to go and she determined that she would go. She prepared the clothes she desired to wear, and after dark took them under her arm and went to the river. She placed the clothes in a sugar trough she hauled to the river and shoving the little boat ahead of her, she swam the river, dressed herself in the dry clothes, and proceeded to the house and enjoyed the pleasure of the evening's entertainment as if nothing unusual had taken place. She was heard to say that she had done so often. She lived not far from Charleston, on the South Side, now in the lower part of Kanawha City, in a large brick farm house. She had no children.

Carroll Morris, son of Major William (A—5)
We know not whom he married. His children were:
Maria Morris; married John Hansford.
Letitia Morris; married ————. Whittaker.
Parthenia Morris; married ————.
Catherine Morris; married Dr. Sutherland.
Michael and Carroll, Jr.

169

Carroll Morris lost his life in attempting to swim acoss the Kanawha, just below Upper Creek Shoals.

*John Morris*—(A—6), born Aug. 24, 1783. His wife was Polly Duke.

He sold his place to Aaron Stockton and removed to Missouri. He had a son, Granville Morris, who was killed in the Black Hawk war.

When John determined to go further west, he went to work to build a boat, into which he took his family, negroes, wagons, tools and some cattle, &c.

The entire Baptist congregation assembled at the river and a prayer was offered for his safe journey and he launched his boat and left the Kanawha valley.

*Cynthia Morris* (A—7), was born Jan. 5, 1792. She married Isaac Noyes, who came from some of the northern states, and become one of the leading merchants and salt manufacturers of this county. For some time he lived on a farm, which is now included in Kanawha City, and was the adjoining farm of Chas. Venable.

This couple lived to be very old and were known and respected by the people of Charleston.

They were the ancestors of the Noyes and Smiths and Rands, Arnolds and Rubys, who compose a large part of the inhabitants of Charleston.

Col. Benjamin H. Smith, and his son, Maj. Isaac N. Smith, and his son, Harrison Brooks Smith, were all lawyers of prominence, and the latter is yet so engaged.

To write of Col. Smith would require a large volume, and the space will not permit to go further into the later families.

### HENRY MORRIS.—B.

He was the second son of William Morris, Sr.

He married Mary Bird of Bath County, Va.

She was, with her sister, captured by the Indians and taken to Chillicothe and for seven years kept there, until she was sixteen years of age. When she and her sister were departing for their home, an Indian child cried for her sister. They retained the sister, and she was never heard of again.

Henry built his cabin on Peters creek of Gauley river, in 1791, and his only neighbors were Conrad Young and Edward McClung.

Henry and Mary had eight children; seven girls and one son. They were Leah, Catherine, Margaret, Polly, and Betsy. There were two other girls, whose names we can not give.

The only son was John Morris.

The incident of the murder of two children of Henry Morris is given as follows:—There were two Indians and two white men, said to be Simon Gerty and Saul Carpenter, who went near to Henry Morris' house on Peters creek, and while Margaret, aged 14, and Betsy, 11, were going to drive in the cows, when the Indians attempted to capture them; Margaret tripped on a vine while running, and was caught and scalped, and died soon after her father found her.

Betsy also endeavored to make her escape, but in getting over a fence, her dress, of home-made linsey, caught on a splinter on the rail, and held her until the Indians came up and she was likewise scalped and killed, and was found by her father with her dress still fastened on the rail in the fence. This was in 1792. The children were taken by the father, wrapped in a blanket and placed in a box and buried together in one grave, and the family went to the Fort on the Kanawha.

Henry Morris then and there swore eternal vengeance on all Indians. His neighbor, Conrad Young, had several sons, and each had a gun, while Morris had but one gun, and the Indians were supposed to have been watching a path that lead to the two houses, but they were not seen any more by the neighbors.

Henry was a large, stout, healthy man, and had no fear of anything and when aroused was a desperate one. He determined to kill every Indian that he could find, and it was not long afterwards that he heard of one being in the neighborhood and he took his gun and started to find him, and followed him up Elk river and killed him early in the morning, the particulars of which are published in the Magazine for January, 1904, page 52.

And as long as Henry Morris lived, he never recognized any Indian as a friendly one, and if there were friendly Indians in the neighborhood, they had to keep the information from Henry, and get them out of the way before he learned thereof, for he could not be persuaded to treat them other than as sworn enemies.

Henry Morris was at the battle of Point Pleasant, and was with the men that went around on Crooked creek to attack the Indians on the flank and rear.

He was an athlete and no man could cope with him in any game, where strength, skill and endurance were required, such as running, jumping and wrestling.

He cleared out a good farm on Peters creek, and there he raised his family.

One of his girls married William Bird, of Bath County. They settled on the Twenty Mile of Gauley, but afterwards settled on Sycamore, where they remained all their lives. Another daughter married Jesse James, of Bath County. They settled on Otter creek, where they had a good farm. After their children grew up, Jesse moved on to Elk river, not far above Charleston, and remained there all their lives. One of the James girls married Arch Price, who lived on Elk river.

Another daughter of Henry married one of the sons of his neighbor, Conrad Young.

Henry Morris remained on his Peters creek farm until his death in 1824.

John Morris, the only son of Henry, married Jane Brown in 1807, and they had seven sons and five daughters, viz: Henry, Leonard, Thomas, Ryan, John, and Silas. The girls were, Mary, Mattie, Jane, Margaret and Sarah. Of these boys Silas is the only remaining one, and he lives in Missouri. Mattie married W. B. Summers, and lived on Peters creek until her death in 1903. Jane married Rev. A. N. Rippetoe and she died in 1904, at the Cross Lanes. Thomas Morris married Leah Ellis, and their oldest son was John Silas Morris, and one of the sons of John Silas was Alfred N. Morris, who was born in 1875; he was baptized and joined the Jordan Light Baptist church in 1894; licensed to preach in 1897; married Virginia Belle Given in 1899, and was ordained a minister in 1899.

Rev. A. N. Morris, of Anstead, Fayette County, was in possession of much of information concerning the Morris family of late date, and the same can be secured through him.

Henry Morris secured a Patent for 600 acres of land on Peters creek in 1793.

There was a grand-son of Henry Morris, who lived at Summersville, Nicholas County, and he had a sweetheart on the Kanawha. He would leave home after dinner and go down Peters creek, up Bell creek, over Little Gauley mountain, down Hughes creek to the Kanawha, swim the Kanawha, march to Henry Jones', where he found her, and afterwards married her. She was a grand-daughter of Franky Morris Jones, a sister of Henry Morris. Some one in speaking of Henry Morris, said that he was a physical giant, an athlete and daredevil. That he was as fearless as he was powerful and as determined as fearless.

## LEONARD MORRIS.—(C.)

Leonard was the third son of William Morris, Sr.

It has been said that he was the original first settler, but as far as is known, he came with the others. This statement probably grew out of the fact that he was one of the first Justices, and attended the County Courts and was probably more and better known to the visitors than the others. In a controversy between the claimants of the Burning Spring 250 acre tract, patented to Gen. G. Washington and Lewis, it has been said that he was one of the witnesses who testified that he saw, in 1775, the surveyors making the survey of this tract. There is nothing in the file of the papers to show this, and we give it as tradition. It is more than probably true.

He was in 1798 the sheriff of this county.

His home was at the mouth of Slaughters creek, and his neighbor was John Flynn, who was killed by the Indians on Cabin creek.

Dr. Hale writes that a son of John Flynn was captured and taken to Ohio and burned at the stake.

Lens creek perpetuates the name of Leonard Morris.

Leonard Morris married first Miss Price and afterwards, he married Margaret Likens.

The first set of children were:—
1. John—he went to Missouri and died prior to 1831.
2. Meredith—he went south and was never heard of.
3. Mary—married Lawrence Bryan in 1794.
4. Sarah—married Fleming Cobb in 1794.
5. Elizabeth—married Robert Lewis.
6. Leonard, Jr.—married Mary Austin in 1805.
The second set of children were:—
7. Charles—married Lucinda Crocket of Ky.
8. Nancy—married John D. Shrewsbury.
9. Parthenia—married J. B. Crocket.
10. Joshua—married daughter of Jonathan Jarrett.
11. Hiram—never married.
12. Peter—married daughter of Jonathan Jarrett.
13. Andrew—never married; died 1822 in Indiana.
14. Cynthia—married Samuel Hensley.
15. Madison—married Nancy Spurlong.
16. Dickinson—married Susan, daughter of Jas. Morris.

Hiram Cobb, a grand-son of Leonard's, like most of the Morris family, was hale and hearty and was proud of his strength. He made a bet of one gallon of peach brandy that he would come in a canoe from Point Pleasant to Charleston between suns, and he won the bet. Some incredulous person made the remark that he had secured the help of a negro man to help him through the Red-House shoals. Cobb heard of the remark and he proceeded to give the slanderer a threshing for his falsehood.

Charles Morris—(C—7), one of the sons of Leonard, was born in 1790 and died in 1861.
His wife was Lucinda Crocket, of Ky.
Their children were:—
1. Leonard—born in 1819; married Courtney Walker.
2. Hamilton—born in 1821.
3. Francis—died young.
4. Andrew—born in 1828; went to Texas; died in 1875.
5. Charles—born in 1827; married Miss Foster; died 1875.
6. Margaret—born in 1829; married —— Samuels, attorney.

174

7. Parthenia—born in 1831; married Thos. Swindler.
8. John—born in 1833; married Miss Abton.

Leonard Morris, born 1819, resides at Brownstown, and although he is eighty-six years of age, has the appearance of being only sixty.

He has been an active, busy man of business all his life, and remembers people and incidents of his early days, from whom we have learned much here given.

Hamilton Morris, brother of the above Leonard, was born in 1821, and resides in Charleston, and but for the fact that he has lost his eyesight, would be as active as ever. "Ham Morris," as he has been called, was elected Clerk of the County Court of Kanawha County, and was one of the most popular men in his county, and one of the most efficient and reliable clerks that ever filled the said office.

Long may they both live.

## JOSHUA MORRIS. (D.)

Joshua was the fourth son of William Morris, Sr.
He married Frances Simms of Virginia.
Their children were—
1. William Morris—lived at Gauley Bridge; married Sarah Hansford.
2. Edmund Morris.
3. Henry Morris.
4. Elizabeth Morris.
5. Lucy Morris.
6. Nancy Morris—married John Harriman.
7. Thomas Morris.
8. Mary Morris.
9. John Morris—born in 1794 in Culpepper County.

Joshua first settled in Teays Valley, but the Indians became troublesome and he removed back to the Virginia settlements, east of the Alleghenies, but he did not remain, but again came and settled on his lands on Mud river. William, his son, married Maria Hansford.

175

They lived near the Falls of Kanawha, and removed to Missouri. They had Fenton, Joshua, and John.

## JOSHUA MORRIS' WILL.

This will was dated July 31, 1824, and was recorded on the 13th Sept., 1824, in Will book No. 1, page 46 in Kanawha county. He directs his debts to be paid and the residue to go to her surviving children and children of deceased children, viz.: William, John, Edmund, Henry, Elizabeth and Lucy Chapman and Nancy Harriman, each, in equal parts, the estate being divided into nine parts, and the above named seven, and the children of Thomas, deceased, to have one-ninth, that is, Armstead, Geo. K., Malon Morris and and Frances Thompson and Polly, Kitty, Juliana, Cassandria, and Jennett Morris, children of Thomas, and children of daughter Mary Chapman, viz.: Joshua M. Chapman, Malon Chapman and Frances, Mary and Nancy Chapman. My beloved wife to have the profits of one third of his estate and Edmund and John Morris and Joshua M. Chapman to be his executors.

## JOHN MORRIS OF CABELL CO.—(D—9.)

The youngest son of Joshua Morris, was John Morris, who settled in Teays Valley, in the upper part of Cabell County.

As we stated that his father, Joshua Morris, found the Indians so badly disposed that he left this settlement and returned to Virginia, and there remained until peace was restored.

John was born in Culpepper County, Virginia, in 1794, and was brought with his father's family to Teays Valley, while quite young.

His first wife was Mary Everette, and their child was,

1. Eliza, who married William Love.

    The wife of John died, and he then Mary Kinard, in 1819, who was born in Culpepper Co.

    The children were:—

2. Charles K. Morris, who married Martha A. Kilgore.

3. Albert A. Morris, who died unmarried.

4. Joseph W. Morris, married Sarah A. Russell, he was a Capt. in C. S. A. and was killed at Frederick, Md.

5. Edna E. Morris, married Addison T. Buffington.
6. James R. Morris, married Helen M. Russell.
7. Mary S. Morris, married first Ira T. McConihay, and then John P. Sebrell.

John Morris was an extensive farmer, and stock raiser, and owned many slaves. His home was east of Milton. He was more than once elected to the Virginia Legislature, and was well known throughout Cabell and adjoining counties, as a man of wealth and influence.

When the civil war came on, he took his family to southwest Virginia, and while there he died in 1862, and his wife died after her return home in 1876. While he was absent, his house was burned by some of the Union Army and a great loss inflicted upon him and his family.

His son Charles K. Morris was also a farmer and stock raiser, and a man of influence in his county.

Joseph and James, both attended school at Marshall Academy, and they married sisters, who lived between the town of Guyandotte and the Academy, on the Ohio river. They were the daughters of John Russell, of whom more may be learned in our October, 1901, Magazine.

Joseph Morris died in the service of C. S. A.

James R. Morris, was also in the C. S. A., and is yet living to tell the tale; his residence is at Milton, W. Va..

The daughters of Mrs. Addison J. Buffington, reside at Parkersburg, W. Va. Their mother was Edna E. Morris. Mrs. Sebrell lives in Putnam county, W. Va., and she is the mother of Dr. J. M. McConihay, of Charleston, and from her we learned much, and also from Mrs. Reynolds, a daughter of James R. Morris.

## JOHN MORRIS.—(E.)

John was the fifth son of William Morris, Sr.

His wife was Margaret Droddy, and their children were, *John, Edmund, Levi, William* and *Thomas Asbury,* and if there were others they are not known to us.

Of what we know of John, is gathered principally from the life of Bishop Thomas Asbury Morris, his son.

John was a captain of the Kanawha Militia in its earliest days; he was one of the executors of his father's will; he lived about five miles above Charleston, on the South Side of the river, and afterwards removed to Cabell county. He was, as was all the Morris family, a strict Baptist. His son Edmund was a Clerk of Cabell county court, and was a politician and represented Kanawha county in 1809 in the Virginia Legislature before Cabell was organized, and may have been elected after Cabell county was organized. The older brother removed to Kentucky.

### BISHOP THOMAS ASBURY MORRIS.

He was born in Kanawha just above Charleston, April 28, 1794, and when quite young in 1804, went with his brother, Edmund to Cabell and assisted in the Clerk's office. While there he was drafted for military services in war of 1812, and started on the road when his father secured a substitute, who followed and took his place, while they were at Point Pleasant.

Thomas Asbury studied under William Payne, a teacher who taught him to be a Methodist and he began to preach, and his first sermon was at the house of his father. He continued and was encouraged by the Spurlock brothers, Burwell and Stephen, who were prominent Methodist ministers, and he finally was ordained and placed on the circuit.

His first wife was Abagail Scales, a daughter of Maj. Nathaniel Scales, January 23, 1814, and he lived at his first home, called "Spice Flat Cottage." Their daughter, Jane, born in 1815, married Joseph G. Rush of Cincinnati, and their son, Francis Asbury Morris, was a member of the Missouri Conference.

In 1836 Thos. A. Morris was elected a Bishop of the Methodist Church, and in 1842 his wife died, and he in 1844 married Mrs. Lucy Meriweather, of Louisville, Ky. In 1851 he met the Conference at Charleston, and visited his early home, but it was all changed, so he could not recognize the place. In 1871 his wife died, and in 1872 he married again, and in September, 1874, he died. He was a man of great executive ability, and an earnest, faithful minister.

It was said of him by his cousins that he became a Methodist in order to become a bishop, there being no such office in the Baptist church, but, when he became a Methodist he little dreamed of being a Bishop. He came in contact with a Methodist, whose teaching convinced him and being convinced, he followed the dictation of his own conscience.

In 1808, there was presented to the County Court of Kanawha county the following report on the establishment of a *Ferry across Mud River, near the mouth of Mud River.* In pursuance of a writ of *ad quod damnum,* I have caused to come on the premises the following jury, to-wit: Manoah Bostick, M. Holland, A. Reece, N. Scales, J. Estes E. Morris, T. Buffington, W. Dingess, Jno. Morris, Jos. Hilyard, S. Sanders, and Chas. Alesbury, good and lawful men, who being duly sworn well and truly and impartially to inquire whether public convenience will result from the establishment of a ferry across Mud river between the Merritt mill and the mouth of Mud river, where the road crosses from the Green Bottom and the mouth of Guyandotte, leading to the Falls of the Guyandotte. Upon their oaths do say that a public convenience will result from the establishment of a ferry at the place aforesaid and in the opinion of the jurors aforesaid a ferry ought to be established. In witness whereof the said jurors have hereunto set their hands and seals, this 27th May, 1808.

Manoah Bostick,
Michael Holland,
Allen Reece,
Nathaniel Scales,
Joel Estes,
Edmund Morris,
Thos. Buffington,
Wm. Dingess,
John Morris,
Joseph Hilyard,
Sampson Saunders,
Charles Alsbury.

This report was received by the Kanawha County Court and ordered to be recorded, which was done by A. Donnally, C. K. C. in deed book C, page 306. This order probably was not executed until after the County of Cabell was organized, and it will be noticed that the Court House was not mentioned for the reason that there was none to mention, even the town of Guyandotte was not mentioned but the place was called the mouth of Guyandotte.

John Morris had deeds recorded in Kanawha, viz.:

From Reuben Slaughter, half 1000 acres, Hurricane, 1804.

From A. Bennett, 1780 acres, Mud river, 1804.

From Chas. Brown, 3500 acres, Mud river, 1805.

### COMMONWEALTH VS. JOHN MORRIS, JR.

An interesting case is reported in Virginia Cases, 176, in which Thomas Ward filed an information against Morris, Jr., in which it is complained that Morris wrote a petition to the Legislature, in which he stated that Maj. Ward, sheriff of Cabell county, being desirous of having the seat of justice for said county located on his own plantation, where it was first held, is actuated by selfish and interested motives and not for the welfare and convenience of the majority of the people of the county, and that the place he desires is on his own land, almost inaccessible by reason of hills and mountains, not near the centre of population or territory, and being sheriff has the collection of the revenue, he persuades ignorant men to sign his petition and for so doing frequently stating that he will indulge them for a time, which indulgence is a great favor, &c., &c. The defendant Morris plead that what he had written of Ward was true, and he was ready to prove the same.

This raised a question of law which the Court referred to the general court and the general court on June 12, 1811, decided that the truth might be given in evidence in justification, &c.

The County of Cabell was established by Act, January 9, 1809, and in the Act it provided that a commission should locate the public buildings. On May 9, 1809, the commission reported that they do fix the mouth of the Guyandotte, on the upper side thereof, in the middle of a field, &c., to be the place for said buildings, and this was signed by John Shrewsbury, Wm. Clendenin, John Reynolds, Jesse

Bennett and David Ruffner. The town of Guyandotte was established by Act, June 5, 1810.

When was the C. H. removed from Guyandotte and to what place was it removed, are questions yet unanswered.

## CARLOS MORRIS.—(F.)

Carlos Morris, the sixth son of William, Sr. We are unable to give information of this son, or of his family.

## LEVI MORRIS.—(G.)

The seventh son of William Morris was Levi.

His wife was Margaret Starke, and after her death he married Peggy Jarrett.

His children were:—

1. Cynthia Morris, married L. Brannon, a hatter.
2. William Morris, married Sarah ———.
3. Benjamin Morris, married Amanda Hamilton.
4. James Morris, married Sarah Shelton.
5. Geo. Washington Morris, married Sarah Hamilton.
6. Frances Morris, married Wm. Spurlock.
7. Elizabeth Morris, married Levi Spurlock.
8. Martha Morris, married ——— Burgess.

Levi was born in 1768 and died in 1834.

*James Morris*—(G—4)—son of Levi Morris, married Sarah Shelton—they had four boys and eight girls, viz.:

George Morris—killed by fall on the ice, a boy.

Levi Morris—married Mary Voirs and went to N. C.

Benjamin Morris—married Ann Montgomery.

James D. Morris—married Alice L. Hammaker.

Susan Morris— married Dickinson Morris.

Amanda Morris—married E. F. Flagg.

Sarah Morris—married Wm. Hamilton.

Ellen Morris—married Silas Custer.

Eva Morris—married Dr. Mauser, of Ky.

Margaret Morris—married Joshua Harriman.
Emma Morris—married Dr. Early, and 2nd Wm. Riggs.
Mary Morris—died young.

## BENJAMIN MORRIS.—(H.)

Was the eighth son of William Morris, Sr.
He was born in 1770, and died July 6, 1829.
His wife was Nancy Jarrett, who died in 1832.
Their children were:—
1. Achilles Morris—who went as Capt. to Mexican war and died.
2. Frances Morris—married Wm. Shelton; they went west.
3. Virginia Morris—married J. Kincaid of Ohio.
4. Catherine Morris—married Miles Mauser of Ky.
5. Jane Morris—married Jacob Johnson, of Monroe county.
6. Celia Morris—married Capt. John Harvey.
7. Eden Morris—married Miss Edgar, of Greenbrier county.
8. Leah Morris—married ———— Purdy.

Benjamin built the brick house in 1824, which is now known as the "Dunn place."

Morris Harvey, of Fayetteville, now more than eighty years of age, was a son of Capt. John Harvey; his wife was Miss Dickinson, daughter of Hon. H. M. Dickinson, of Fayette county. His sister Fanny, married Capt. Snelling C. Farley, of steamboat fame.

## ELIZABETH MORRIS-SEE.—(I.)

She was the ninth child of Wm. Morris, Sr.
She was married to one Mr. See, whose name does not appear.
It appears, however, that in 1792, there was an administrator oppointed for one Michael See, in Kanawha county, and Shadrack Harriman, Ed. McClung and Roland Wheeler were the appraisers of his estate.

Michael See and Adam See, the sons of Geo. See.
Adam was born November 29, 1764, and they came from the South Branch of the Potomac, near Moorefield. Whether the husband was

Michael, and whether he was a brother of Adam See, we cannot, with assurance now determine. Michael See was the only one of the name mentioned among tithables in 1792. They lived near Witchers creek.

They had a negro boy, Jonathan, who was carried away by the Indians and he was afterwards made one of their chiefs, in Ohio. Dick was a younger brother of Jonathan, who had grown up, and both Jonathan and Dick, were sons of Dick Pointer, of Donnally's Fort. Dick belonged to Leonard Morris and expressed a desire to go and see Jonathan. Mr. Morris gave his consent and furnished Dick with horse bridle and saddle, and gave him such instructions as he could. Dick started off to the Indian Chief Jonathan, and was gone but two or three days, when he returned home and in explanation of his return said that he had concluded that it might be safer for him to remain at home and let Jonathan come and visit him, and no doubt this was a wise conclusion.

Frances Morris-Jones—(J.)—was the tenth and last child, of William Morris, Sr.

She married John Jones. He was born in 1755, and died in 1838. He was in the Battle of Point Pleasant.

Their children were:—

1. Gabriel Jones, who went to Culpepper county.
2. William Jones, who went to Indiana.
3. Nancy Jones, married ———— Huddleston.
4. Thomas Jones.
5. Levi Jones, who went to Indiana.
6. Frances Jones, married Sand. Shelton.
7. Edward Jones, went to Indiana.
8. John Jones, went to Indiana.
9. Hilliary Jones, lived in Fayette county.
10. Benjamin Jones, went to Texas.
11. Cynthia Jones, married Mr. Funk, and 2nd Jabez Spinks.

For the history of this family, see the October, 1903, Magazine, 285-288. John Jones came from Culpepper also, and was one of the soldiers of Gen'l Lewis' army and was in the battle of Point Pleasant, and afterwards in the Revolutionary war. He settled and lived above Paint creek on the Kanawha river, and he was thrifty and had a good home and farm and acquired considerable land. He was a member of the Baptist church, located at Kellys creek.

His wife survived him.

Before her death, she had prepared monuments for herself and husband.

She was the youngest of William, Sr., and was known as "Franky." Col. B. H. Jones, of the 60th Va. Infantry, C. S. A. is said to be a grand son of John and Franky Jones. He died at Lewisburg, and had written much of the late war.

### MARRIAGES OF THE MORRIS FAMILY.

We take the following list of marriages from the records of Kanawha county. Owing to the fact that there are so many of the same name, we are not able to designate the person or to locate them in the proper family.

1793 Sarah Morris and Chas. Young—Mar. 20, by F. Watkins.
1795 Sarah Morris and Fleming Cobb—by Jas. Johnson.
1796 Elizabeth Morris and Joseph Hilyard—by Jas. Johnson.
1796 John Morris and Mary Ann Coleman—by Jas. Johnson.
1794 Mary Morris and Lawrence Bryan—Nov. 9, by F. Watkins.
1800 Catherine Morris and Chas. Venable—by Jas. Johnson.
1802 Lucy Morris and Joseph Chapman.
1803 Edmund Morris and Sally Estill—11th Sept.
1804 John Morris and Jane Jordan—Apr. 20.
1805 Leonard Morris and Mary Heister—July 13.
1806 Polly Morris and Jas. Ellison.
1807 Cynthia Morris and Isaac Noyes.
1807 Miriam Morris and Eason Hannon.
1807 John Morris and Jane Brown.
1802 John Morris and Hannah Morrison.
1824 Maria Morris and And. Slaughter—May 5.
1824 Parthenia Morris and Absalom Walls—Feb. 29.
1824 Roxalena Morris and Joel Alexander—June 7.
1824 James C. Morris and Polly Webster.
1832 Letitia Morris and Norris Whittaker.
1834 Leonard Morris and Eliza Ann Jones.
1834 Geo. W. Morris and Sarah A. Hamilton.

We have given a start on the history of the Morris family and of their genealogy.

We can not go further in the line of descent, and we have now taken much space.

No doubt but we have omitted some and may have located some names in the wrong families, but we have endeavored to learn the facts and give them as we have learned them.

We can but notice that all the descendants have not remained loyal Baptists, and no doubt "Major Billy" will require of those who have dared to deny the family faith, some satisfactory explanation.

To those who would pursue the subject of the genealogy of the descendants, we refer them to Rev. A. N. Morris, Anstead, Fayette county, West Virginia.

---

## JAMES NOURSE AND ST. GEORGE'S CHAPEL.

It has been asserted that James Nourse erected the old church, the ruins of which stands near Charlestown, Jefferson County, W. Va., and whose history has heretofore been regarded a mystery.

185

It is stated of late that James Nourse was the man who built it; that he had the pulpit and other wood work sent from England, and that he had a vista cut through the forest so that he could see the church from his bed room and that the vista was still in evidence in 1859; that the Rector of the church lived at Piedmont, the name of the home of Jas. Nourse—That Mrs. Briscoe believed the above story and that the said ruins is part of her property.

That a Mr. Smith has in his possession papers of a Mr. Trussel, among which is a bill for hauling the stone to build the church and that for each days hauling he was to have one acre of land. On this it is concluded that it was built in 1771 or 1772.

We have been permitted to see a book entitled "James Nourse and his Descendants," published in 1897 by Miss Lyle, for the use of the family. From this we gather the following facts:

James Nourse, third son of John Nourse, was born at Weston-under-Penyard house, county of Hereford, England, July 19, 1731.

His brother John wrote a letter to James, dated Nov. 29, 1751, on his finances, as James is about to come of age and John evidently was his guardian, in which John says he can on next July receive his fortune, three hundred pounds. James Nourse married Sept. 30, 1753. Miss Sarah Fouace, of London, whose father left France at the time of the revocation of the Edict of Nantz.

After his marriage, James Nourse went into trade in the city of London as a woolen draper. He continued in that business for fifteen years which brought him to the fall of 1768, at least. In 1768 he was a church warden of St. Paul's church.

In April, 1768 he wrote of his leaving London and going to America —that his business afforded him a comfortable livelihood, but little provision for a large family—that he was in want of no necessaries and in the enjoyment of some conveniences of life, but with little improvement of fortune, so as to enable his children to set up for themselves. By removing he expected to purchase land sufficient for their maintenance, if employed with industry.

James Nourse, with his wife Sarah, and their children, on the 16th of March, 1769, left London, and arrived at Hampton, Va., on the 10th of May, 1769. He resided one year at Hampton, in the Sheldon House, and thence he removed to Piedmont, a plantation, which he purchased, near Charlestown, Va., (now in Jefferson County, W. Va.)

There is a record of his list of household effects brought with him, consisting of 116 bundles, crates, boxes, cases etc., every one number-ed. This list seems to have included his entire household effects, even to his clocks and lanterns, family pictures, an escretoir, a ma-hogany cupboard, a spinnet, a bureau with books, globes, furniture, plows, chaise, groceries, beds and bedding, etc., etc.

It is said in his book, written in 1774, that he owned eighty-four head of "Horn-cattle" valued at 151 pounds and 56 hogs worth 26 pounds.

In 1775 he visited Kentucky, with a company of which he was the leader, to locate lands. On Easter day, 1775, he wrote back from Fort Cumberland to his wife.

He kept a journal, giving particulars of his trip, to Pittsburg and down the Ohio.

On the 10th of May, 1775 he writes "from our camp at Smith's Point, at the mouth of Great Sandy, about 40 miles below the Great Kanawha. He says Captain Smith and ten others were there in camp, from their part of the country."

These parties were the owners of lands awarded to Virginia Soldiers under the Savage Grant, which extended from below Sandy up to and above the Guyandotte. Capt. Chas. Smith was the owner of a part of said lands.

*See Oct. 1901, W. Va., His. Mag.*

The Journal continues until July. On Oct. 1776, he was appointed one of the Trustees of Berkeley Springs, when Bath was laid out. During the Revolutionary war, he was an ardent patriot.

There was $3,333.33 advanced to him for the use of the militia of Berkeley and Frederick County, Va., who was about to march to re-inforce Gen. Washington. The said James Nourse to be accountable for the expenditure.

He was a member of the Virginia House of Delegates in 1778 from Berkeley County.

In 1781 he was appointed to settle the claims of Maryland against the United States and removed to Annapolis for this purpose.

It seems that he went back and forth from Annapolis to Piedmont, attending to his duties in making settlements, etc.

He made a drawing of the improvement he intended to make in

the Piedmont house, which he thought would not be expensive and would make it both cool and convenient.

September 9, 1784 he writes to his son Joseph that his wife had died on September 7.

His will was made in March, 1784. He gives to his seven younger children, one hundred pounds each, and the rest of his estate to be equally divided among all his children.

The appraisement of his personal estate, at Piedmont, was one thousand and thirty-six pounds; at Annapolis, three hundred and thirty-three pounds.

The personal estate was insufficient to pay his debts, writes Joseph, but that they were all paid. His real estate was divided among his children, by order of the Court of Berkeley County.

### Children of James Nourse.

1. Joseph—born in London, July 16, 1754.
2. Elizabeth—born in London, July 7, 1755.
3. Sarah—born in London, August 14, 1756.
4. James—born in London, November 11, 1758.
5. Catherine B.—born in London, May 9, 1759.
6. Charles—born in London, May 8, 1760.
7. William—born in London, August 16, 1761.
8 and 9. Robert and Sara—born in London, September 25, 1762.
10. William—born in London, October 30, 1763.
11. Elizabeth—born in London, January 23, 1765.
12. Susanna—born in London, February 9, 1766.
13. John—born in London, January 17, 1768.
14. Gabriel—born in Virginia, January 24, 1770.
15. Philip—born in Virginia, June 30, 1771.
16. Sarah Anne—born in Frederick county, Va., July 16, 1773.
17. Horatio—born in Frederick county, Va., July 24, 1774.
18. Michael—born in Frederick county, Va., September 1, 1778.
Three children died unnamed—21 in all.

1. Joseph Nourse, attended school until 1767, when he was taken into his father's business. After they went to Piedmont, Va., in 1770, he assisted his father on the farm until 1772, when he went to Philadelphia. In 1776 he went South with General Charles Lee, as his

military secretary. In 1777 he was appointed deputy secretary to the board of war, with salary $780 per annum. In 1778 he was elected Secretary of Ordance and paymaster to the board of war, at salary of $90 per month. In 1779 he was elected assistant Auditor General, with salary $10,000 per annum. In 1781, he was elected Register of the Treasury, which office he held until 1829.

It was said that there were five of the Nourse family held positions in the Registers office, and when President Jackson was elected, he avowed his intention *"to sweep out the Nursery."*

Joseph married Maria Louise Bull, in April, 1784, in Berkeley county, Va., and he had six children and he died in 1841.

4. James Nourse went to Kentucky, married Sarah Benois in 1789; he died in 1799, leaving three children.

5. Catherine B. Nourse married John Esten Cooke, April, 1778 and they lived near Piedmont. They removed to Kentucky in 1794. He died in 1817 and she then removed to Lexington.

8. Robert Nourse settled in Woodford county, Kentucky, but removed to Logan county. He married Rebecca Jameson and they had nine children. He died in 1836.

10. William Nourse was in the U. S. navy during the revolutionary war from 1780. He was captured by the British, carried to England and put in dungeon. In 1784 he was a clerk in his father's office in Annapolis, Md. He was sent to England in 1787 to settle some family matters of estate. He married Elizabeth Jamison in 1789; in Mercer county, Kentucky. She died in 1811, and he then married Rebecca Kyle. He had ten children. He died in 1836.

11. Elizabeth Nourse married Jeremiah Chapline, March 20, 1786. She died in Clark county, Mo., 1846, leaving a large family.

Susanna Nourse married William Riddle in 1793. She died in Ralls County, Missouri, in 1848.

14. Gabriel Nourse was the first born in Virginia, at Hampton, in January, 1770. He married Ann Double in 1790, at Winchester, Va; he died in 1839.

18. Michael Nourse was born in Frederick county, Virginia, in September, 1778. Married Mary Rittenhouse in 1800, and died in 1860, at Washington, D. C.

The family was a large one and the members were all good, religious people, educated and refined. The father and mother were

189

pious Episcopalians, though some of the children were Presbyterians, Methodists and Baptists and others Episcopalians.

The main question in this case, however, is, did James Nourse build St. George's Chapel?

Rev. Dr. Gibson, of Huntington, W. Va., thinks that the church was built in 1771 or 1772, and says this is his conclusion for the reason that in 1775 James Nourse addressed a letter to his wife, "Mrs. Nourse, Berkeley Church," and that this implies that the church was well known.

While this shows that the church was there in 1775, we see nothing to prove that it was not there a long time before that, unless it is assumed that James Nourse built it.

We do not think the circumstances show that James Nourse was of sufficient financial ability to construct a building of this dimension and style of architecture and finish. It would have required the outlay of more money than he could have afforded at that time. The church was a large one and was well finished and well furnished. It might have been called on extravagant church for the entire parish to have built. It must have cost many thousand dollars. From the foregoing facts James Nourse was not possessed of sufficient funds to thus construct such a building. He was not wealthy and he comes to Virginia to purchase land on which with industry they could be maintained. His fortune was limited and he had to make considerable outlay to purchase land and to remove his family and effects thereto and then to stock his farm, which must have left him without funds.

He was a man that kept his accounts and there is no mention of any expenditure for church purposes and this is strong proof of his having nothing to do therewith.

When he became settled at Piedmont, there must have been quite a settlement at Charles Town, for the settlement on Evetts Run and Bullskin creek began at a very early date, from about 1734, and at Charles Town not later than 1760.

It would have been more economical to have located the building in the vicinity of the largest number of people, and not away from them.

For all these reasons, it would seem that James Nourse did not build the church, and that it was built before 1772-1773.

. As to the fact that the Vista was in evidence in 1859, we do not suppose that this will be claimed as any evidence of when the church was built or by whom built. Neither does the credulity averred of Mrs. Briscoe add much strength to the claim. And as to Mr. Trussels contract to have one acre of land for each day's hauling stone for the church, this of itself does not prove anything. Produce the contract and with it the conveyance of land in the execution of the contract, and then the evidence will be worth consideration. As it is, it does not show with whom the contract was made, not when it was made, nor that anything was done under the contract, nor when done.

As to the family tradition—It would seem that in such a family when there has been so much information made a matter of record, so much written by different members of the family, of a matter of so much importance as the building of this church had been done, there would have been much said thereof in such records and it would not have been left to tradition. Of all the records, one letter to be sent by hand, was addressed to Mrs. Nourse, Berkeley Church, and that is the only mention made in writing known. All of the tradition that we have is *"that James Nourse caused the said Church to be built,"* and this by no means indicates that he built it.

In 1752 the General Assembly dissolved the Vestry of Frederick and ordered a new election and the reasons assigned were that the Vestry had made large levies with pretence of building and adorning churches and chapels and had left the same unfinished and some had gone to decay—6 Hen 258.

In 1769 Frederick was divided into Norborne and Beckford Parishes—8 Hen 425.

In 1772 Frederick County made into Frederick, Berkeley and Dunmore, and the Parishes to be Frederick, Norborne and Beckford, same boundaries as counties—8 Hen 597.

And afterward Commissioners were appointed to value the churches and chapels in said parishes.—8 Hen 623.

Norris writes that St. George's Chapel was once grand for its time, that its walls were 22 inches thick, of stone, its roof of sheet lead, its windows and door frames of cedar wood, its floors of tiling, its pews and pulpit of oak elaborately carved, and its furnishing of the best, tasteful and harmonious—and that no one could tell when it was built, but is supposed to have been begun by the Vestry and afterwards finished by private subscription.

Perhaps Mr. Norris had some influence with the Vestry and perhaps he had influence with the Vestry and people of St. Paul's in London, and secured the help necessary to complete the same. Who knows?

W. D. Briscoe in October, 1903, W. Va., Hist. Mag., says that so far as he knows the erection of this church is clothed in mystery, that he thinks it was built by the Church of England between 1760 and 1770—See picture of ruins in said Magazine, page 274.

We hope that the subject will interest some one sufficiently to investigate the records, hunt up the Parish Register and obtain facts that will enable the mystery to be solved.

W. S. Laidley.

---

# GENEALOGY OF MRS. VIRGINIA HARVIE PATRICK.

### BY REV. ROBT. DOUGLAS ROLLER, D. D.

In the April number of the WEST VIRGINIA HISTORICAL MAGAZINE appeared an excellent sketch of Gabriel Jones, the first lawyer who ever practiced his profession in what is now the State of West Virginia. Some of his descendants are now living in this State. The city of Charleston claims one, most worthy in life and character, in the person of the venerable widow of that honored and esteemed practitioner of medicine the late Spicer Patrick, M. D.

Mrs. Patrick's ancestry is so distinguished in every line, and so interwoven with the rise and progress of the two Virginias and, in fact, with the whole republic, that some succinct statement must be of more than local interest.

I am aware of the modesty of this family which shrinks from public notice, but as this sketch, prepared principally by a non-resident member of the family, came into my possession in a casual, yet legitimate, way, I am sure of no offense to modesty, because we claim that the lives of all good people are public property, in so far as they relate to the fundamental principles of good government, good society, good order and true religion.

Before each individual or family sketch, is given the lines of ascent leading to that particular excursus. This is done for the sake of perspicuity. This genealogy contains sketches relating to the following families:

| | |
|---|---|
| Harvie, | Jacquelin, |
| Jones, | Cary, |
| Marshall, | Burwill, |
| Willis, | Carter, |
| Ambler, | Higginson, |
| Randolph, | |

Virginia, widow of Spicer Patrick, M. D.,
daughter of
Jacquelin B. Harvie and Mary Marshall,
son of
John Harvie and Margaret Morton,
son of
John Harvie and ——— Gaines.

The Harvies are of Scotch descent, coming to Virginia from Stiolingshire, Scotland. John Harvie, son of John and ——— Gaines, was born in Albemarle county, 1742; married Margaret Morton, daughter of Gabriel Jones, and Margaret Strother. He became early in life a successful lawyer, was delegate to the House of Burgesses from West Augusta; was a member of the Convention of 1775-6; signed the Bill of Rights; member of Continental Congress, 1778-9; signed articles of confederation; received commission as colonel of Virginia forces February, 1777; Registrar of Virginia land office from 1780 to 1791; Mayor of Richmond 1785; member of Virginia Legislature at various times; died at "Belvedere," his county seat, near Richmond, 1807.

[Council Journal Hist. Convention, 1775-6, Henings' Statutes.]

The inhabitants of West Augusta wrote to the convention requesting that John Harvie and John Neville be allowed to represent them, to which the convention agreed. The people of West Augusta afterwards returned thanks to John Harvie for the way in which he represented them. He was one of the committee appointed to prepare and bring in an ordinance for raising and embodying a sufficient force for the defence and protection of this colony. It was resolved in convention that John Harvie, gentleman, be appointed commissioner to receive the money due to the several claimants in the counties of Berkeley, Frederick, Dunmore, Hampshire and West Augusta, from the public, on account of the late expedition against the Indians, and pay the same to them, and the said John Harvie is required to settle and state all the accounts of the said expedition that remain unsettled, and advise those already settled in West Augusta, and make report thereof to the next convention.

Mr. Harvie's report was referred to the committee of which Mr. Richard Lee, as chairman, acknowledged them as having been examined and found correct. The convention allowed him 200 pounds for his services and all his expenses. John Harvie and Thomas Walker were appointed to decide whether they should engage such Indian warriors of the neighboring tribes as are willing to march to the assistance of this colony. May 24, 1776, Mr. Harvie was added to the Committee of Propositions and Grievances, and to the committee to prepare a declaration of rights and such a form of government as will be most likely to maintain peace and order in this colony and secure substantial and equal liberty to the people, to be called the "Bill of Rights."

*Jacquelin Burwell Harvie,* son of John Harvie and Margaret Morton Jones, was born in Richmond, Va., October 2, 1788; married September 18, 1813, at "Oak Hill," Fauquier county, Mary, daughter of John Marshall and his wife, Mary Willis (Ambler). He was prepared for the navy, and was serving as a midshipman when the terrible tragedy of the burning of the Richmond theatre occurred. On that occasion, he lost a brother, a sister and a niece. The loss of so many of his family required him to resign the navy that he might assist in the management of the large estate. During his life he filled many places of honor and trust. He was for many years a State Senator, and at the time of his death was Major General of Militia for the Eastern District of Virginia.

He was full of enterprise, and the Richmond Dock and Water Works and Belle Isle Nail Factory attest his public spirit. It was remarked of him that he was too far in advance of his time. He died in Richmond, February 9th, 1856.

Virginia, widow of Spicer Patrick, M. D.,
daughter of
Jaquelin B. Harvie and Mary Marshall,
son of
John Harvie and Margaret Morton Jones,
daughter of
Gabriel Jones and Margaret Strother,
son of
John Jones and Elizabeth.

For the purpose of this excursus we repeat a few facts mentioned in the sketch of Gabriel Jones, and add several not there mentioned.

John Jones and his wife Elizabeth came to Virginia from Montgomery county, North Wales, Great Britain.

*Gabriel Jones* was born in the County of York, three miles from Williamsburg, May 17th, 1724. He married October 16th, 1749, the Rev. James Keith officiating, Margaret Morton, widow of George Morton and daughter of Major William Strother and Margaret Watts, of King George County, in the Colony of Virginia.

Gabriel was educated in England, and studied law with Mr. John Houghton at Lyons Inn. On his return to Virginia, he settled in Frederick County. Became Private Secreary to Lord Fairfax. No lawyer was known in the bailiwick of Augusta County until 1745, when we find Gabriel Jones. Queens Attorney Court was formed in this year, when he qualified to practice in it. In 1778 he was appointed Deputy Commonwealth's Attorney. He was elected member of Confederate Congress, 1774, and of the State Convention 1788. He was one of the most prominent men of the Colony and a man of wealth and culture. He was a member of the House of Burgesses from Frederick County 1748-1751, Augusta County, 1757-8-64, 69, 71. He was appointed with Lord Fairfax and others, trustees for the towns of Stevensburg and Winchester, they or any five of them at any time, to establish such rules about building houses and laying off towns as they deem best and convenient. He was commissioned to ascertain the pay and subsistence of Militia, and damage done by Cherokees and Catawba Indians. He was also appointed with Samuel Washington and George Read, by the Congress and also by Virginia to go to Fort Pitt to look into the condition of affairs there in 1777.

(Waddell's History of Augusta County, R. A. Brock, History of

Convention 1788. Vol. II., page 16-19- Va. Hit. Coll; Meade, Vol. II., p. 324-5. Hennigs Stat., Vo. VII., pp. 230, 282; Vol. IX., p. 374.)

Virginia, widow of Spicer Patrick, M. D.,
daughter of
Jacqulin B. Harvie and Mary Marshall,
daughter of
John Marshall and Mary Willis Ambler,
son of
Thomas Marshall and Mary Randolph Keith,
son of
John Marshall and Elizabeth Markham,

The Marshall family were of British descent, having come from Wales to Virginia. They were distinguished by their intellect and force of character. John Marshall, son of Thomas Marshall was born in Westmoreland County, Virginia, in 1700; died 1752. Married, 1724, Elizabeth Markham, daughter of a wealthy Englishman, who for political reasons had recently come to the Colony. He was a Militia officer and of influence in his neighborhood. He left four sons, the most distinguished of whom was Thomas, who was regarded by his children with veneration.. He was born in Westmoreland, April 2nd, 1732. Moved to Fauquier, 1753. Married, 1754, in Fauquier, Mary Randolph Keith, daughter of Rev. James Keith and Mary Isham Randolph, of Tuckahoe. Thomas Marshall was appointed by Washington his assistant in surveying the land of Lord Fairfax. "They had been neighbors from birth, associates from boyhood and were always friends." Thomas Marshall was a man of extraordinary vigor of mind and of undaunted courage. He was Lieutenant of Volunteers in the French and Indian wars. He was repeatedly elected to the Virginia House of Burgesses, never failing to obtain the suffrages of the people, whose respect and confidence he held in the fullest measure, and he warmly participated in all the earliest movements to encourage the Colonists in resistance to British tyrrany. When the call to arms was made in Virginia, he was one of the first to offer his services and was a field officer in the first regiment raised. Was active in raising a patriotic company known as the Culpepper Minute men. This was the earliest organization in the cause of freedom. He was a member of the

Convention of 1775-6, but left the Convention to take an active part in the field. When his name was proposed for the office of Major he was elected by acclamation in the Convention. In his first engagement at the battle of the Great Bridge, the first engagement on Virginia soil, he was distinguished for valor and good conduct— afterwards he successfully commanded in the Continental line, the Third Virginia Infantry and the First Virginia Artillery as their Colonel. He was in the battles of Germantown and Brandytown, having three horses killed under him, and in the latter engagement contributed largely by his courage and skill to save the American army. He endured all the hardships of Valley Forge with three of his sons. In 1779 he was sent with his regiment to join the army in South Carolina and with part of his regiment was taken prisoner in Charleston. During the term of his parole he made his first visit to Kentucky. Returning to Virginia he remained to the close of the war, and in 1785 moved with the younger members of his family to Kentucky. He died in 1806, at the home of his son, Captain Thomas Marshall, in Mason county, and lies buried in the family cemetery near Washington, in that State. In token of his great bravery and patriotic services the House of Burgesses through their Speaker, Edmund Randolph, presented him with a sword, which descended to his son Thomas, and by his descendant was presented to the Maysville Historical Society. The wife of Colonel Thomas Marshall was Mary Randolph Keith. Her father, James Keith, was an Episcopal clergyman and cousin german to the last Earl Marshall, and to Field Marshal James Keith, one of the most valued of the great Fredericks Lieutenants, who saved the Prussian army and fell at Hutchkirch, "as poor as a Scott, though he had had the ransoming of three cities." James Keith, the father of Mary, had to leave Scotland on account of taking part in the rebellion of 1715, and took refuge in the Colony of Virginia.

Thomas and Mary Marshall had fifteen children, seven sons and eight daughters, all of whom arrived at mature years. The oldest was John.

(Horace Binning Eulogy, &c.; Story, J. Marshall. Campbell Hist., Henning; Magruders Hist. of Marshall.)

*John Marshall*, son of Thomas and Mary Marshall, was born in Fauquier county, September 24th, 1755. His father was a man of fine mind and great intelligence, who devoted himself personally to the training of his children. He had a private teacher from Scotland, Mr. James Thompson, a clergman, who came to this country and took up his residence in the family of Colonel Marshall, and instructed his children. John early displayed a strong love for English literature, especially poetry and history. At the age of twelve he knew by heart a large portion of Pope's writings and was familiar with Dryden and Shakespeare and Milton. He was sent to the classical academy of the Messrs. Campbell in Westmoreland county. After his return home he pursued his study of Latin with his old preceptor, Mr. Thompson, who was an accomplished classicist. He was fond of athletic sports and exercise in the open air. He began the study of law at eighteen, but his mind became so excited over the impending war with Great Britain that his studies were put aside.

At the age of nineteen he was chosen Lieutenant of a company of Minute men. His first experience was at the battle of Great Bridge. July, 1776, he was appointed First Lieutenant in a company of the 11th Virginia Regiment. In May, 1777, he became a Captain. He was at the battle of Brandywine, September 11th, 1777; at Germantown, October 4th, 1777; at Monmouth, June 28th, 1778; at Stony Point, and endured the hardships of Valley Forge.

One of his contemporaries says at this time his judicial capacity and fairness were held in such estimation by many of his brother officers, that in many disputes of a certain description he was constantly chosen arbiter. In argument, disputed points were often submitted to his judgment, which, given in writing, and accompanied as it commonly was by some reasons in support of his decision, obtained general acquiescence.

At this period, besides his field service, he acted as Deputy Judge Advocate of the army, and thus came into personal relations with Washington, securing confidence and regard of life-long duration. One of his messmates, Slaughter, says: " He was the best tempered man I ever knew. During his sufferings at Valley Forge nothing ever disturbed him. If he had only bread to eat it was just as well; if only meat, it made no difference. If any of the officers murmured at their deprivations, he would shame them by good natured railery, or encourage them by his own exuberance of spirits. He was an excellent companion and idolized by the soldiers and his brother officers, whose gloomy hours were enlivened by his inexhaustible fund of anecdote.

There were more officers than were needed in the army, and in 1779 he returned to Virginia for a time and attended a course of law andp hilosophy at William and Mary College. He was licensed to practice law in 1780, but the courts were closed and he returned to the army. After the surrender at Yorktown he entered on the practice of law. His success was marked from the beginning. In 1782 he was sent to the Legislature from Fauquier, and was appointed a member of the Council of State.

At Yorktown he met Miss Mary Willis Ambler, daughter of Treasurer Jaqulin Ambler. They were married January 3rd, 1783, at the " Cottage," in Hanover county, a family country place.

In 1785 his father moved to Kentucky, and gave him the family place, "Oak Hill," but he removed to Richmond to carry on the practice of law. In 1787 he was in the Legislature. In 1788 he was a member of the Convention that ratified the United States Constitution. In 1789-90-91 he represented Richmond in the Legislature. He now devoted himself to law and became distinguished for his clear and comprehensive grasp and logical analysis of the legal and political questions of the day.

Though gentle in his manner and careless of his dress, his intellectual powers placed him at the head of his profession. Washington offered him the place of Attorney General and afterwards the Ministry to France, but both positions were declined. In 1797 he was sent as Envoy to France by Mr. Adams. On this mission he acted with such dignity, ability and manly spirit, that on his return he was received with warmest enthusiasm. A public dinner was given him by both Houses of Congress then in session "as an evidence of affection for his person and of their grateful approbation of the patriotic firmness with which he sustained the dignity of his country during his important mission.

On his return to Virginia he was not less warmly welcomed by all parties. He was elected to Congress in 1799. Was Secretary of State under John Adams. Whilst in this office was appointed Chief Justice of the United States, January 31st, 1801, which office he held till his death in 1835. In 1829 he was a member and presiding officer of the State Constitutional Convention. Shockoe cemetery, Richmond, Virginia, contains his remains. He wrote this inscription for his tombstone: "John Marshall, son of Thomas and Mary Marshall, was born September 24, 1755, intermarried with Mary Willis Ambler, the 3rd day of January, 1783, departed this life the 6th of July, 1835."

Virginia, widow of Spicer Patrick, M. D.,
daughter of
Jacquelin B. Harvie and Mary Marshall,
daughter of
John Marshall and Mary Willis Ambler,
son of
Thomas Marshall and Mary Randolph Keith,
daughter of
James Keith and Mary Isham Randolph,
daughter of
Thomas Randolph and Judith Churchill,
son of
Thomas Randolph and Mary Isham.

William Randolph came to Virginia from Warwickshire, England, about 1669. On July 29th of that year he was Clerk of Henrico County. He held at different times the offices of Justice, High Sheriff, and Colonel of Militia, and was a member of the House of Burgesses from Henrico, from 1684 to 1699, and Speaker of the House in 1698. Was Attorney General of the Colony in 1696. In 1693 by the charter was appointed one of the first visitors and trustees for founding William and Mary College. He died April 11th, 1711, and was buried at his country seat, "Turkey Island." His tombstone bears his coat of arms.

By his wife Mary, a daughter of Henry Isham, of Bermuda Hundred, Henrico county, he had with other issue, Thomas Randolph, of Tuckahoe, Goochland county, who was appointed one of the first Justices of that county in 1728. He was the father of Mary Isham (Randolph), who married James Keith.

(Henning's Stats., Vol. III., p. 167; Campbell's Hist. of Virginia.)

Virginia, widow of Spicer Patrick, M. D.,
daughter of
Jacquelin B. Harvie and Mary Marshall,
daughter of

200

John Marshall and Mary Willis Ambler,
daughter of
Jacquelin Ambler and Rebecca Burwell,
son of
Richard Ambler and Martha Jacquelin,
son of
John Ambler and Elizabeth Burkadike.

*Richard Ambler*, son of John Ambler and Elizabeth Burkadike, of the city of York, England, was born December 24th, 1690, died 1756. Came to Virginia, 1716, settled at Yorktown; was Collector of Customs and naval officer for District of York river, an office both lucrative and honorable, and which he discharged with great integrity. In 1724 he married Elizabeth Jacquelin, daughter of Edward Jacquelin, and Martha Cary, a daughter of William Cary, of Warwick. Elizabeth was born 1709; died 1756.

*Jacquelin Ambler*, son of Richard and Elizabeth Jacquelin Ambler, was born in the town of little York (Yorktown), August 7th, 1742. Married Rebecca, daughter of the Hon. Lewis Burwell, of Gloucester. Was Collector of the port at Yorktown and naval officer of York river, which office he resigned in 1777. Member of the Privy Council, 1780. Treasurer of the State, which office he held until his death. He stood so high for character·that he was called the Aristides of Virginia.

In a small handwriting below the records in the family Bible this is written:

‘ ‘ I will have mercy unto a thousand generations of them that love
and keep my commandments,
Let this be remembered now in the fifth generation,
We boast not that we declare our births,
From loins enthroned or rulers of the earth,
But higher far our proud pretentions rise,
Children of parents past into the skies.’’

Virginia, widow of Spicer Patrick, M. D.,
daughter of
Jacquelin B. Harvie and Mary Marshall,
daughter of
John Marshall and Mary Willis Ambler,
daughter of

201

Jacquelin Ambler and Rebecca Burwell,
son of
Richard Ambler and Elizabeth Jacquelin,
daughter of
Edward Jacquelin and Martha Cary.

*Edward Jacquelin*, of Jamestown, Virginia, son of John Jacquelin and Elizabeth Craddock, of the County of Kent, England, descended in the direct line from the noble family of La Roche Jacquelin. They were Protestants, and fled from La Vandee in France to England a short time previous to the massacre of St. Bartholomew. They were eminently wealthy, and converted a large portion of their wealth into gold and silver, which they transported in safety to England. He was born in 1663; died 1739. Was born in Kent County, England; came to Virginia, 1697; settled at Jamestown; married Martha Cary, daughter of William Cary, of Warwick. Member of the House of Burgesses and Justice of the Peace. His wife was born 1686; died 1738.

Edward and Martha (Cary) Jacquelin had one son born in 1716; died 1734; aged 18 years. This Edward and his mother gave the silver baptismal bowl to the James City Church. It is now used at the Monumental Church, Richmond, Virginia.

Virginia, widow of Spicer Patrick, M. D.,
daughter of
Jacquelin B. Harvie and Mary Marshall,
daughter of
John Marshall and Mary Willis Ambler,
daughter of
Jacquelin Ambler and Rebecca Burwell,
son of
Richard Ambler and Elizabeth Jacquelin,
daughter of
Edward Jacquelin and Martha Cary,
daughter of
William Cary and Martha,
son of
Miles Cary and Anna Taylor.

*Miles Cary* was descended from the Carys of Devonshire, England; his great-grand-father being William, Mayor of Bristol in

1546.  Miles was the son of John Cary, of Bristol, England, who was born there in 1620; came to Virginia in 1648, and settled in the County of Warwick.  Member of House of Burgesses, 1658-9-60.  Of the Council, 1663.  March 29th, 1666, superintended the erection of defences at Point Comfort against the Dutch.  There lost his life in 1667.  Married Anne Taylor, daughter of Colonel Thomas Taylor, of York; also a member of the Council.

*William Cary,* son of Miles and Anne (Taylor) Cary; was a member of the House of Burgesses, 1692, 1708, 1710; died August, 1711.  He was the father of Martha, who married Edward Jacquelin.  His will was made August 25, 1711.

(Meade; Hennig's Stats; Brock.)

Burwell,                       Carter,
Higginson,                    Armstead.

Virginia, widow of Spicer Patrick, M. D.,
daughter of
Jacquelin B. Harvie and Mary Marshall,
daughter of
John Marshall and Mary Willis Ambler,
daughter of
Jacquelin Ambler and Rebecca Burwell,
daughter of
Lewis Burwell and Mary Willis,
son of
Nathaniel Burwell and Elizabeth Carter,
son of
Lewis Burwell and Abigail Smith,
son of
Lewis Burwall and Lucy Higginson.

The Burwell family is of very ancient date, upon the borders of England and Scotland.  According to tombstones and epitaphs, the Burwells of Virginia are descended from an ancient family in Bedfordshire and Northamptonshire in England, but the first to whom we trace is Edward Burwell, of Haslington, Bedfordshire, England, (probably the Edward Burwell, of the Virginia company, 1616), and his wife Dorothy, daughter of William Bedell, in Huntingtonshire, by whom he had a son, Lewis Burwell; born 1625, who at an early age came to Virginia.  His mother married for her second husband Roger Wingate Masurer, of the Colony of Virginia. By a record in York County, 1648, she conveyed a certain property to her only and beloved son, Lewis Burwell. This Major Lewis Burwell acquired a very large landed estate, and settled on the present Carter's Creek, in Gloucester County. In 1640 he married Lucy, daughter of the "valiant Captain Robert Higginson." Lewis Burwell died in 1658; had an only son, Lewis Burwell, of Gloucester and Queen's Creek, York County; was member of the Council for many years, from which body he retired in 1702. He marriel Abagail Smith, niece and heiress of Nathaniel Bacon, Sen., President of the Council. He was grand-son of Sir James Bacon, of " Triston," and cousin of the great Lord Bacon. The eldest son of Lewis and Abagail Burwell was Nathaniel, who married Elizabeth, daughter of " King" Robert Carter. They had one daughter and three sons. Their eldest, Lewis Burwell, was born in 1710; married 1736, Mary Willis, daughter of Colonel Francis and Anne Willis, of Gloucester. He was educated in England; matriculated at Cain's College, Cambridge in 1731; was a man of genius and learning. He was Burgess as early as 1736; a little later became member of the Council, and as President of that body acting Governor of the Colony, 1750; died 1752.

(Meade; Brock's Virginia and Virginians; Burk's History of Virginia.)

Virginia, widow of Spicer Patrick, M. D.,
daughter of
Jacquelin B. Harvie and Mary Marshall,
daughter of
John Marshall and Mary Willis Ambler,
daughter of
Jacquelin Ambler and Rebecca Burwell,
daughter of
Lewis Burwell and Mary Willis,
son of
Nathaniel Burwell and Elizabeth Carter,
son of
Lewis Burwell and Abagail Smith,
son of
Lewis Burwell and Lucy Higginson,
son of
Robert Higginson.

Colonel Robert Higginson, in his daughter's epitaph, is said to have been one of the first commanders who conquered the Dominion of Virginia from the power of the "Heathen." The York County records state that Captain Robert Higginson received gifts of land from the county for his services against the Indians. Captain Higginson commanded the forces raised to protect the Colony after the second massacre; was still on duty in 1646, and received land from the General Assembly for his services. His only daughter and heiress, Lucy, married first Major Lewis Burwell; second, Colonel William Bernard, of the Council; third, Colonel Philip Ludwell, of the Council and Governor of North Carolina.

(Meade, Vol. I., Records of York County.)

Virginia, widow of Spicer Patrick, M. D.,
daughter of
Jacquelin B. Harvie and Mary Marshall,
daughter of
John Marshall and Mary Willis Ambler,
daughter of
Jacquelin Ambler and Rebecca Burwell,
daughter of
Lewis Burwell and Mary Willis,
son of
Nathaniel Burwell and Elizabeth Carter,
daughter of
Robert Carter and Judith Armstead,
son of
John Carter and Sarah Ludlow.

John Carter came from England; settled in Norfolk County, which he represented in the House of Burgesses in 1642; commander against Rappahanock Indians in 1654; Burgess for Lancaster for a number of years; died 1699; married for his third wife Sarah, daughter of Gabriel Ludlow; had a son who on account of his large landed possessions was known as "King" Carter. He was Speaker of the House of Burgesses for six years, 1694-1699. Treasurer of the. Colony many years. Member of the Council, 1699-1726, and as member of that body acting Governor of the Colony. Married first, Judith Armstead, eldest daughter of John Armstead, of "Hesse" Gloucester. Their daughter, Elizabeth, married Nathaniel Burwell. Robert Carter died 1732.

(Campbell's History of Virginia : Meade.)

*John Armstead,* of "Hesse" Gloucester, was the son of William Armstead, and the father of Judith, who married Robert Carter. He was long a Justice of the Peace in Gloucester, High Sheriff in 1676, and member of Council from 1687 to 1691.

(Burk's History of Virginia; Hening, Vol. III., page 565; Sainsburg's Abstracts.)

--- --- ---

# THE RUFFNERS.

## By Dr. Wm. Henry Ruffner.

### I. Peter.

The Ruffners having constituted an important element in the make-up of Kanawha county, especially in its earlier decades, their origin may be a matter of public interest.

The Ruffners of Virginia, West Virginia, and most of those who are scattered in the States farther west even to the Pacific Ocean, are all descendants from Peter Ruffner, who emigrated from the German border of Switzerland to America in 1732, whilst still a young man. He sojourned for seven years in Lancaster County, Pennsylvania. There he married Mary Steinman, the daughter of a wealthy German landholder, who assigned to him a patent obtained from King George II for a baronial estate in Virginia on the waters of the Shenandoah River, in what was then Frederick County, afterwards Shenandoah, now Page. Thither he came with his wife, and as has been suggested, with live stock and other conveniences. He certainly brought either money or the means of making money, as was proved by his rapid accumulation of additional property. His original patent covered a belt of land beginning at the mouth of Hawkbill Creek, a mill stream which passes close by Luray, and continuing up the creek including both branches for eight miles. His lands were afterwards extended four miles farther up the two branches of the creek, which additions greatly improved the character of his estate.

Peter established his dwelling at the "Big Spring," now on the edge of Luray where he and after him his son Peter, and after him a grandson Jonas, lived, reared large families, and died. After whom came Forrer, and after him the widow Chapman whose heroic sons distinguished themselves in Mosby's command. At the time when Peter Ruffner came there was a small settlement of Germans in the neighborhood, among whom were Stover, Strickler, Roller, Heistand, Beidler, etc.

It is quite certain that Peter Ruffner came from Switzerland, yet there is an important statement made by Wm. S. Marye which brings him from the Kingdom of Hanover in Germany. Marye, one of the Fredericksburg Maryes, and an educated man, came in 1794 to the German settlement and lived for a time with a Scotchman named Mundell, who was engaged in merchandizing. In 1802 he married Mary Ruffner the daughter of Peter the second, and soon came into possession of the family records and traditions. In 1835 Marye wrote a history of the Ruffner family which contains a number of statements not found elsewhere, but which does not contradict the prevailing family tradition except on the one point in locating the paternal home of the first Peter in Hanover. Marye bore so high a reputation for probity that we may ascribe his error to inadvertence. With this remark I will quote from his narrative:

"Peter Ruffner the elder is the first of the Ruffner family of whom we have any intelligence in this country. He was a native of the Kingdom of Hanover in Germany; was of the Teutonic-German stock; was the third son of a German baron, who owned large landed estates in Hanover. He spoke the High Dutch language (Hoch-Deutsch) and was in religion a Protestant of the Martin Luther school.

"He was at an agricultural college, and before he got through his studies (with other students), he left college without the knowledge of his parents, and came to this country, having been attracted hither by the then glowing descriptions of America published in the German States. On arriving in this country, he located in one of the interior counties of Pennsylvania (Lancaster county, I think it was), where he very soon thereafter became acquainted with and married Miss Mary Steinman, the daughter of a very wealthy German farmer there, who owned a large landed property in the Valley of Virginia. Said Steinman was a native of the Kingdom of Wurtemburg in Germany; was of the Slavonic-German stock; he spoke the Low Dutch (Platt-Deutsch) language; he emigrated some years previously to this country, with considerable means, and had made a considerable fortune by farming and grazing, and had invested much of his surplus funds in those valuable wild lands in the Valley of Virginia, along the Shenandoah River, and on both branches of the Hawksbill Creek, in Shenandoah County.

Steinman gave to Ruffner a large body of very valuable land, situated on both branches of the Hawksbill Creek, to which said Ruffner and his wife Mary removed, and settled on the plantation now owned by and on which Jonas Ruffner resides, on the Hawksbill Creek, adjoining the town of Luray, where he lived many years with his wife Mary, and by her he had the following children, viz:

1. Joseph.
2. Benjamin.
3. Reuben.
4. Peter.
5. Emmanuel.
6. Elizabeth.

The said Peter Ruffner was only about nineteen years old when he came to America. He was a tall, fine looking man, being 6 feet 3 inches, of strong mind and with great energy of character; was a man of mark and of much influence in his neighborhood and county. His wife was said to be possessed of equally good parts; and they were both well calculated to do well in the world. They were industrious, thriving and prosperous farmers for many years and acquired much additional landed property. They lived to a good old age, and died and were buried on the plantation on which they had first settled, having raised all their children, and settled them on good farms near to them, as they respectively got married.

At the time Peter Ruffner the elder migrated to and settled in Shenandoah, there was a considerable settlement there of Slavonic Germans, mostly from Pennsylvania, the stock being of that extraction of Germans, with some few foreign Germans, all who spoke the Low Dutch (Platt-Deutsch) language. Indeed at that early day, that part of the Valley of Virginia was almost exclusively settled by this class of Germans, and it was with that class of Germans that the said Peter Ruffner became identified and inter-married afterwards."

Had Marye located the Ruffner barony in Switzerland his narrative would have harmonized with some known facts. I am creditably informed that Judge Drew of Kanawha, when a student at Heidelburg University made the acquaintance of a Baron Rufnier (also a student) from Switzerland, and that their acquaintance is still continued by correspondence. No doubt this name is but another form of Ruffner. In 1876 at the Philadelphia Exposition a Ruffner from Berne, Switzerland, exhibited chemicals. From various quarters it is reported that the name is now common and influential in the region about Berne.

But evidence is accumulating which indicates that neither Germany nor Switzerland was the original fatherland of the Ruffners; but that they originally came from Italy. A tradition to this effect exists among at least three lines of people bearing the name in America, who are not known to be related to each other, and in a book entitled "Noblesse Francaise," which I examined in the old Philadelphia library, is to be found the name of Ruffiniere. In a similar book of Italian notables occurs the name of Ruffiniar. The same name with the exception of the final "r" occurs very often among the Latin people both ancient and modern. Ruffinianus was a Roman rhetorician; Ruffinus was a son of Poppaea by her first marriage to Rufus Crispinus. In the Gallic War there was a General Ruffinus. A number of others might be mentioned. The radical name of them all was probably Rufus, red, so named from the color of the soil.

But the etymology of the name is of less consequence to us than the doings of the people of the Hawksbill. The man who brought the name certainly had enterprise and good judgment, for as heretofore said, large as was his tract of land on the Hawksbill he largely and rapidly added to it. Beautiful though partial views of his possessions may be obtained from the car windows for several miles south of Luray, looking east toward the Blue Ridge. We have no detailed information as to Peter's additions except as to the purchase from Lord Fairfax of 196 acres of land on the Hawksbill in 1761. The original deed in a somewhat mutilated condition is now on deposit in the State Museum at Charleston. The handwriting is quite legible, but parts of the document are gone including the signature. The antique style of the deed, I think, possesses interest enough to justify the making of the following quotations from it, to-wit:

"The Right Honorable Lord Fairfax, baron of Cameron, in that part of Great Britain called Scotland, proprietor of the Northern Neck of Virginia: to all whom this present writing shall come, sends greeting.

Know ye that for good causes, for and in consideration of the composition to me paid, and for the annual rent here-inafter named, I have given, granted and confirmed, and do hereby give, grant and confirm to Peter Ruffner of Frederick County, a certain tract * * * adjoining other land of Ruffner * * * on the branches of the Hawksbill. * *
* Bounded as follows * * * To have and to hold * * * Royal mines excepted * * * and a full third part of lead, copper, tinn, coals, iron mine and iron ore.

"Said Ruffner shall pay yearly and every year on the first day of St. Michael the Archangel the Free Rent of one shilling sterling money for every fifty acres.

"Given at my office * * * the fifth day of May in the first day of his Majesty George the third, 1761."

At that time the market towns of the producers of the Shenandoah County were Fredericksburg and Alexandria. Peter Ruffner continued to live and prosper where he first settled for 49 years. His death occurred in 1788 at the age of 76 years. His wife lived 10 years longer, and died at 84. They left five children, four sons and one daughter.

The Big Spring home place was inherited by Peter's fourth son and namesake, whose daughter Mary became the wife of Marye. This Peter the second had eleven children, one of whom Jonas succeeded to the ownership of the home-stead. He built the brick residence occupied by the Chap-man family. He donated the site of Luray, and is jestingly reported to have said "the land is poor and much of it too steep to plough—so you may have it!" I mentioned Jonas particularly because all of his fourteen children except one went to Kanawha about 1840, though the most of them passed on farther West. One of the daughters, Rebecca, married Frank Ruffner, and another, Mary Ann, married John B. Davenport. Descendents of these two families still live in Kanawha.

To return to the immediate family of the first Peter, his eldest son Joseph was the progenitor of all the Kanawha Ruffners except the few just mentioned; but I postpone the full account of him until my next number, in order that I may mention a few miscellaneous items.

The celebrated Luray cave is so much a matter of pub lic interest that I will mention some facts concerning it. The hill in which the cave is situated belonged in early days to the Ruffner family. So far as I can learn the first discovery of a cave in the hill was made by one of the sons of Joseph Ruffner, who went out soon afterward to Kanawha, and became one of its most prominent citizens. This cave is entered near the top of the hill, and is not the same as the one now so much visited; though there is scarcely a doubt but they are connected. It was probably in 1793 or 4 that Ruffner, then not grown, and a companion, chased a fox into a hole. Ruffner digged for him, and to his astonishment uncovered the mouth of a cave, the opening to which descended vertically into the earth a distance of perhaps 30 feet. The hole remained open, but was not explored immediately on account of the formidable look of the entrance. After a time, however, the cave was entered by a Ruffner. As to this point the testimonials are unanimous, but I have not been able to determine just which of the Ruffners it was. The best account we have of the attempt at exploration was published in the Shenandoah Herald in 1825. This account was copied in the Virginia Gazetteer, and in the Lexington, Virginia, Intelligencer the same year, and has formed the basis of most of what has been said about it. In 1880 two college-bred gentlemen visited Luray, and published what they could gather in their little book of travels under the names of "Ego" and "Alter." They were thoroughly trustworthy, and I will quote their account of the adventure, as follows:

"A Mr. Ruffner who was nearly as much celebrated for deeds of Sylvan prowess as the renowned Putnam, in passing this cave some thirty years ago, namely, in 1795, conceived the bold and hazardous design of entering it alone. He accordingly placed his rifle across the mouth to indicate, in case of accident to his friends in case they should happen to see it, that he was in the cave. He descended, but soon fell and put out his light, and as must have been expected, was soon bewildered and lost in its labyrinth of passages. It happened that some of his friends in passing the cave discovered his gun, and rightly concluding that he had gone into it, they procured lights and entered in search of him. They found and brought him out after he had been in for forty-eight hours. This brave fellow was among the pioneers who were foremost in exploring and settling our Western frontier; and was at last killed by the Indians after having performed deeds of valor which would have done honor to the character of a hero."

This cave was long known as "Ruffner's Cave," and was so put down on the old maps. I have a map now with the cave thus marked. One feature of the tradition is not mentioned by "Ego" and "Alter," namely, that Ruffner dropped a pine sapling into the vertical mouth of the cave, and used it as a ladder.

With regard to the Ruffner who is above mentioned as the first who entered the cave—it could not be Daniel, for he was not an Indian fighter, and was not killed by the Indians. The early Ruffners were Mennonites, an anti-war sect, and could not be expected to furnish many fighters; but Schuricht in his history of the Germans in Virginia names a number of noted Indian fighters among the early settlers, and among them "George Ruffner." But I have no other knowledge of him. In fact the first three generations of Ruffners were so prolific that there is no record in existence of all their names.

So far as my information goes, I should incline to assign the early fighters to the family of Emmanuel, the youngest son of the first Peter. He had a large family and was himself a giant in size and strength. His arm is reported to have been as large as the leg of a common sized man. In 1805 he removed to Fairfield County, Ohio. Concerning his family history I have almost no accurate knowledge; but I always suspected that it was one of his sons who performed a remarkable feat, which was reported in the newspapers many, many years ago under the caption of "Ruffner against Crockett." In order that the story may not be wholly forgotten I will tell it here as I remember it.

Ruffner, who lived on the bank of the Ohio, was roused from sleep one winter night by the violent barking of his dogs which were driving some animal into the River. Ruffner dashed down the bank, thinking the animal was probably a deer, and when he found that the dogs and their game had taken water, he plunged in after them. Ice was running freely in the river, but on he went, and when he reached the other side he found his dogs in fierce conflict with a large black wolf. But the wolf slashed the dogs so savagely as to clear the space around him, and there he stood ready to fight the master. Ruffner was in his night-clothes and without any sort of weapon, but he set the dogs on him again, and whilst they were scuffling in the edge of the water, he seized the wolf by the hind legs and tried to drown him, but failing in this he swung him high in the air, and brought his head down upon a rock, crushing his skull. Such a man as this would consider the exploring of a cave an easy venture.

Peter Ruffner the elder had one son and a daughter who were content with their Hawksbill farms, and never went West; but he had another son who possessed the adventurous

212

spirit of the early Ruffners, and went off with his family to Kentucky.

Peter Ruffner's posterity now considerably exceed one thousand in number, a goodly increase in one hundred and sixty-five years.

Lexington, Va., April 10, 1901.

# THE RUFFNERS.

## II: JOSEPH.

### BY DR. W. H. RUFFNER

Joseph Ruffner, the eldest son of the first Peter, was the head of the large Kanawha family. He was born in 1740, on Hawksbill Creek in Shenandoah, now Page county, at the Big Spring mentioned in former article. At 24 years of age he married Ann Heistand (or Hiestand), daughter of Henry Hiestand, of the neighborhood. She is reported as having been a tall, comely woman of good sense and German virtues. Joseph had the maternal characteristics of raven black hair, black eyes, dark complexion and stature above medium. Though full of energy, and occasionally vehement, he had usually a quiet manner and amiable temper. They had eight children, all of whom, except one who died young, ultimately went to Kanawha.

213

Joseph Ruffner's farm lay next above his father's, on both sides of Hawksbill creek. It consisted of 1,200 acres of fertile land, and included the north fork where the two branches of the creek united. Here were his family and farm buildings erected, and also a grist mill and saw mill, which are now known as the Willow Grove Mills. He operated extensively and successfully. Among other things, he is reported to have dealt largely in bear skins for the French army. In those days the skins of deer, beaver, otter, raccoon and other animals also constituted an important item of trade. Flour, Whiskey, butter, beeswax, dried fruit, wool, flaxseed, etc., constituted the bulk of the outgoing domestic products..

Fredericksburg was the chief market town for the people of this neighborhood, and Joseph Ruffner kept on the road a large wagon covered with bear skins and drawn by six gigantic horses, most probably the Lancaster County (Pa.) Conestogas. This turnout was not only "famous over all the earth for ten miles around," but famous in all the country from Shenandoah to Spottsylvania. What freight was brought back in this lumbering ship of the mountains I cannot even guess, except the item of salt. Nearly everything used in the German settlement was made at home. There was Pennebacker's combined iron furnace, forge and foundry, within two miles of of Willow Grove Mills. Screws and nails were made in the blacksmith shops. Wagons, farm and domestic tools and implements and furniture were made in the neighborhood. Carpets, beds and clothing were made in the families. Tan-yards supplied all needed leather. Tea and coffee had not yet supplanted bean and potato soup for breakfast, and mush and milk for supper. Maple trees gave them "sweetening," both long and short. Herbs gave the old women their materia medica. Even guns were made in the settlements, and there were small lead mines then that have since been lost sight of.

But nevertheless there came gradually to be some demand for store goods, as is shown by the fact that the Scotchman, Mundell, opened a store at Willow Grove Mills in 1794, which was continued long enough for the growth of a village, which was called Mundellsville.

For thirty years Joseph Ruffner pursued his prosperous career, filling his barns year after year, raising and marketing cattle, hauling to Fredericksburg and back. Meanwhile his stalwart sons, David, Joseph, Tobias, Samuel, Daniel and Abraham, and his daughter Eve, were growing up around him with sober, industrious habits, and, excepting the unfortunate Samuel, showing the long-headed business sense which in due time exhibited itself in other fields.

This scene of prosperity was suddenly marred by an event which changed the course of the family history. Ruffner's great Switzer barn, crammed with the crop of 1794, in the basement of which were stabled seven cows and the six big horses, was burned; causing the loss of four of the horses and all the cows, besides the entire building and crops. Not long after this another stable was burnt and two more horses perished. Insurance was unknown in those days. It was the work of an incendiary, and no one doubted that the guilty party was a certain free negro man, against whom Mr. Ruffner had given testimony in court; but legal evidence against the fellow could not be obtained, and as Judge Lynch had not yet arisen, nothing was done with the scoundrel.

It is thought that these fires created in Ruffner's mind such a sense of insecurity that he determined at once on some important change, and he seems to have thought of engaging in the iron business at some distant point. This seems evident from the fact that in the same autumn in which the fires occurred he set out on a hunt for iron ore lands. Judging from the route he took it is probable he had heard of the ample beds of iron ore on the upper waters of the James river, which are now feeding so many enormous furnaces. He reached a point on the Cow Pasture which may not have been more than twenty miles from Clifton Forge—namely, the house of Col. John Dickinson, who, if I mistake not, was 'the head of a large and worthy family, some of whom are still to be found in the same region. This no doubt was the same Col. Dickinson who was in the battle of Point Pleasant. And it is not an extravagant surmise to suppose that what he (Ruffner) saw and heard of the Kanawha Valley during that famous march led him to get possession of the great Buffalo Lick.

At any rate Joseph Ruffner found Col. Dickcinson in possession of the deed for 502 acres, including the Salt Spring— a survey which was destined to become the most famous in the Kanawha Valley. It fronted on the river and extended up Campbell's Creek. Dr. Hale has made the public acquainted with the early history of the little briny swamp on the north bank of the river five miles above Charleston, which, by courtesy, was called a spring, and in truth was the most frequented of all the watering places ever known in Virginia. Buffalo, elk and deer came in great numbers and scored the river bank into deep gullies which long continued visible.

Col. Dickinson found that his visitor had money, and was just in a state of mind to listen. Before leaving the house Ruffner, who had foresight of his own, bought the sur-

215

vey, including the salt spring, for 600 pound sterling. The amount is commonly stated to be 500 pounds, but by reference to the deed it will be seen that 600 pounds is the true figure, which was about $2,000. But the price was to be increased according to the subsequent production of salt. If this should reach 50 bushels per day the price was to be increased to 10,000 pounds. How this increase of price was avoided will appear in my next number. This transaction with Dickinson seems to be iconsistent with Ruffner's reputation for good practical sense, but the future showed that all his anticipations were correct.

As soon as this purchase was made Ruffner gave up his thought of making iron and immediately returned home. The next spring (1795) he rode out to Kanawha on horseback alone; and from Greenbrier he followed the track for 100 miles, along which only six years before Mad Ann Bailey had run the gauntlet of the Indians in carrying ammunition to lite Clendennin Fort. When he reached Gauley river he found it booming, and undertook to cross it in very peculiar style. I have the incident as recited to me by that devoted antiquarian, John L. Cole, who got it from the lips of Paddy Huddlestone, Sr., who lived a few miles below Kanawha Falls, and who witnessed it. Cole, in repeating impersonated Huddlestone, who said:

"One day I walked up the river and found Gauley very high; drift running. I travelled on up stream and when I got about seven miles from the mouth of Gauley I saw a man on the opposite side of the river leading his horse down a steep place to the bank of the river. There was no trail to this point, and I don't know how he got there, but he looked as if he meant to cross the river, but I didn't think he would be fool enough to try to ford it, or to swim it with all the load he had on. I couldn't imagine what he was going to do. But presently he took a short-handled axe from his saddle and went to work on a dry chestnut tree that had fallen against the cliff. The trunk he cut into lengths and split. He then took a rope and tied the pieces to his horse's tail and dragged them to a place to suit him. Then he took from his saddle bags some wrought nails and made a raft, which he put into the water and loaded his things onto it. He tied the raft to his horse's tail and pushed him into the river, jumped on the raft and started over. He guided the horse by speaking to him and got over safely. Then he knocked the raft to pieces and put the nails back in his saddlebags and came home with me for the night. This man was Joseph Ruffner."

At Huddlestone's the traveler was within 25 miles of the

Salt Spring, or "The Licks," as it was generally called then and for a long time afterward. It is quite likely that the new owner was disappointed in the quantity and strength of the water, but his faith was not shaken in the underground supply. Daniel Boone was then living on the opposite side of the Kanawha river, attracted thither by the big game that resorted to The Licks. But Boone's interest went down as Ruffner's interest went up. The old hunter saw that his occupation there would soon be gone and that he must follow the rolling buffalo and high-stepping elk, and leave the nimble deer to hide in the brush. In three or four years Boone's canoe flotilla glided through Elk shoals toward the setting sun. The people wept as they saw him go, but the time had come when the hunter and red man must give way to the farmer and the manufacturer.

When Joseph Ruffner went on towards Clendennin's Fort another sight greeted his eyes. It was that beautiful plain of 1,000 acres on which now stands the capital of West Virginia. It was still almost covered with virgin forest, made up of trees of a size much beyond those of the country east of the Alleghany. The assemblage of flat land, trees, hills and rivers evidently roused the enthusiasm of the dark-eyed German. And here he found a little company of men congenial in spirit with himself.

Seven years before (1788) a colony of about a dozen men, headed by George Clendennin, had come from the East, established themselves on the north bank of the Kanawha, where they had built a fort, a residential blockhouse and six small dwellings, and had laid off a town of 40 acres in extent in the angle made by the junction of Elk river with the Kanawha. George Clendennin, with his brothers William, Robert and Alexander, and their father, Charles Clendennin, for whom the town was named, made up nearly half the colony.

The Clendennins were Scotch-Irish people who were living in 1753 in Borden's grant, which is now a part of Rockbridge county, Va. The tradition is that three brothers Clendennin came together from the north of Ireland. Two of them, Archibald and Charles, settled in Virginia. Charles ultimately went to Greenbrier. He was the father of George, who became a prominent citizen, and who bought the Charleston bottom in 1787, from Cuthbert Bullitt, who had acquired it from his brother, Col. Thos. Bullitt, the original owner. The fort said to have been built by Clendennin was occupied by a garrison in 1789, and in that year Mad Ann Bailey made her trip to Lewisburg. Her husband was one of the garrison.

By this time the fort had received the name of Fort Lee, in honor of Light Horse Harry.

Ruffner's visit to Clendennin's Fort was the arrival of a new power in the Kanawha Valley—a power which was to create, to strengthen, to develop and to abide. He at once saw rich resources of many kinds. There were hundreds of acres of the finest saw mill timber, there was the land fat with vegetable matter, loose and easily cultivated, there was the beautiful Kanawha or Woods river, alive with fish, navigable for large boats, and communicating with a vast system of navigable streams pouring their water into the Gulf of Mexico, and in spite of the departure of the elk and buffalo, there were still deer, beaver, otter and raccoon, and bears enough to bed all the armies of Europe. Who can doubt that the penetrating eye of Jeseph Ruffner saw all this, and perhaps more? At any rate, before he left the place he owned everything from Elk river to the "head of the bottom," about three miles. The bottom was owned by three of the brothers Clendennin—George, William and Alexander—from each of whom he received a deed. As to the pioneer history of this locality the reader is referred to the detailed and reliable historical sketches which have been published from time to time by Dr. J. P. Hale.

Besides the fort close to Charleston, there was at the time of the purchase by Ruffner another and smaller fort on the river bank about one mile above the settlement; said to have been built by Clendennin for the protection of men who were engaged in clearing land at that place. This fort stood in front of the present site of Holly Grove brick mansion, built in 1815 by Daniel Ruffner, son of Joseph. At this time besides the seven families at the lower fort there was not a family living between Charleston and Point Pleasant—60 miles, and a very few living in the upper end of the valley.

In a few days after his purchase Joseph started back to Shenandoah, and in the autumn of the same year (1795) he removed his family to Kanawha, excepting his oldest and only married son, David, who remained another year in Shenandoah. Five unmarried, grown sons came with their parents, namely, Joseph, Jr., Samuel, Tobias, Daniel and Abraham. The only daughter, Eve, was married about this time to Nemiah Woods, who settled in Ohio.

Joseph sold his landed property in Shenandoah to Forrer, and he afterwards sold to Gibbons. When he brought his family to Kanawha his first care was to provide a home and the conveniences and necessaries of living. It is believed that he sojourned for a time in the Clendennin house, but he fixed upon the location of the small fort as his permanent home.

218

Immediately behind the fort, on a site about midway between the fort and the site of the present brick house he erected a comfortable hewed log house, and moved his family into it. There he spent the remainder of his days, which, alas! were not to be many. Here they all went to work and "lifted the axes against the thick trees." Ah, let us not forget what heavy labor, what patient endurance, what rough living, characterized the life of the men who first contended with the mighty forests of Kanawha Valley. And this Ruffner family could not forget that within one year murder had been committed by Indians within a mile of where they were living.

Joseph was promptly made overseer of the public road that passed his lands, and the next year he was presented by the grand jury for the bad condition of his road!

Town lots in Charleston sold slowly. There were in the beginning only 40 of them of one acre each. In the deed executed the consideration mentioned usually was nominal. In one deed, however, five pounds sterling is mentioned as the price—about $16. But in 1892 one lot sold for $166.67. The land at the lower end of the bottom was rated at $12 per acre.

Joseph continued to be land hungry, even after he had bought the great bottom, as shown by a deed made to him in 1797 by Wm. T. Taylor, of Kentucky, for 6,660 acres on Sixteen-mile Creek, on the Ohio river below Point Pleasant.

Of necessity, the whole family became riflemen. Panthers screamed around their dwellings at night, bears shared the corn crop, and squirrels sometimes came like Rocky mountain locusts. Hunting was the recreation of the men. Even in my boyhood bears were found about the heads of the hollows. When I first saw my uncle (by marriage) Moses Fuqua, he was riding up to his gate with a rifle in front and a bear behind. This was about 1835.

Whilst waiting for the time when his attention could be somewhat withdrawn from his farm work, Joseph leased to Elisha Brooks, "a droll genius," the privilege of making salt from the brine that was wasting at the edge of the river, and before the lease expired the proprietor had ceased his labors.

David Ruffner had brought out his family in 1796 and lived in the Clendennin blockhouse. Land at the lower end had been assigned to him, but his career was changed, as was the case with the others, by the death of the strong, brave,, upright, far-seeing head of the family.

Joseph Ruffner died in March, 1803, aged 63 years and about 6 months. In his own mind his western career was just beginning, but his unfinished work was left in able hands. The fourth son, Samuel, was the only feeble member, and he became so when in infancy he was nearly burnt to death in his cradle. The other five sons had brain and muscle suited to the rugged development work which lay before them.

The will of Joseph Ruffner is dated February 21, 1803, less than a month before he died. His home "plantation" and all his personal property he gives to his wife, after her death Daniel to become the owner of the farm. By this time Daniel was married and he remained with his mother. Among the personal items are three negroes, six axes, a "Conque Shell" (dinner-horn), and a large German Bible (Luther's version). The Bible, which was valued by the appraisers at five dollars, was a thick folio bound in leather with clasps, and illustrated by numerous pictures. It became an heirloom in the family, and descended to the eldest son bearing the Ruffner name in each succeeding generation, namely, to David, Henry, Wm. Henry, and now turned over to Joel Henry. No debts are mentioned. He probably owned nothing.

In the will Joseph divided the bottom (exclusive of the town) into three parts. The lower division he gave to David, who then lived upon it; the middle to Daniel, after his mother's death, and the upper division to Tobias. Joseph, Jr., and Abraham received outlying lands. The front bottom of the Dickinson survey containing the Salt Spring, was given to David, Joseph, Tobias, Daniel and Abraham; in other words, to all the sons jointly, except poor Samuel, who was to be taken care of by contribution from all the rest. To each son was given a lot in Chahleston. David seems to have fellen heir to all the town lots not otherwise disposed of.

I think that no member of the large Ruffner family has been possessed of a deeper penetration, a sounder judgment, a readier facility for laying hold at the critical moment, and a cooler courage than the head of the Kanawha branch. Better than all, he was both honest and devout. His wife was a fitting companion. She outlived him 17 years, and died in 1820, aged 78 years. She was industrious and active and very benevolent. In her latter years she rode much on horseback, making social and charitable visits. Riding down "Ruffner Hollow" one night with her little grandson, Joel, behind her on the horse, a terrific scream came from a tree they were passing. The old lady simply said "It's a panther," at the same time laying whip to her horse, who shot down the ravine like an arrow, and carried the party safely to the open country.

When the time came to carve the names of these two old

people on the tomb, a large brown sandstone slab was selected, and laid horizbontally on tasteful sidings of light-colored stone, which may now be seen adorning the old Charleston graveyard in the bottom, not far beloy the Holly Grove Mansion. On the top slab is an ample record, ending with these beautiful words: "Let their spotless integrity, useful industry and sincere piety be remembered and imitated by their descendants."

Lexington, Va., May, 1901.

---

## JAMES RUMSEY,

### THE INVENTOR OF THE STEAMBOAT.

We are able through the courtesy of G. A. Rumsey, of Salem, N. J., to give a picture of James Rumsey. This photograph was taken from a portrait painted by Benjamin West, London, 1790, and the original is now in the possession of Mr. Rumsey of New Jersey.

JAS. RUMSEY.

Having the pleasure to give to our readers a look at this famous inventor that lived in Shepherdstown, W. Va., it will not be out of place to give some facts concerning him, even at the risk of repeating some that we have heretofore published.

222

In 1900 this society published a paper prepared by Geo. M. Beltz-hoover, Jr., entitled "James Rumsey, the Inventor of the Steam-boat."—In 1901, in January number of this magazine, there was published an article on "The Inventor of the Steamboat" by Hon. D. B. Lucas, and in the same number of said Magazine, Dr. John P. Hale wrote "Rumsey vs. Fulton."

It is not a question whether he was *one of the* inventors, for there seems to have been more than one, but whether he was *the* inventor; the first one whose invention was proved by actual test.

The only person whose claim appears to have been a rival, was John Fitch, of Pennsylvania.

From what has been written of the latter's claim, it seems he stated that the first time the idea came to him was in April, 1785. He had not perfected his invention in October, 1787, but then he obtained from Virginia Assembly the right to navigate the waters of Virginia.—See 12, Hen. Stat. 616, Oct., 1787.

It only remains for us to show that James Rumsey's invention was prior to the time that Fitch had his vision of a steamboat.

James Rumsey settled at Berkeley Springs in 1783, and in the summer of that year he made known his invention to others. Berkeley Springs was then known as Bath, and was in Berkeley County, and was then a public resort.

John Wilson, of Philadelphia, testified that in 1783, while at these Springs he was told of Rumsey's invention. Rumsey filed his petition in the fall of 1783, with the Assembly of Maryland, which was read and referred to next session. Geo. Washington wrote that he had been convinced by Rumsey's model that boats could be propelled by his invention; this was while at said Springs in Sept., 1784. In October, 1784, the Virginia Assembly passed an Act giving to Rumsey the right to navigate the waters of that State, 11 Hen. Stat. 502. In 1785, Rumsey was at work in his shop on his machinery. In 1786, he gave private tests of his boat. In 1787 he made a public test at Shepherdstown, which was a success.

Of these facts there can be no question.

And we are willing to submit the question of priority to the jury without argument.

There is one circumstance which we do not understand. The Virginia Assembly granted the exclusive right to Rumsey for the

223

period of ten years, in October, 1784, but retained the right to abrogate the privilege by the payment to Rumsey of ten thousand pounds. In October, 1787, the said Assembly gave the same privilege to John Fitch, without mentioning Rumsey or their former Act. And this was just about the time that Rumsey gave his public exhibition of his boat at Shepherdstown.

Who can explain this action of the Virginia Assembly?
It needs explanation.

### RUMSEY FAMILY.

The family became quite a numerous one, as some families do in the course of time. We shall give only that part of the genealogy that bears on the inventor.

Charles Rumsey came from Wales in 1665, and settled at the head of Bohemia river, in Cecil Co., Maryland. He married Catherine ———, Sept. 26, 1675. She died in 1710. Their children were: Prudence, born 1679; Margaret, 1682; Grace, 1685; Elizabeth, 1687; Mary, 1692; Charles, Jr., 1695; William, 1698; Edward, 1703.

Edward married Miss Douglas, from Scotland, and their children were: *Edward, Jr.,* Charles, Margaret, Susan and Mary.

Edward, Jr., married Anna Cowman, or Maryland, and their children were Charles, *James,* and Edward the 3rd. *James Rumsey* was born in 1742-3 and died in 1792. The exact dates according to our calendar, are March, 1743, and died Dec. 21, 1792, in London. He married a Miss Morrow, and their children were, James, Jr., Susan and Clarissa.

James, Jr., through disease, became deaf and dumb.

Susan married, first Mr. Fraley and second Jacob Skiles.

Clarissa married Geo. D. Minor, of Bowling Green, Ky.

Not much is known of James Rumsey in his young days. He was a volunteer in the Revolutionary Army, and in 1783, he was in business as merchant in Berkeley Co., Va., and in 1784 was keeping a boarding house at the springs.

At what time he removed to Shepherdstown we know not. He left home in 1788 and went to Europe, and while in London, died suddenly December 21, 1792, and was buried at St. Margarets.

This family is generally spoken of as the "Three Morrows," brothers, who lived in Shepherdstown.

Charles Morrow seems to have taken an interest in the steamboat and assisted Rumsey in his experiments.

John Morrow was President of the Board of Trustees for the town of Shepherdstown in 1796. He was the Executor of the will of Robt. Rutherford. He purchased War claims for services in the on the Ohio river. One of them was Governor of Ohio, and one a member of Congress.

The daughter of James Rumsey, Susan, married Mr. Fraley. She was left a widow, and she afetrwards married Jacob Skiles, of Greenbrier Co.

## SKILES FAMILY.

Jacob was the son of Henry Skiles, of Lancaster, Pa., and Jacob had brothers, William and Henry, and sisters, Mrs. Vixey and Mrs. Hannah.

Jacob, with others, started down the Ohio river with goods; they were captured by the Indians. Of his comrades, John May was killed; Skiles was wounded; Mr. Flynn and two girls were also on the boat and were also taken prisoners. Flynn was burned at the stake. The girls were ransomed by French traders. Skiles was taken to the Miami of the Lakes. He was blackened preparatory to being burned, he feigned sickness and secured a postponement of the ordeal, and through the help of a squaw made his escape, and made his way back home. He went to Greenbrier Co., Va., and there married Mrs. Fraley, and in 1803 he removed to Bowling Green, Ky. They had four children, James Rumsey Skiles, W. H. Skiles, Chas. M. Skiles, and Elizabeth Rumsey Skiles. He died in 1816.

Jacob Skiles was a large land owner, and part thereof was in Kanawha County, viz., Patent for 32,097 acres on Gauley and 40,000 acres on Kelly's creek, and other tracts in Greenbrier County.

Jas. Rumsey Skiles was born in 1800, married Miss Bell of Tennessee, was prominent in all public matters in Kentucky, was a member of the Legislature, president of the first railroad in Kentucky, president of a Bank, etc. In 1855 he removed to Texas and died in 1886. It was through him that the Portrait of James Rumsey was obtained.

James Rumsey had a brother-in-law, Joseph Barns, who was a carpenter and who made the boats for Rumsey. Joseph had a daughter, Polly Barns, whose mother was a sister of James Rumsey. Joseph Barns, it is said, went to London to look after Rumsey's affairs after his death, and was never heard from afterwards. Polly Barns was raised by one of the Morrows, and she married William Morris.

## MORRIS FAMILY.

William Morris, son of William, of London, married Catherine Carroll, a daughter of William Carrol, of Ireland, May 10, 1768. Their children were, viz.:

Jane, born Nov. 3, 1770, married John Hansford.
Gabriel, born Dec, 27, 1772.
*William*, born Dec. 16, 1775, married Polly Barns.
Catherine, born Jan. 15, 1778, married Chas. Venable, 1800.
Carroll, born Nov. 2, 1779.
John, born Aug. 24, 1783.
Cynthia, born Jan. 5, 1792, married Isaac Noyes.

William Morris, Sr., lived on Greenbrier, where Alderson now is, and the probabilities are that his son William met Polly at Jacob Skiles. After they married, they all moved to the Kanawha Valley and are buried at the mouth of Kelly's Creek.

The Hansfords, Morrises, Venables, Noyes, were the early settlers of the Kanawha Valley and their descendants are and have always been among the best people of the Kanawha Valley.

Is it not rather strange that the Potomac and Kanawha should have been so connected through the Rumsey family and their kindred?

To-day the best boat on the Kanawha river, has been named the James Rumsey, an improvement on steamboats almost as great as

Rumseys on all other boats. Mr. Charles Ward is the inventor and builder of the new boat.

We regret to announce that the Legislature of West Virginia failed to appropriate a fund for a monument for James Rumsey. It will come however, sooner or later.

W. S. LAIDLEY.

## SHEPHERD FAMILY ITEMS.

In the October number, 1902, of your magazine is a very interesting illustrated sketch of Thomas Shepherd, of Shepherdstown, from the pen of Mrs. Fanny Shepherd Allen. It is not the purpose of this note to add to that sketch a line of facts, now in hand, touching him and some members of his family and their descendants, but to correct two of the statements, which inaccurate traditions carried into Mrs. Allen's work.

Susannah Shepherd, born September 1, 1758; married John Eoff, born February 14, 1752, at Shepherdstown, on the 27th day of March, 1777. They crossed the mountains prior to 1800 and settled on land six miles east of Wheeling; later on, that land was sold and a farm purchased on the bank of the Ohio, which embraced ground on which the southern portion of that city now stands. John Eoff, the husband of Susannah, was a farmer all his life and not, at any time, a member of either of the so-called learned professions. He died on his homestead February 13 or 14, 1831.

His son, Dr. John Eoff, born Oct. 2, 1788, who also died there in January, 1859, was the most distinguished physician of that city during days of his active practice from which he retired in 1840. The father and son have often been confused from the sameness of the name and the long overlapping of their lives in the same city. I have the

227

pleasure of a personal acquaintance with a son of Dr. Eoff, born March 26, 1828, resident of Wheeling sixty years, now resident of this city, totally blind for the past seventeen years, a very intelligent, active-minded, well preserved, interesting gentleman, Alexander Quarrier Eoff.

He says that in the great flood of 1832 all his father's papers, including those pertaining to the family, were destroyed by the water rising into the residence to the depth of five feet. "When it subsided the old tall clock was lying on its face on the floor. No one had ever dreamed that the waters of the river could rise into the house."

"Martha married a Mr. McDowell."

The writer's grandmother, Mrs. Col. Joseph Holmes, was a daughter of George McNabb and Martha Shepherd McNabb. These great grand parents were married at Shepherdstown-Mecklenburg, in 1771. In the passage of the traditions the McNabb has doubtless been metamorphosed into "McDowell."

J. T. HOLMES.

Columbus, O., May 15, 1903.

----

Since the foregoing items were written the April number has come to hand. The article therein on Col. David Shepherd states that the Col. had three sisters and one brother. He had four brothers: William, Thomas, John and Abraham, and five sisters: Martha, Mary, Susannah, Sarah and Elizabeth. Sarah married a Mr. Thornburg and Elizabeth married William Brown.

Very truly yours,

J. T. HOLMES.

----

# THE STRIBLING AND HEREFORD FAMILIES OF MERCERS BOTTOM, MASON COUNTY, WEST VIRGINIA.

In the November issue of the Historical Magazine, a map of Charleston was given as found among old Clendenin papers. I waited the next number to see if the mistake would be corrected. It was not, hence my letter. This map was among old papers of Dr. M. W. Stribling (at one time a resident of your city), and a few lines in regard to his family and his pioneer home, may prove of interest to some of your readers.

Dr. Matthew Wright Stribling (son of Thomas Stribling and Betsy Snickers) was born in Berryville, Clarke County, Va., in 1796. He was a graduate of the University of Virginia, and also of Philadelphia Medical College. In 1817 he came to Red House Shoals on Kanawha river (where his father and brother, William, were then living, and where they afterwards died and were buried) and commenced the practice of medicine. In 1828, he was elected to the Virginia Legislature; that same year he married Elizabeth Page Hereford of Mercers Bottom, and, with his bride, rode horse back to Fauquier County where he left her with relatives and proceeded on to Richmond. Their eldest daughter was born in 1829 in Fauquier County. Two years later, on his return to the Kanawha Valley, he located in Charleston, and resumed the practice of his profession. Here the oldest son was born in 1834, while the youngest (O. F. Stribling) was born in 1836 in Point Pleasant, whither the family had moved the previous year. "No one ever possessed a higher sense of honor, no one ever had warmer feelings of friendship, or was more free from vindictive feelings—no more ardently affectionate son, brother or father."

In 1845, failing in health, he and his wife traveled over to Virginia hoping a change would be beneficial, but he steadily grew worse, died and was buried in Fauquier County. She lived until 1872 and died at Atchison, Kansas, where she had gone to visit her daughter. Their children were:—

1. Mary Caroline, married, 1858, Junius Temple Hereford (born 1830 in Charleston) and died 1872, Atchison, Kansas. Their only child, Frederick Stribling was born in Atchison, and died at Mercers Bottom, 1880.

2. Robert Mackey never married. He was educated at Drewen College, Ky., and at Cincinnati Medical College. He was a surgeon in Confederate army. After the war located at Florrissant, St. Louis County, Missouri; died there in 1888. .

3. Otis Francis, was educated at Gallipolis, Ohio, and at Lexington Law School, Va. He is a farmer at Mercers Bottom. He married 1869, Virginia Caroline Neale (daughter of W. P. L. Neale and Catherine Beale Steenberger, gr. daughter of Willam Presley Neale and Ann M. Smith, Loudoun County, Va.—Peter H. Steenberger and Maria Beale Jordan). Their children:

1. Mathew Weightman, b. 1871; m. 1897, Mary M. Hunter.

2. Catherine Beale, b. 1873, m. 1899, James A. Young, (son of Norborne Young and Sarah E. Harper, Magnolia, Arkansas). He is in insurance business with headquarters at Louisville, Ky. They have one son, Otis Stribling, b. 1903.

3. Elizabeth, V. C., b. 1875; d. 1902.

4. William Neale, b. 1877.

Shortly after the death of her husband, Mrs. Stribling, with her three children, moved to her father's home, afterwards inherited as her portion of his estate.

He (Robert Hereford) born in Loudoun Count, Virginia, 1769, was a man of wealth, and in 1805 purchased 1000 acres of the Mercer grant in lower part of Mason county. He moved thither in 1807, to an unbroken wilderness farm, save a few acres on which stood a double house of round logs. In this he lived until 1811, when, with the aid of his own servants trained as carpenters, masons and blacksmiths, he built the present structure—the oldest brick house now standing in Mason county. His wife was Mary Mason Bronough, (born 1770, Stafford county, Virginia, daughter of Dr. John Bronough, and Ann Carter of "Cleves"; grand daughter of Jeremiah Bronough and Simpha Rosa Enfield (Mason) Dinwiddie, who was daughter of Col. Geo. Mason of "Gunston Hall"). Their children were:

1. William Amsby, b. Loudoun county, 1791; m. Emily Chinn and had, Dr. John Robert, Eliza, Mary Catherine, Andrew Chinn, Major in C. S. A., Thomas and Emily.

2. John Bronough, b. 1794; m. Catherine M. Stirling (daughter of Lewis Stirling and Mary Trumbull, La.), and had Dr. Robert Francis, Sarah Trumbull, Lewis Sterling, Ann M., John Bronough, James Stirling, Catherine M., and Isabella Semple.

3. Robert Ammon, b. 1796; m. Virginia Lewis (daughter of Howell Lewis and Ellen Hackley Pollard), and had: Robert Lewis, Brooke Gwathmey, Frances, Kate Bronough, Bettie Washington and Lawrence Berry.

4. Ann Maria, b. 1798; m. John Beale (son of John Beale and Margaret Skillern—grand son of Taverner Beale and Elizabeth Hite), and had: Dr. John, Mary Margaret, Julia, George Robert, who was Major in Mexican War, and afterwards Judge in Louisiana, Charles, William and Thomas.

5. Elizabeth Page, b. 1800; m. Dr. M. W. Stribling as above.

6. Thomas Ammon, b. 1802; m. Mary Cumberland Wilson, daughter of James Wilson and Mary Prentice—grand daughter of Cumberland Wilson and Janet Allan of Glasgow, Scotland) and had: Dr. James Wilson, Robert Prentice and Junius Temple.

7. Margaret Mason, b. 1805; m. Alonzo Cushing, b. Fredonia, N. Y.

8. Mary Ann, b. Mason Co., 1807; m. Capt. —— Cain, Miss. No issue.

9. Katherine Ellen, b. 1810; m. Dr. Daniel Couch (son of Daniel Couch and Sarah Richardson) and had: Mary, Edward, and Margaret.

10. Francis Marion, b. 1814; m. Harriet Fort, La., and had: Mary, Happie, Adele, Alice, Frank, Jennie and William.

The old house of nearly a century past (though some changes have been necessary) is unique in one particular—it has been lived in by six generations and is still unfinished—walls not plastered and rough and pioneer like in many ways. The rooms were ceiled with walnut plank, and in one, never white washed, shows plainly bare foot prints of many sizes. While the lumber was piled up in the yard, it must have been played over by children whose feet were wet with dew and stain of weeds. Mrs. Hereford's mother (Mrs. Bronaugh), in the latter years of her life, would stay six months with this daughter, and there made comfortable, in a pirogue, with feather bed, pillows and quilts, would be rowed by servants up the Ohio and Kanawha rivers to Buffalo, where her son William was living. This was repeated each year until her death. Thus she (Mrs. Bronough) Mrs. Hereford, Mrs. Stribling, O. F. Stribling, Mrs. Kate Young and her little son, Otis, make the six generations who have lived in this house. In the yard is an old-fashioned white-rose bush, set out in 1810—some of the largest locust trees in all the country around—a beautiful walnut tree planted by one of the daughters in 1818. In the house are many relics—a tall hall clock, and solid mahogany tables from England—a cherry bedstead with high posts beautifully carved in pine apple design—a wine buffet, etc., from Scotland.

The garret was a store house of papers, not only of the family, but of those connected by ties of of intermarriages. Some were destroyed by the mice—still many of interest remain—among the family papers, an Almanac of 1764; The Gentleman's Annual Pocket Remembrances for the year 1803; Continental money (Four dollars) and (2s. 8 p., etc., etc.

Mr. Robert Hereford was a man of piety—true and sincere in his convictions of right and duty—a member of the Methodist church, but not bigoted. On one occasion, when present at a communion service in a Baptist church, he advanced to the table, but was met by the preacher with: "Hold on, brother Hereford, this is our table." Mr. Hereford stepped back, replying, "I beg pardon, I thought it was the Lord's."

Feeling the need of a house of worship in this frontier wilderness, he built a church on his farm, and, in the church yard surrounding it, he, his wife, Virginia Lewis Hereford and other members of his family are buried. Not a vestige of building remains—only a grove of trees and a few tomb-stones.

He was a son of John Hereford of Fairfax County, Virgina, who had bought property in Lewisburg as far back as 1759. Will dated 1783; probated 1794. The family were originally from Hertfordshire, Eng. His wife was Peggy ————, and their children were John, William, James, Thomas, Francis, Robert, Ann, Peggy, Kitty and Elizabeth. Two of these sons, John and James, were attending school in Alexandria, Virginia, when the War of the Revolution began. They ran off and joined the army, but their father followed and brought the u back, as too youthful for service. They remained in school but two or three months, when they left again. The father visited them again, but not to withdraw them from the army—his parting advice was: "never to turn their backs on a red coat." John died in Mason county, 1846, aged 88 yrs., 3 mos., 11 days. He married Betty Patterson, related to the Bonapart—Patterson family; married 2nd, Sarah Massey. of Alexandria, Va. They moved to this count' after his brother Robert came west, and lived on an adjoining farm. She died, 1855, aged 73 yrs., 11 mos., 1 day. Both are buried not far distant on an isolated noll in the low grounds of the Ohio Sixteen Creek—their graves neglected. A relative, who knew him well, says it was his request the following couplet should mark his grave:

"Stranger, pause and shed a tear,
A Revolutionary soldier is buried here."

It is thought such was done on a sandstone which crumbling by time, was replaced by a descendant with the present white marble on which is inscribed:

He served in War of 1776.
As Adjutant under Gen. Geo. Washington.

One of the delights of his declining years, was to muster with the militia at Point Pleasant—he and Major Waggoner riding ahead. He has numerous descendants in this county—also west and south—people of strong minds and presonalities.

Ellen S. Neale.

Mercers Bottom, W. Va.

233

## THE TEAYS FAMILY OF KANAWHA.

In the year of 1750 a party was organized in Germany consisting principally of pleasure seekers, to make a visit to the colonies of America, and among this party was a young refined and wealthy lady, Miss Adelaide Lee, a daughter of Mr. Lee, whose wife was a Miss Inocence, a highly educated and refined family, and of the German Reformed Church. There were six daughters in this Lee family —Miss Adelaide who came on this visit with her friends, who was taken ill in Philadelphia and died there. The father Lee, not hearing from her for some time, determined to come and learn of his daughter, fearing that something had happened that prevented her from writing as usual. With father Lee and his next two daughters, Maria and Rosamend, and a young kinsman of the Duchy of Grueirsucken, by the name of Frederick Conrad took ship and also sailed for Philadelphia to find Adelaide, and also prospecting and looking for a proper place for a home in the new world. Soon after their arrival they learned of the death of Miss Adelaide, and the father decided to travel through the colonies and then select his place of residence.

He soon settled in Frederick, Maryland, and there his daughter Rosemond married a Mr. Waters, and her father gave to her his possessions, consisting of a farm, tan yard, vineyard, etc., and Father Lee, with his daughter Maria, then moved on to Winchester, Virginia, where he again invested in a tract of land, made a tan yard, planted a hop garden, etc. Tan yards were valuable in those days.

234

On the 29th of September, 1759, Maria married Frederick Conrad; he of the age of thirty-four and she of twenty-one, and Conrad and Father Lee went into business as partners.

Mr. Lee then sent for his wife and family in Germany. They soon arrived, bringing the old family bible chained to the leg of a table. Miss Charlotte remained in Frederick, Md., with her sister, Mrs. Waters, while the mother and Katherine made their way on to Winchester. Charlotte afterwards married a Mr. Balster, and her father purchased for her a property to represent the "German Dot." Afterwards father Lee took his wife and Katherine with him on a visit over the Blue Ridge to New London, and being pleased with this country, he there invested in real estate for his daughter Katherine, who had met a Captain Thomas Teays of the Colonial Army, who had asked her to become his wife and who had assented to the proposal.

Capt. Thomas then spelled his name Tass, but afterwards changed the spelling to Teays, the pronunciation being the same, and the latter spelling better adapted to the English pronunciation, although many of the family in Virginia retain the original spelling of Tass, to this day. Captain Thomas Tass and Katherine Lee were married about 1760, in Bedford county, Va.

Thomas Teass is said to have been with Capt. Wm. Crawford when he was surveying out west for George Washington, and was captured by a band of marauding Indians, out on what is now known as Teays Valley, near Scary Creek, now in Putnam county, and he was taken by the Indians to their settlements in Ohio and where he was condemned to be burned. One historian states that he was saved by an Indian who recognized him as one who had divided his salt with the Indian, and secured his release—Others say he was saved by an Indian woman, and others that he was scalped, but survived.

Be that as it may have been, he was held for many years, but finally made his escape and made his way back to the Kanawha Valley and to Winchester, where he called to see his brother-in-law, Frederick Conrad.

Thomas Tass had not used razor or shears for many years and his clothing was not of the dudish order of store clothes, he was not recognized by Conrad and who refused to believe his story, but insisted that Thomas Tass had been killed many years before, and he turned down the brother-in-law as an impostor. So he moved on over the Ridge.    He had no difficulty in making himself known at home, although his children had grown out of his knowledge.

Captain Teays remained at home with his family, consisting of three boys and four girls, viz: Katherine, Martha, Mary, Lucy, John, William and Stephen.

In 1800 about, when he was about sixty years old, he desired to secure land for his family and for his service in the army he was entitled to the same.   He set out west to locate land, and arrived again in the Kanawha Valley, which was down in the vicinity of Coalsmouth, on the Kanawha and on Coal river, and he then returned to his home in New London, Va., where he remained the rest of his days.

He was born on the James River, and he had two sisters—one married a Mr. Leiws and the other a Mr. Reives.

Mr. Lee gave to his daughter Katherine, his possessions at New London and he proceeded to Stanton and there for a fourth time made an investment for a home and when his youngest daughter, Louisa Christina, married Dr. John Sharp Watkins.

Stephen Teays, the youngest son of Capt. Thomas, about 1795 or perhaps earlier, went to the west and located on his fathers land.

Stephen Teays in the year 1796 was married to Miss Mary Carroll, in Kanawha, by the Rev. Jas. Johnson.

Miss Carroll was a niece of Catherine Carroll, who had married Major William Morris, and settled at the mouth of Coal river, on the lower side thereof and erected a two-story, double-log house on the lands of his father.   Stephen cleared up a farm and established a ferry and kept the weary travelers that desired to stay with him.

Stephen was born in 1774, and died March 20, 1823.   Mary Carroll was from Maryland, and was of the same family of Charles Carroll, of Carrollton, who signed the Declaration of Independence in such way that there would be no mistake as to which of the Carrolls it was, when King George offered the reward for the heads of the signers.

Mary Carroll was born in the year 1777, and died January 2, 1834.

Tacketts Fort stood on the Teas' land about one-half mile from Coalsmouth and one-fourth of a mile out from the Kanawha river, and on that portion of the land that was afterwards allotted to my Aunt Parthenia Wilson, who was the grand-mother of the Wilsons of

Kanawha today. The location of the fort is visible today, after a century of cultivation, of which I shall write more hereafter.

Stephen Teays set out a row of peach trees from the mouth of Tacket's creek to the mouth of Scary creek, about four miles long, one in each corner of the fence.

The 1000 acre survey of land near Hurricane Bridge went in the partition of the estate of Thomas Teays to two of his maiden daughters, Martha and Polly Teays, who remained at the old home in Virginia. Martha Teays after visited her brother Stephen Teays' family, coming all the way on horse-back, a distance of some five hundred miles and made as many as four of such trips in her life-time.

The children of Stephen and Mary Carroll Teays were:

(1) Katherin, born 1798; married Henry Thomas in 1821, and she died August 11, 1830.

(2) John, born 1800; died 1845 in Missouri; never married.

(3) Mary, born September 14, 1802; married John Capehart, October 26, 1826. She died May 18, 1838. He died August 5, 1846.

(4) Parthenia, born September 15, 1803; married Sam B. Wilson, December 23, 1830. She died July 10, 1878.

(5) James T., born in 1805 or 6; married Elizabeth Everett, 1831. Died in 1867 in Missouri.

(6) Elizabeth, born December 25, 1809; married John Hansfard, 1828. Died, 1829.

(7) Martha, born 1811; married Joe Capehart, 1822. Died, 1832 in Missouri.

(8) William, born 1813; died 1818.

Mary Teays, daughter of Stephen, known as Polly Teas, married John Capehart, October 22, 1826. They had the following children:

William Henry, Charles Carroll, Stephen Philip and Parthenia Jane.

When Charles Carroll was named, he received the congratulations of Major William Morris and Katie Carroll Morris, wishing the dear babe all the goodness and greatness of his Maryland namesake,Stephen Philip—the writer, was named for both of his grandfathers, and Parthenia was named for her Aunt, Mrs. Parthenia Wilson.

Parthenia Teays married Samuel B. Wilson, December 23, 1830. Jas. T., the only one of the family that had two names, married

Eliza Everett, daughter of Col. John Everett, of Guyandotte, and a man of note in his day. They had nine children—Stephen, Oliver, William Carroll, Frances Asbury, Sarah Elizabeth, James Henry, Edward and Jennie.

Elizabeth Teays, 4th daughter of Stephen, married John Hansford, a grandson of Wm. Morris, and son of Maj. John Hansford, of Paint creek. They left one child, Mary Jane, who married first Dr. J. W. Walls, of Winchester, and next V. R. Rust, of Poca—

Martha, the 5th daughter of Stephen, married Jo Carpehart. Their children were Silas, Aaron and Mary; twins, Elizabeth, Katherine, James, John, Oliva, Parthenia and Martha. They went to Henry county, Missouri.

The children of Parthenia and Sam'l. B. Wilson were Mary Elizabeth, who married W. E. Chilton, Sr.; Hannah Katherine, who married Capt. George S. Chilton; Parthenia Jane Wilson, Oliver Teays Wilson, and Sarah A. Burnet, of Huntington, W. Va.

The lower end of the 1000 acre tract of Thomas Teays was sold to John Lewis, known as Coal River John Lewis, a grand son of Genl. Andrew Lewis, who married a daughter of Col. Andrew Donnally. He settled his brother, Samuel Lewis, in a log house, near the mouth of Scary and an older brother, William Lewis, on what was called Dogwood hill, in a pioneer double log house, who had two sons, William and Andrew, who located in St. Louis. Their father, William Lewis, died and was buried on the farm of his brother, John Lewis, known as "Valcoulon," where he built a large two-story brick mansion, just back of Tackets Fort. John Lewis came to the neighborhood very wealthy, the owner of many slaves, had a park on hill for his deer and elk and kept a colored man whose duty it was to keep away the dogs from molesting his herds of deer, one of which I well remember was snow-white.

I also remember his family with whom I was intimate as schoolmates, viz: And. D., John W., James V., and Margerie, the daughter, who married Edward Kenna. She urged my stepmother to be sure and come to her wedding as she never expected to marry but one Irishman. Her son was the Hon. John E. Kenna, and she afterwards married Richard Ashbey and her son, Walter L. Ashbey, of Charleston, is her other son.

John Lewis established the first race track in the Kanawha Val-

238

ley, on the bottom just below where Tacketts Fort stood. A brother-in-law, Engles, managed and looked after the racers, the Medoc Stock, beautiful sorrels.

Mrs. Emily Engles afterwards married for her second husband, James Capehart, of Point Pleasant, my uncle, and father of ex-Congressman James Capehart, of Mason County, W. Va.

I will relate here an incident I always heard of Mr. John Lewis, whose fields was large, his force great and his stock in abundance, and there was an old man, Jerry Wells, who lived on the Hurricane waters, who was known as very light fingered. Mr. Lewis could never catch up with him, but Jerry received the blame for everything that was lost, and Lewis proposed to Jerry that if he would not steal anything from him for a year, he would give to him fifty dollars. The old man stood and studied for some time before answering, but finally said "No, Mr. Lewis, I could not afford that, I would be loosin by it"—and the trade fell through.

Extravagance and bad management brought Lewis almost to want before his death, or at least, he was not worth half so much.

S. P. CAPEHART.

239

## A GLANCE AT THE VAN METER FAMILY IN THE UNITED STATES OF AMERICA.

Centuries ago a part of the province of Gelderland, in the Netherlands was called Meteren. The origin of the name is not known. It is suggestive of a personality and may have come from one or more of the French Huguenots who there found a refuge from persecution. Others have thought the people who left that town, or village, adopted Meteren as a surname, with the addition of "Van," which represents the preposition "from," as well as a mark of nobility. However that may be, the name has been borne by people who have distinguished themselves in religious and literary labors. Jacob Van Meteren, of Antwerp, caused the first complete edition of the Bible to be printed in the English language. This book was published in Zurich, in 1536, and was a great and expensive work. It is supposed that Van Meteren made the translations himself, employing Miles Coverdale to supervise the printing to guard against errors. In 1597, Joost Van Meteren, born in Antwerp, wrote a history of Holland. In 1875, Van Meters were living in that country, respected, educated and wealthy. The description of the family coat of arms, given in J. B. Rietstap's "Armorial General," is in French (the polite language of Holland).

Meteren (van) Hollande ecartele: aux 1 et 1-4 d'argent a une fleur de lis de gueules: aux 2 et 3 d'or a'deux fasces de gueules, accompagne de huit merlettes du meme, rangees en orle. Cimier la fleur de lis.

The baptismal and marriage registers of the Old Dutch Church of Kingston, Ulster County, New York (formerly Wiltwych and familiarly known as Esopus or Sopus), are said to show Van Meterens, Van Maitres and Van Meters on their pages. They have been transcribed and edited but, unfortunately, the compiler Mr. Roswell Randall Hoos, has never answered any question on this subject. Abraham and Jacob Lamiater are among those who took the oath of allegiance in Ulster County in 1689. Delameters and De Lametres are found in Kingston as early as 1739. They seem to indicate a French branch, if not the original family.

In the lists of passengers on the ships of olden days the name of Jansen is conspicuous. It may have been to avoid confusion that Joost Janz (also written Jansen), j. m. (young man), of Meteren, in Gelderland, Holland, living then in what is now Marbletown, New York, came to write his name Joost J. Van Meteren. In 1682, he married Sara Du Bois, j. d. (young woman), of Kingston, in the same county, a daughter of Louis and Catharine (Blanshan) Du Bois. A touching story is told of the almost miraculous escape of Catharine Du Bois from burning at the hands cf the Indians. (Letters of Rev. Allen H. Brown, 1899.)

Bommel, in the Netherlands, (province of Gelderland) was the birthplace, March 10, 1650, of Kreijn, son of Jan Gysbertsen Metrn (as he wrote his name). In 1663, he came with his father a widower, to New Amsterdam. Although the father used a different spelling, in the old records of Kings county, Long Island, and on the records of the First Dutch Church of Monmouth County, New Jersey, the name is spelled Van Meteren, Van Metra, Van Metere, and in other ways. The father was well-off, financially. He married a sister of Jan Van Cleef. In 1673, he was comfortably settled at New Utrecht, Long Island, and one of the magistrates of that town. In 1683, he was a deacon in the Dutch Church. There is a tradition that "Jan Guysbertsen Metrn" refused to take the oath of allegiance in 1687, and soon after went back to his fatherland. Children may have been born after the marriage to Miss Van Cleef but, as yet, they are an unknown quantity. His son, Kreijn Janse, took the oath of allegiance to the English government in 1687. He is then mentioned as a resident of New Utrecht. He was married September 9, 1683, to Neeltje (Eleanor), daughter of Jan Van Cleef and Engeltje Pietersen, residents of the same town.

Kreijn is on the assessment roll of New Utrecht from 1675 to 1709 when he removed to Middletown township, Monmouth County, New Jersey. Kreijn J. Van Matre (a later spelling) and his wife are among the first members and organizers of the Dutch Church of Monmouth. His name is entered on the church records as Kriin Jansen, and, in 1716, when elder, as Kriin Van Metra. He purchased a large tract of land in what (in 1899) are Holmdel and Atlantic townships. His first dwelling, a log cabin, was erected on the farm where William Jones now resides in Atlantic township. The old family burying ground is on this farm, only a part of the original tract, and in it he and his wife, and many others of the past generations of the Van Maters, are interred. Kreijn died March 10, 1720, and his wife January 1, 1747. They are reported to have had the following children:

Jan, b. April 26, 1687, died young.

John, b. April 17, 1688, at New Utrecht, L. I., m. October 17, 1718, Ida daughter of Ryck Hendrickse Van Snydam. He was a communicant in the Dutch Church in 1713 and his wife in 1731.

Ydtje (Ida), b. August 24, 1691; m. Jan, a son of Adrian Bennett and Barbery, his wife. Communicants in Dutch Church in 1731. She died September 13, 1774.

Gysbert (Gilbert), b. February 24, 1694; m. Maijke (Micha), daughter of Daniel Hendrickson and Kaatje Van Dyke, his wife. He was a communicant in the Dutch Church in 1721 and his wife in 1740. It is not known where he died or is buried.

Engeltje (Angelina), b. September 30, 1696; m. John Anderson.

Benjamin, b. January 22, 1702; m. Elizabeth, daughter of Jacob Laen (Lane) and Elizabeth Barkalow, his wife. Both were members of the Dutch Church in 1737. He died July 21, 1775, and is buried in the Van Mater cemetery.

Cornelia, b. May 24, 1704; m. Hans (John) Van Cleef.

Syrenius (Cyrenius), b. August 28, 1706; m. Abigail, daughter of Auke Lefferts and Maria Ten Eyck, his wife. Both are buried in the Van Mater cemetery. His grandson, Joseph C. Van Mater, called "big Joe Van Mater," is distinguished for freeing 100 negro slaves.

Joseph, b. in Monmouth County, February 5; baptized August 13, 1710; m. December 1, 1734, Sarah, daughter of Roelof

Schanck and Geesie, or Ghesye, Hendrickson his wife, Joseph Van Mater and his wife rest side by side in the Van Mater cemetery. A number of deacons and elders will be found among the different generations of this branch of the family. Joseph lived on the old homestead where Kreijn Janse first settled. The family graveyard is reserved forever for that purpose by the will of Joseph Van Mater. To this branch of the Van Maters, Monmouth County is largely indebted for the blooded stock of horses for which the county became celebrated during the first half of the nineteenth century.

John Van Mater (son of Kreijn Janse) and his wife had eleven children: Cryn Jans; Ryck (Richard); Gilbert; Jannetje; Neeltje; Marya; Eyda (Ida); John; Cornelia, or Catharine; Cornelius; Geertje.

In 1899, there were no male descendants of John Van Mater in Monmouth County, N. J., bearing the name of Van Mater. Kreijn gave real estate to his other sons; to John, he gave money; Kreijn died in 1720, but his will was not proved until March 21, 1729. Was the delay owing to John's absence?

Nearly twenty-eight pages of "Early Dutch Settlers of Monmouth County New Jersey," much of it in fine print, are devoted to the Van Mater family; genealogies, wills, etc. The book has been freely quoted here by permission of the compiler, Judge George Crawford Beekman, of Freehold, Monmouth County, New Jersey. The reader is referred to this valuable publication for fuller particulars. The children of John are mentioned because the claim has been made that the Salem County, New Jersey, and the Virginia Van Meters are descended from him.

Let us return now to Ulster County, New York, to look after Joost J. Van Meteren and his wife. Their daughter, Rebecca, was baptized April 26, 1686. It is improbable that she was the only child and here is a line of inquiry. September 3, 1704, Rebecca Van Meteren married Cornelis Elting, a son of Jan Elten and Jacomyntje Slecht. A sister and brother by the name of Van Meteren married two of the Eltings. Rebecca may have been the Miss Van Meteren. This theory would make the Mr. Van Meteren her brother. The indefinite Mr. and Mrs. Elting had seven children: two sons and five daughters. The fourth daughter had the interesting name of Youchamanchi; one of her great, great granddaughters married Mr. William C. Van Meter, Sr., of Moorefield, Hardy County, West Virginia, The baptisms of three of the children of Cornelis Elting and Rebecca Van Meteren reveal the names of Isaak, Zara and Alida (Eleanor). Jan Van Meteren was one of the four sponsors for Zara in 1715. Who was this Jan Van Meteren? Sara married John Hite; Eleanor married Isaac Hite and Rebecca Van Meter, daughter of Isaac Van Meter, married Abraham Hite (three of the eight children of Hans Jost Heydt and Anna Maria Du Bois). As late as 1710-11,.the names of Van Meter, Elting, Du Bois and Hite—all kindred—were found in Kingston, New York. In 1899, no traditions of the Van Meters were obtainable in the county; the name was not in the Kingston directory.

Between 1712 and 1714 the region now known as Upper Pittsgrove, in Salem County, New Jersey, and beyond it, began to be settled by people from New York State (including Long Island), New England and East Jersey. John and Isaac Van Meter, Jacob Du Bois and his sister, Sarah Du Bois, from Esopus, Ulster County, New York, located 3,000 acres of land, purchased in 1714, from Daniel Cox, of Burlington, New Jersey. They divided the tract by the compass; the Du Boises taking on the north side of the line, the Van Meters on the south side. The Van Meters continued to purchase until they owned about 6,000 acres; and most of the titles to the lands held by the present occupants go back to the Van Meter titles. The name, as first recorded in the Clerk's Office, at Salem, in 1714, is spelled Van Meter and, ever since, it has appeared the same way, with and without the capital M for Meter.

A first-class school, for that period, was established by the new arrivals, and religious services (presumably after the Dutch Reformed order) were not neglected. The first house for public worship stood near Woodstown. It went down soon after 1740. The date of its building and even the memory of its site have passed away. May 22, 1739, application was made by Isaac Van Meter to the Philadelphia Presbytery, in behalf of himself and others, for the establishment of the gospel in Pilesgrove. April 30, 1741, a Presbyterian Church was organized; 49 members signed the covenant beginning with Isaac Van Meter, Hannah (his wife), Henry Van Meter (their son), Sarah Van Meter (their daughter). The Nienkirks, Du Boises, and others followed. (History of the Presbyterian Church of Pilesgrove, or Pittsgrove, in Salem County, N. J.)

John Van Meter's name does not appear in the covenant. Is he the Monmouth County John and where did he go after locating land in Salem County? What degree of consanguinity existed between him and Isaac? There is a tradition that the Monmouth County Van Maters and the Salem County Van Meters were related. They visited each other until Time, with its inevitable changes, brought newer and stronger ties.

At this point it may be well to take up the history of the Van Meters as it has been gathered by some of the southern members. James M. Van Meter, of Martinsburg, West Virginia, (an aged man), writes in 1898: "All I know I got through my father, from the original ones, and the old V.'s never lied. The first Van Meter (from New York), John, passed through here about 1725 with a tribe of Indians going to the south branch to fight the Catawba tribe. The Catawba tribe killed all of the northern tribe except John Van Meter and two of his Indians. When John got home, he told his sons if they ever went to Virginia, they must go to the Wapapatoma and take up land for it was the prettiest land he ever saw. That is the Indian name for south branch of the Potomac. About the year 1730, four of his sons came over. Their names were Abraham, Isaac, Jacob and John. John and Isaac got permission from Governor Gooch, of Virginia, to put settlers on 40,000 acres of land (Mss Journals of the Governor and Council 1721-1734, pp. 363-4). They soon sold out to Jost Hite. Abraham, my double great grandfather, died in 1780. He married Ruth Hedges, daughter of Joseph Hedges, of Annapolis, Md., and granddaughter of Sir Charles Hedges, of Oxford, England. My two grandfathers, Abraham and Jacob, were his sons. I have the history of my family down to 1880. My grandfather Abraham died December 29, 1838. He married Elizabeth Barns, a Scotch-Irish girl. My grandfather Jacob married Isabel Evans, a daughter of the Isabel Evans who fought the Indians at the Big Spring, a little south of Martinsburg.

"Isaac went to the south branch of the Potomac. He had about the third trial before he could settle, the Indians running him

245

away and burning his cabin. At last, when he succeeded and started his family, the Indians killed him.

"Jacob settled on the Opequon Creek, about three miles from my great grandfather Abraham. His descendants are here.

"John settled near Shepherdstown. Thomas Shepherd married his daughter Elizabeth."

Garrett Van Meter, of Moorefield, W. Va., believes, with B. F. Van Meter, of Kentucky, that the pioneer John. of Virginia, was a son of Kreijn, of Monmouth County, N. J., and a noted Indian trader. Alludes to his removal to New York and his explorations in Virginia at the head of a band of Indians. Upon his return, he urged his sons to lose no time in possessing the land. "Four of his sons: Abraham, Isaac, Jacob and John, came to Virginia, I think, in 1736, although some put it later and others at an earlier date. Abraham and John settled in Berkeley County, Jacob at the lower end of the south branch, Isaac in Hardy County. * * * Other Van Meters emigrated at the same time."

D. S. Van Maitre, of Parkersburg, W. Va., writes in 1878: "The first settlement of the Van Matres, or Van Meters, was in the vicinity of the present town of Martinsburg and was by John Van Meter and family consisting of five sons and six daughters (MSS Journal of the Governor and Council 1721-1734, p. 363). I feel pretty well satisfied that the Isaac associated with him in the 40,000 acres grant was his son, Isaac, as he had a son Isaac. * * * These Van Meters were from Salem, N. J. The Isaac V. M. who a few years later settled on the south branch of the Potomac could not have been this son of John, for I find that the Christian name of the wife of the former was Esther, while the name of the latter was Hannah."

Here a letter from J. P. Wilson, of Romney, to Miss Annie E. Van Meter (now Mrs. Williams) of Moorefield, W. Va., (1876) comes in appropriately. He states that Isaac, the pioneer, was twice married. "The second wife was the widow Sibley, who had one son, Henry Sibley, I think."

Dr. Foote, in his "Sketches of Virginia," states that "Isaac Van Meter, the founder of Fort Pleasant, came to the South Branch of the Potomac in the year 1740, in company with some Cayuga Indians and laid a tomahawk right on what has been known for the last century as the Old Fields; he went back to his home and, in 1744, he moved there with his family."

Samuel Kercheval in the "History of the Valley of Virginia," published in 1833, when writing of the settlements on or near the Cohongoruton (ancient Indian name of the Potomac, from its junction with the river Shenandoah to the Alleghany mountains), gives the names of many of the first settlers on this water course and its vicinity. Among them, are Jacob Van Meter and brothers. He says the Van Meters were a numerous family and that they came from New York.

Judge Beekman in a private letter (1902) writes: The "fur trade" with Indians was very profitable and an easy way to make money and get confidence of the Indians. * * * Monmouth coast was prolific of shell fish out of which Indian money was made, or wampum. Many of our white people were engaged in making this shell money. * * * With the shell money anything could be bought of the Indians. As the red men were driven back from the coast, they became dependent upon the whites for their "belts of wampum." Thus the Indian traders from Monmouth and Long Island had an unlimited supply of Indian money and we find them slowly following up the Indians as they receded inwards."

A copy of the will of "Isaac Van Meter of the South Branch of Potowmach in the county of Frederick, Virginia," executed February 15, 1754, is recorded at Trenton, N. J. It was presented at court held in Hampshire county, Virginia, by Henry and Garret Van Metre, surviving executors, December 14, 1757. They qualified before the Salem county surrogate November 30, 1758 (where the name is written Van Meter). The will provides for his "dear wife, Hannah," and mentions the following children: Henry, Jacob, Garrett, Sarah (the wife of John Richman), Catharine Van Metre, Rebecca Hite (the wife of Abraham Hite), and Helita Van Metre. The lands in the province of New Jersey are to remain under their respective leases; at their expiration, to be sold at public vendue to the highest bidder; devises lands in Virginia, slaves and money. The children are to have the privilege of selling their land, but, in that case, the other children are to have the first offer, so they may keep it amongst them.

Garret Van Meter, born in New York, in 1732, was married to Ann Markee April 3rd, 1757. He was killed by the Indians near Fort Pleasant, Va., in April 1788. Three of his seven children lived to marry and raise families: Isaac, Jacob and Ann. The two sons married sisters, the Misses Inskeep. The daughter married Abel Seymour. He and Isaac Van Meter represented Hardy county in the Assembly when the constitution of the United States was adopted. Isaac had five sons and four daughters. Jacob, who is said to have been a Colonel in the war of 1812, had three sons who lived to raise families. Twenty-six years ago, some of the descendants from Isaac and Jacob had spread out into Maryland, Pennsylvania, Ohio, Indiana, Illinois, Kentucky and Texas. The years, as they roll by, find them still increasing and farther and farther west.

A Van Meter (a daughter of Jacob and Louisa Van Meter, of Hardy county, W. Va.,) possesses the original location where the first settlement was made by Jost Hite. She literally lives in the "house that Jack built" (Col. John Hite). Her first marriage was to a Mr. H. R. Hack. After his death in 1887, she married Mr. Arbuckle, but her pride in her maiden name is not lessened.

The writer of this chronicle has no facts to present concerning Sarah Richman, Rebecca Hite, Jacob, Catharine and Helita Van Meter (five of the seven children of Isaac, the pioneer) or their descendants, except that the Hite descendants were among the first settlers of Kentucky.

Henry Van Meter seems to have retained his interest and lands in New Jersey yet he, also, is associated with Virginia. George Washington, while surveying for Lord Fairfax, in 1748, says he went to the South Branch of the Potomac to Henry Van Meter's. At another time, said he stopped at Mr. Van Meter's, near the "Trough." Henry died soon after his father (Isaac) and it is supposed that he was buried in the beautiful valley so dear to the family, because his grave cannot be located in Salem county. His will recorded at Trenton, N. J., is dated May 2, 1752; proved December 8, 1759. The following children are named in it: Joseph, David, John, Ephraim, Fetters, Benjamin, Jacob, Elizabeth and Rebecca. All the land, 2,400 acres, was left to the sons. Joseph was one of the elders chosen by the Pittsgrove Church, Salem Co., N. J., in 1762, to assist in improving the methods for raising the minister's salary. He is said to have been a Colonel in the war of 1812 and a comrade of James Monroe. When the latter became President of the United States, Col. Van Meter spent two weeks with him in the White House. (This story comes from West Virginia.)

Little is known of Henry Van Meter's children, and their descendants, with the exception of the line of Benjamin, a child of the last wife, Mary Le Fevre, daughter of Erasmus Le Fevre, a French Huguenot. (This name was corrupted to Fetters.) Henry is said to have been married four times.

Benjamin Van Meter was born October 1, 1744, married April 1, 1766, to Bathsheba Dunlap, daughter of Captain James Dunlap, of Pittsgrove. Captain Dunlap died September 19, 1773. Her mother was Anne Hunter, daughter of Robert Hunter. One of the nieces of Mrs. Anne Hunter Dunlap, a Miss Purviance, married William P. Leigh of Virginia. Benjamin and Bathsheba (Dunlap) Van Meter lived on his ancestral estate in what is now Upper Pittsgrove township, Salem county, N. J. The husband was a ruling elder in the Presbyterian Church. He liberated all his slaves before his death, but some of them refused to leave him. He died October 15, 1826. His wife died November 7 1831. Their children w^ ˳: James, Mary, Ann, Sarah, Erasmus, Fetters, Robert, Hunter and Bathsheba. Sarah and Fetters died in their infancy. James married Ruth Jones; Mary, Matthew Newkirk; Erasmus, Mary Burroughs; Robert Hunter was twice married, first to Rachel Buroughs, second to Sarah Leake Whitaker; Bathsheba married William Mayhew.

James and Robert Hunter Van Meter were physicians. They settled in Salem, N. J., and were identified with the First Presbyterian Church as founders and elders. The line of Dr. James Van Meter is extinct on earth, yet the bequests of that family to the First Presbyterian Church of Salem, N. J., will keep their memory green while time endures. Dr. Robert H. and Sarah L. W. Van Meter were the parents of eight children: Emma, Mary, Robert, James, Edward, Mason, Josiah and Harriet. Robert, James and Josiah died in their infancy. Mary married Enos R. Pease, of Connecticut; Harriet, Rev. R. J. Cone, of New York; Edward, Caroline Whitaker, of Deerfield, N. J. Mason (unmarried) is President of the Fenwick Club. Edward died January 4, 1875. His wife and daughters: Mary Caroline, Harriet F. and Anna Hunter, are all living. Shourds' "History of Fenwick's Colony," and Lewis' "History of the First Congressional District of New Jersey" give fuller genealogies, etc., than space will permit here.

ANNA HUNTER VAN METER.

Salem, New Jersey, March, 1902.

————

## ADDENDA, BY W. S. LAIDLEY.

When it is known, or remembered, that the Van Meters were the first to make a move towards the settlement of the country west of the Blue Ridge, in the Colony of Virginia, the above sketch by Miss Van Meter, will be read with more than ordinary interest.

In 1709 the people of Virginia did not know that the Potomac river went through the "Great Mountains," as the Blue Ridge was then called, and had no knowledge whatever of said mountains except what they obtained at long range, as far as the eye could reach.

In 1716 Gov. Spottswood, moved by an unbounded curiosity, or in expectation of great promotion from his King, collected a great company of friends, with armed men, and Indian guides, &c., saying nothing of his provision for jolly picnic he proposed to make of the undertaking, and started in June, for the discovery of the land beyond and to see what was to be seen west of the Blue Ridge. There is a report of his travels and route, but it is not yet settled where the point is that he crossed the Ridge.

In Lewis' history of West Virginia, he gives the route, but as this account takes him into Pendleton county, West Virginia, on the top of the Alleghany, we fear to follow him so far. And as the said Governor discovered the river Euphrates which ran into Lake Erie, we are a little backward about taking his own account of his discoveries.

In 1721 the Virginians thought so little of the said country and so much of their own peace and safety that they entered into a treaty with the Indians, by which they abandoned to the Indians all the territory west of the mountains and the Indians were to keep off the land south of the Potomac and east of the mountains. John Van Meter was an Indian trader, was well acquainted with the Indians of the north, and especially with the Delawares, and traditiớn says he had a band of Indians equipped at his own expense, which went with him on expeditions when required by him.

While it is true that William Penn tried to retain peaceful relations with the Indians, in 1728 the people within thirty miles of the borough of Philadelphia, were praying for protection from the ravages of the Indians by a petition to the Governor of Pennsylvania. John Van Meter takes with him Isaac Van Meter in 1730 and makes his way to Williamsburg, Va., and there meets Governor William Gooch and his Council of State, and while we cannot tell the conversation that took place, we know that the Van Meters wished to obtain the ownership and title to a large portion of the fair land that was situate west of the Blue Ridge, and that the Governor desired him to own it, or any one else, that would move thereto and reside thereon. Consequently there was not much time spent or words wasted before an understanding was reached whereby the said Van Meters were to have 40,000 acres of this choice land, the best in the world, and the Governor was to secure a living human wall between him and the savage Indians, in addition to the great mountains, so that both were made happy in the execution of the following paper, which speaks for itself:

At a Council held at the Capitol the 17th day of June, 1730:

Present

The Governour.

| | |
|---|---|
| Robert Carter, | John Carter, |
| James Blair, | Rd. Hitzwilliam, |
| Wm. Byrd, | John Geymee, |
| John Robinson, | Wm. Dandridge, |
| — — — — — — — | John Custis, Esqrs. |

Several petitions being this day offered to the Board for leave to take up land on the River Shanando on the North West side of the Great Mountains, Robert Carter, Esqr. Agent for the Proprietors of the Northern Neck moved that it might be entered that he on behalf of the sd Proprietors claimed the land on the sd. River Shenando as belonging to the sd. Proprietors & within the limits of their Grants it belonged sole to the Proprietors to grant the sd. Lands wch. Moven at his request is entered and then the Board proceeded to the hearing of the sd. Petitions.

On reading at this Board the Petition of John Vanmeter setting forth that he is desirous to take up a Tract of land in this Colony on the West side of the Great Mountains for the settlement of himself & Eleven Children & also that divers of his Relations & friends living in the Government of New York are also desirous to move with their families & Effects to Settle in the same place if a Sufficient Quantity of Land may be assigned them for that purpose & praying that ten thousand acres of land lying in the fork of Shenando River including the places called by the names of Cedar Litch & Stony Lick and running up between the branches of the sd. River to complete that Quantity & twenty thousand acres not already taken up by Robert Carter & Mann Page, Esqrs or any other lying in the fork between the sd River Shenando and the River Cohongaroola & extending thereto Operkon & up the South branch thereof may be assigned for the Habitation of himself his family & friends. The Governor with the advice of the Council is pleas'd to give leave to the sd. John Vanmeter to take up the sd first mentioned tract of ten thousand acres for the Setlmt. of himself & his Family. And that as soon as the petitioner Shall bring on the last mentioned Tract twenty Families to inhabit or that this Board is satisfied so many are to remove thither Leave be & it is hereby granted him for surveying the last mentioned Tract of twenty thousand acres within the limits above described in so many Several Dividends as the petr. & his sd. partners shall think fit. And it is further ordered that no person be premitted to enter for or take up any part of the afsd. Lands in the meantime provided the sd. Vanmeter & his family & the said twenty other families of his Relations and friends do settle thereon within the space of two yeares according to his proposal. *MSS. Journal of the Governor and Council* (1721-1734.), p. 363.

Isaac Vanmeter of the Province of West Jersey having by his petition to this Board set forth that he & divers other German

Families are desirous to settle themselves on the West side of the Great Mountains in this Colony he the Petitioner has been to view the Lands in those parts & has discovered a place where further Such settlement may Conveniently be made & not yet taken up or possessed by any one of the english Inhabitants & praying that ten thousand acres of Land lying between the Lands surveyed for Robt. Carter Esqr the fork of Shenando River & the River Operkon in as many several Tracts or Dividends as shall be necessary ffor the Accomodation & settlement of ten ffamilies (including his Own) which he proposes to bring to the sd. Land. The Governour with the advice of the Council is pleas'd to order as it is hereby Ordered that the sd. Isaac Vanmeter for himself & his Partners have leave to take up the sd. Quantity of ten thousand acres of Land within the Limits above described & that if he bring the above Number of Families to dwell there within two yeares Patents be granted him & them for the same in Such Several Tracts & Dividends as they shall think ffit & in the Mean time that the same be referr'd ffree from the entry of any other pson. *MSS. Journal of the Govenor and Council* (1721-1734.), p. 364.

No one will accuse these Dutchmen of being either fools, crazy or even reckless men. They knew more of the Indian character than did the Virginians or even the Pennsylvanians, they knew what could be or had been secured by treaty or contract in relation to the settlement of this country. We do not pretend to have seen the same in writing or of having heard of its execution, signed sealed and delivered, but we know no sane man would have undertaken this contract unless he had had some assurances of his peaceful holding of the land he had contracted to place his family and the families of his friends upon. It was not intended to go upon the land and enter upon a war with the Indians with these forty families. This historic sketch brings us down to 1730, and will naturally lead us to the subsequent events that took place under and by virtue of the above contract in relation to the settlement of the Shenandoah Valley.

# RECORDS RELATING TO THE VAN METRE, DUBOIS, SHEPHERD, HITE AND ALLIED FAMILIES.

S. GORDON SMITH.

In the latter part of the 17th century French Huguenot refugees together with a number of Dutch families from the Netherlands, and some palatines from the German provinces, came to America, and arriving at various points in the vicinity of Manhattan, ultimately found their way up the North river to the lowlands south of the Catskill mountains, 80 odd miles above the Bay. Here in the little fertile valleys watered by the Wallkill and the Eusopus; comprising in area, not more than 3000 acres, and running a few miles into the interior, these pioneers founded five small settlements, collectively, called the New Paultz region, but made up of the individual villages of Esopus, Marbletown, Hurly, Kingston and New Paltz.

These pilgrims driven from their home beyond the sea by a common religious persecution that was then devastating their native land, found a safe and permanent abiding place on the Hudson.

'As a result of the peaceful communal intercourse while in those little Ulster county valleys, they soon forgot social and religious differences; became further united by intermarriage and with its resultant kinship, and harmonious social and business relations; the end of a generation found the two types happily blended, until, at this time by mutual agreement, the Dutch language was spoken only in the domestic circles, while the French tongue served for public use in business, educational and religious intercourse.

Among the French exiles who came were the families of du Bois, Le Fevre, Ferree, Deyou, Vernoy, Hasbroque; some of the Dutch surnames were Jansen, Etten, Bogard, Paaling, Wynkoop, Ten Brock, Gerritsen, Van Meteren, and so on. All these names under the conditions I have named, underwent same change and many came to be written with a radical variation from the original. Take, for instance: Joost Janz Van Meteren (i. e. of Meteren—so-called, from the village of Meteren, a short distance southwest of Buren in the province of Gelderland, in Holland), whose name has been variously written or expressed in these forms: Van Meteren, Van Metre, Van Meter, La Meeter, Lameeter, La Maetre, La Maitre, de la Meter, &c., &c., and that of Dubois, as: D'boy, Debois, Dibois, Deboys, du Bois, Duboy, and so on. This explanation will answer for a host of others of the first settlers whose spelling of the family name today may hardly be identified with the original.

In the church registers of Kingston, to which place it was the custom of parents to take their children for baptism before they were a month old, the names were written by different pastors who officiated from time to time, each of whom spelled and wrote the surnames as be thought proper.

The earliest records relating to the Van Metre family in Ulster county, N. Y., are those taken from the marriage and baptismal registers of the church at Kingston; to-wit:

Abraham La Matre, j. m. of Midwound (Flatbush, L. I.), resid. in Kingston, and Ceeltje Vernoy, j. d.,.from the Esopus. m. 17th. June, 1682.

Joost Jan., j. m. of Meteren, in Gelderland, resid. in Marbletown, and Sara du Bois, j. d. resid. in the Nieuw Pals (New Paltz), m. in the Paltz, 12 Dec. 1682.

Jacobus le Maitre, j. m. b. in Nieuw Haarlem, and Geertje Elsenteen (Elten), j. d. b. in Schenecktede, m. 23d Sept. 1688.

It is not unlikely that these three men were kinsmen, altho' the surnames vary and hailing from different localities, they seem to have converged here and settled among their kindred. The baptismal record of their children is as follows:—

Issue of Abraham and Ceeltje (Vernoy) La Matre: Comelis, b. 1683; Susannah, b. 1685; Johannes, b. 1688; Isaac (?), b. 1689; —by Elsje Tappan, 2d wife: Ariantje, b. 1694; Johannes, b. 1697; David, b. 1701; Jacobus, b. 1705; and Abraham, b. 1707.

Issue of Joost Jan and Sara (du Bois) Van Metren: Jan. b. 1683; Rebekka, b. 1686; and Lysbeth, b. 1689.

Issue of Jacobus and Geertje (Elten) La Maitre: Isaac, b. 1694; Martha, b. 1696; Jacobus, b. 1699; Marten, b. 1701; Bata, b. 1703; Hester, b. 1706; and Jannetje, b. 1711.

It is possible that other children may have been born in these families between the baptismal periods recited, if so, their names do not appear upon the register. In the record of the baptism of Joost Jan's children, his name, as one of the parents, is written as: Joost Jans, Joosten J. Van Meteren, and

Jooste Jansen; while that of his wife: Sara du Bois—remains unchanged. The name of du Bois appears twice among the sponsors of the children, while none of the name of Van or La Metre occur in any form, as might be expected if the Van Metres and La Metres et als were related; but, on the contrary appear other names, which prompt a query,—! could not Joost Janz have been the son of Jan Joosten? I find the custom obtained here, of transposing names, as it did more extensively, perhaps, among the Welsh!

Jan Joosten and his wife Macyken Hendrickse, were sponsors to Joost Jan's first child: Jan, along with Jacob du Bois, the next older brother of Joost Jan's wife Sara. Jan Joosten and his wife were sponsors also, to Joost Adriansen's child; Jannetje, bap. 1672; and again in 1682,—for another child, Sara, the dau. of Joost Adrian. This Jan Joosten was evidently a man of prominence in the religious community, as may be inferred from the fact, that Thomas Cook—in January, and a dau. of Thomas Garton, in February, 1682,—were "Baptised at Jan Joosten's in the presence of the whole Consistory." Joost Adrian may hae been a son of Jan Joosten. His wife's name was Lysbeth Willem—se. Joost Jan's first and third child was named respectively, Jan and Lysbeth, a safe inference is that they may have been named for Jan Joosten and Lysbeth Willemsee.

After the birth of Lysbeth in 1689, Joost Jans' name seems to have dropped from the record; it reappears again along with his wife Sara's at the baptism of Rebecca (Van Meteren) Elten's child Zara, 6th Febr., 1715, when they were sponsors. Rebecca *m.* Cornelis Elten in Sept. 1704, this couple had nine children by the end of the year 1728, and nowhere among the sponsors of any of these children, occurs the name of Joost Jan, except in the instance noted.

There appears to be no mention either, of the marriage of Jan, Jr.. or of Lysbeth Van Meteren, upon the Kingston records.

It is possible that this Joost Jans came to be known later as John Van Meter, of Berkeley county, Va., the Indian trader who first trod the Valley of Virginia with the Delaware Indians between 1724-1730; and who, according to various writers, as well as by tradition, was credited with being so well pleased with that country, that upon his return to New York in 1725, "he settled his boys here."

It was in 1714 that John and Isaac Van Metre, Jacob and Sarah lu Bois (the sister of Jacob du Bois and probably the wife of John Van Metre,) came to Salem, N. J., from Ulster county, N. Y., and took possession of 1600 acres of land located on Alloway's Creek, which they had purchased of Daniel Coxe of Burlington, N. J., agent of the West Jersey Proprietors. In 1716, John and Isaac Van Meter, and Sara du Bois sold their portion of the above tract (i. e. 1200 acres) to Jacob du Bois, who remaining settled at Pilesgrove. Isaac Van Meter remained also in Salem county, and while there married: circa 1717; Annetje (Ann or Hannah), dau. of

257

Gerritt and Helena (Folker-Elten) Wynkoop, of Moreland Township, Pa.

John Van Meter and Sara du Bois, after the sale of the above land disappear from our view as far as New Jersey is concerned; they probably returned to New York—temporarily at least, and went out with one of the family groups migrating to other parts. Isaac and Hannah Van Metre continued to reside in Salem county. They are prominently mentioned in connection with the organization of Pilesgrove church, their names appearing in the covenant roll in 1741, also the names of their elder children Henry and Sarah. Henry the son, m. in 1744, his cousin Rebecca du Bois, dau. of Isaac du Bois of Perkiomen, Pa. The dau. Sarah m. John Richman; both of whom: Henry and Sarah and their families— removed afterward to Virginia.

Jacob Dubois the grantee of the Van Metre tract in 1716 m. circa, 1690, Gerritje Gerrittsen probably at Kingston. She was the sister of Tryntje Gerrittsen, wife of Solomon du Bois—the brothers having married sisters. Solomon was the father of Isaac who settled on his father's lands at Perkiomen and died there in 1729, leaving five daughters. The children of Jacob du Bois of Salem, most of whom were born in New York, were: Magdalena, Barent, Louis, Geeritje, Sarah, Isaac, Gerritt, Catharine, Rebecca, Neeltje and Johannes.| Brent m. in 1715, his cousin Jacomyntje, dau. of Solomon du Bois, of Kingston; Louis m. 1718, Jannetje, Van Vlied, and Gerritt m. Margerat ———. When Jacob their father, divided his lands at Pilesgrove, in 1733, into four equal parts, the above sons received each his respective fourth interest, and settled upon their lands. In the church covenant which I have referred to,—of 1741— are found among the signers thereto, these names: Isaac Van Metre, his wife Hannah; their children Henry and Sarah. Barent du Bois, his wife Jacomyntje; their son Garret and his wife Margerat, and *their* son Jacob, Jr. Sometime after this date Isaac and Hannah Van Metre, their children Henry and Sarah and their families emigrated to the South Branch of the Potomac, and no doubt, it was this Isaac, son (?) of John and Sara Van Meter who was associated with his father (?) John in procuring the grant of 40,000

258

acres of Valley lands from Governor Gooch, some years before. In their respective petitions, John Van Meter states that he is from the "Govt. of New York"; to him was allotted 30,000 acres for 20 families, including his own (of 11 children), relatives and friends. To Isaac, who probably absented himself from New Jersey about this time,—who states that he is from the Province of West Jersey; is allotted 10.000 acres, for 10 German families including his own; provided; that by 1732 the Van Metres will have settled the 30 families upon the granted lands. For some reason which does not yet appear, the Van Meters transferred or assigned their holdings to Jost Hite; and it is evident, that as far as Isaac was concerned— he did not remove his family to Virginia till about 1744, and then settled at Point Pleasant in Hardy county. John Vanmeter with his contingent from New York and Penna. proceeded at once, by way of the old Indian trails through Pennsylvania—to Opequon, Virginia, and settled there under new grants from Jost Hite.

Before dismissing the subject relating to the New Jersey Van Metres, it may be well to say that Kryn Jan Van Meteren, sup. son of Jan Gysbert, could not possibly have been the Indian trader. It seems clear that he was of another family that came from New Utrecht, L. I., to Middletown, N. J., about 1709, and remained in Monmouth county, N. J.

There were also in New Utrecht, in 1698, four families of Jansens, having from one to five children each. They were: Lawrens Jansen, Andries Jansen, Hendrick Jansen and Cryn Jansen. In the same year, Gysbert Jantz, with four children, was living in Flatbush, L. I. Kriyn or Cryn Jansen's son Jan b. 1687 d. y.; his next son John, b. 1688, m. 1718, Ida, dau. of Ryk Hendrickse von Suydam and their descendants for the most part, lived and died in Monmouth county. Both John and Ida are buried on the farm upon which they had settled now in Atlantic Township.

As the children of the first settlers of the Paltz grew into maturity and married, and the latter to a considerable extent, among their own kinsfolk, they sought new homes in distant parts. Family groups from Ulster county, N. Y., made their way to the German communities in Penna. To Germantown, Perkiomen, Bensalem, Pequea and other localities where their compatriots had preceded them. In the settlements named were found younger branches of the du Bois, Wynkoop, Ferre, Neukirk, Hoogland, Paaling, Heydt and other families, mostly related by marriage; but whether or no John Van Meter dwelt among them after leaving New York, does not as yet appear.

One of the most prominent persons connected with the early Virginia colonists of the Valley, was Hans Jost Heydt, (i. e. John Joseph Hite). His name has been subjected to all sorts of contortions. Jost Hite, as I shall call him, was a native of Strasburg in Alsace. It is said that he married Anna Maria du Bois, a dau. of Louis, one of the Patentees of New Paltz, and therefore must have been a brother-in-law of Joost Jan Van Meteren *alias* John Van Metre. The date of his marriage is uncertain, nor is it yet clear what number of children were in his family when living in the Paltz. Two daughters were baptized in Kingston—Elizabeth in 1711 and Magdalena in 1713. For these, Cornelis and Rebecca (Van Meteren) Elting, and Jacob and Madelena Capsesyen were sponsors respectively. These are the only items referring to Jost Hite on the Kingston records. He next appears in Pastorius Colony at Germantown, in 1716, and in the following year, 1st mo. 15, 1717 a record is found where he paid quit rent on 174 acres of land at Schippack, to the Penna. Land office. He is thus located in the Perkiomen region.

On the 17th, Dec., 1718, he bought of Joseph and Mary Kirkbride, and Thomas and Sarah Stevenson of Bensalem, in Bucks county, Pa., two tracts of land, 100 and 500 acres each respectively, for £175; it was also located in Schippack. Francis Daniel Pastorius drew the deed. In 1719 Jost Hite and his wife Anna Maria, conveyed 141 acres of his holdings to Peter Tysen, shoemaker, of Philadelphia. An additional grant of 50, acres adjoining his other land, was made to Jost Hite in 1725, by the Proprietaries Commissioners. Hite disposed of 100 acres of his Perkiomen plantation, in 1728, to Jacob Markley; and one the 10th of May, of the same year "Yost Hyt", name appears with those of Powling, du Bois, Froman, Fry and others of "Falckner's Swamp, Schippac and Goshenhoppen, in Colebrookdale," in a numerously signed petition to the Prov. Council, praying for protection against the depredations of the Indians in those parts.

Jost Hite while living in Skippack, seems to have been very thrifty. In addition to farming he carried on weaving and milling, having built a mill on Perkiomen creek; the weaving industry he seems to have brought from Germantown, apparently.

In January 1730, Hite sold the 600 acres, including the mill— still, at what is now Schwenksville—to John Paaling (Pawling) for £540. Paaling, three days later conveyed a half interest in the mill and 58 acres of land to Isaac du Bois (previously referred to), son of Solomon du Bois, who had now located in the neighborhood on his father's lands. Isaac, who was a nephew of Jost Hite and Joost Van Meteren, died in 1729. In 1747 his heirs sold the property to Peter Pennypacker, ancestor of the Hon. S. W. Pennypacker, Governor-elect of Pennsylvania, who now owns and makes his summer home upon the property. It was on these lands, too, that General Washington and the American army encamped for several days both before and after the fateful battle of Germantown, in October, 1777. The property was then known as Pennypacker's Mills and was in the possession of Samuel Pennypacker.

While a resident of the Perkiomen country, among those whom Hite had for neighbors, were the families of Froman, Fry, Conrad, Jones and others whose names afterward became familiar in the Valley of Virginia. Paul Froman m. Hite's dau. Elizabeth. Robert Jones m. Mary, dau. of John Van Metre.

After 1730 we lose sight of Hite in Pennsylvania; but in 1732 his name appears among the Dutch settlers in the Shenandoah valley, where he seems to have bought out the interest of the Van Metres in the 40,000 acre grant and opened it to settlement. At this time Hite was said to have been well advanced in years. He had a large family—at least eight, probably ten, in number. Many of his children were married, and grandchildren born before the "trek" of the Germans led them through Pennsylvania, and Maryland to the banks of the Potowmack.

261

The names of Jost Hite's children, which I have compiled from various sources were: John, m. Zara Elting; Jacob, m. a Mary Van Meteren; Isaac m. Helita Elting; Abraham m. a Rebecca Van Meteren; Elizabeth m. Paul Froman; Magdalena, m. Jacob Chrisman; Maria, m. Geo. Baumann; Susannah m. Abraham Weissman, Joseph (?) and Thomas (?). I have the baptismal record of sixteen of the grandchildren of Jost Hite, by the Rev. Johann Caspar Stoever, which occurred at Opequon between the years 1732 and 1739. During the sa  le period Jost Hite and his wife were sponsors not only to these children but for those of his friends: Peter Stephan, Ulrich Bug﬇r, Blank and others.

Mr. W. S. Laidley is a lineal descendant of Jost Hite through his oldest son John, and by his only son John's eldest son Jacob, whose eldest dau. Mary Scales Hite m. John Laidley, who were the parents of the editor.

There lived at Lebanon, Pa., contemporaneous with Jost Hite, Peter and Abraham Hite and their families. Possibly these may have been relations of Jost. In 1747, the Rev. Stoever baptized several of their children.

With regard to the identity of John Van Metre, the Indian trader, it seems impossible to reconcile the various statements made about him and his family; or to determine positively the relationship, if any, existing between him and Isaac Van Metre of Salem, N. J.; or to set aside the feeling that the Rebecca Van Meteren who m. Cornelis Elting was probably the daughter of John. It is possible, if it were true that she was the dau. of John, of Berkeley county, Va., that she may have lost her husband by death and afterward m. Solomon Hedges, albeit she had nine children for a second wedding dowry.

In his petition to Governor Gooch for the Virginia lands, John Van Metre informs us that he is of the "Govt. of New York," and has a family of eleven children; of whom, says D. S. Van Metre, in West Va., Magazine, April 1902; there were five there were five sons and six daughters. John Van Metre's will proved at Winchester, Va., in 1745, proves this to be correct, and gives the names of his children. They were: Abraham, Isaac, Henry and Jacob, sons; Sarah, Mary, Rebecca, Elizabeth, Magdalena and Rachael, daughters. Johannis and Joanna, grandchildren; son and daughter of his *eldest* son Johannes (the German form of Dutch Jan), deceased; both under age Johannes, being deceased, the order in which the names are written may not have been the same as of their birth. Three of these names agree with the baptismal names of Joost Jan Van Meteren's children, at Kingston. Jan, the eldest b. 1683; Rebecca, b. 1686; Lysbeth, b. 1689. Sarah *m.* James Davis, probably the same who was killed by the Indians in 1752; Mary *m.* Robert Jones; Rebecca *m.* Solomon Hedges; Elizabeth *m.* Thomas Shepherd, and Rachael *m.* John (?) Le Farge. (Le Farge).

The late J. B. Kerfott of Martinsburg, Va., supplies the following: Abraham *m.* 1st Ruth Hedges, 2d, Mrs. Wheeler, nee Roberts, Johannas *m.* Rebecca Powelson. He also says, that according to tradition the first wife of John Van Metre was Sara Berdine, of a New York Huguenot family. Evidently the name has been confused and du Bois is probably meant. John Van Meter *m.* 2nd, Margerat ————. The will mentions her name. It also disposes of about 3,400 acres of lands, some of which had been bought of Jost Hite, some acquired of others, and some that lay in Maryland, that was probably bought before he settled in Virginia. He signs his name "John Metor."

There is some reason to assume that John Van Metre after settling his son (?) Isaac, at Salem, N. J., in 1716, resumed his business relations with the Indians of New York, and as they made frequent incursions into the country of their natural enemies the Catawbas and Cherokees in the Carolinas, Van Metre often accompanied them south to the Holston.

At Monocacy, Md., where a number of German and Quaker families from New Jersey and Pennsylvania, had settled about 1725 —John Van Meter, and possibly Isaac, too, bought considerable land and here John may have established his family—Jan's in particular—where they would be centrally located on the trail of the trading expeditions between New York and the Carolinas. His sons

Johannas and Isaac both owned land at Monocacy, here Johannes lived and died, perhaps a few years after his marriage as he left only two children. This would account to some extent, for the absence of any mention of Johannas in the accounts and traditions of the Virginia family. Here too, it is possible, that Abraham Van Metre met and married Ruth Hedges; Rebecca, Solomon Hedges, and Elizabeth Thomas Shepherd. Both the Hedges and the Shepherd families were prominent in Maryland before they appeared in Virginia. Even prior to 1725, the Hedges, Shepherds, Zanes and others were among the early Quaker settlers in Salem, N. J., and it is unlikely that the genesis of the families of that name in the valley of Virginia, may be traced to an origin in Fenwick's Colony, Salem county, N. J.

Elizabeth Shepherd received as a part of the legacy from her father John Van Meter, a plantation called "Pelmel," on the Potomac, in Prince George's county, Maryland, a fact which has important bearing upon the subject, since it indicates a possible prior residence in Maryland, before the Van Meters came to Virginia.

—*Samuel Gordon Smyth.*

West Conshohocken, Penna., Nov. 15, 1902.

————————————

————————

## THE YATES AND AGLIONBY FAMILIES, OF JEFFERSON COUNTY, WEST VIRGINIA.

I have been asked to write a brief account of the Yates and Aglionby families, which have been connected with Jefferson county, then Berkeley county, since the year 1786.

It is in reality but one family, that of the Yateses, a branch of it having in 1854 assumed the name of Aglionby, from which it is descended in the female line.

It may be well to begin with Charles Yates (1728-1809) the first of the name to acquire land in the Valley of Virginia. His father was the Rev. Francis Yates, rector of Gargrave in Yorkshire, but formerly of Whitehaven, in Cumberland, being the son of another Francis Yates, incumbent of St. Nicholas, in that town, 1694-1720.

I was able some years ago to trace the descent of the Yates family a generation further back, viz., to William Yates, who was living at Shackerley, in the parish of Donnington, Shropshire, in 1656. He was the great grandfather of Charles Yates.

It will be convenient to set down here some information concerning the Yates family in its earlier period, which I have been enabled to collect from various sources.

Boschobel is in the parish of Donnington, Shropshire, and in the account of the escape of King Charles II. from the battlefield of Worchester, the Yateses are mentioned along with the Penderels, their relatives, as having conveyed the King to a place of safety after his adventure in the Oak.

William Yates, living there about that time, had a number of sons. Two of these, Robert and Bartholomew, emigrated to Virginia, where they became professors in the new college of William and Mary at Williamsburg, the Rev. Bartholomew Yates being subsequently its president. These distinguished men were also rectors of parishes, and Bishop Meade gives an account of them in his book on "Old Churches and Families in Virginia," where they have left numerous descendants in the female line.

Francis Yates, the son of William, b. 1666, and educated at Christ's College, Cambridge, was ordained by Bishop Frampton at Gloucester 1686. In 1694 he was chosen minister of St. Nicholas, Whitehaven, and is said to have been nearly related by marriage to the Saintly Bishop Wilson, of Soder and Man, who ordained his son Francis Yates (the 2nd) September 25, 1720.

An anecdote of the Rev. Francis Yates, of Whitehaven, may be given here. He was six feet five inches high; and it is recorded that once, at an assize trial, he was to give evidence in favor of a prisoner against whom the judge was violently prejudiced, and endeavored to give the business an unfavorable result. Upon Mr.

Yateses' entrance, My Lord exclaimed, "And now, Caiaphas, what have you to remark?" "I have only to remark, My Lord, that when Caiaphas was high priest, Pontias Pilate was judge."

His son, the Rev. Francis Yates, the father of Charles, who went to Virginia, was educated at Queens College, Oxford, and married in 1725 Ansie Orfeur, who belonged to one of the oldest families in Cumberland. The Orfeurs had been settled at High Close for fourteen generations, and through them the Yateses became connected with the Howards, the Lamphephs, the Dykees, the Lowthers, the LeFlemmings and other families of worship and renown in Cumberland and Westmoreland. The late Miss A. E. Terrill, in her delightful "Memorials of a Family in England and Virginia" (printed for private circulation in 1887) has preserved a romantic account of the marriage between William Orfeur, of High Close, and Elizabeth Howard, the granddaughter of Belted Will, of the Border, about the year 1654. A son of theirs, General John Orfeur, fought under Marlborough at Blenheim, as a Major of Dragoons.

The Rev. Francis Yates, rector of Gargrave, and Anne Orfeur, his wife, left three sons and one daughter, viz., Charles, Lowther, Jane and John Orfeur. Charles will be spoken of later on. Lowther was educated at Sedbergh and St. Catherine Hall, Cambridge, of which he became a Fellow and finally Master. He was Vice-Chancellor of the University and Canon of Norwich Cathedral at his death in 1798.

Jane married John Mathews, a retired lieutenant of the Royal Navy.

John Orfeur, the youngest son of the Rev. Francis Yates, of Gargrave, married Mary, daughter of Henry Aglionby, of Nunnery, and Anne, his wife, daughter of Sir Christopher Musgrave Bart, of Edenhall.

We now return to Charles Yates the eldest surviving son of the Rev. Francis Yates and Anne Orfeur, his wife, who emigrated to Virginia and settled at Fredericksburg in 1752, where he became a member of the business firm of Payne, Moore & Co. After the Revoluton he was associated in business with William Lovell, Esq. Miss Terrill has given selections from the correspondence of Charles Yates, with his family in England and also with some of his friends, who were officers in the American Army at Princeton and elsewhere. In 1786 he describes to his brother, John Orfeur Yates, the acquisition of a tract of land "forty miles from Alexandria and four miles from the Potomac." For many years he spent his summers, a pleasant change from the tidewater region of Virginia, at Walnut Grove, where he had built a substantial house.

After a life of sixty-one years in Virginia, he died January 11, 1809, greatly esteemed amongst persons of all classes for his probity, his kindness and charity. He was buried in the Masonic burial ground at Fredericksburg. He never married, and, wishing for the society of his kindred, he proposed that one of his nephews should be sent out to him. This wish was gratified by the arrival at Fredericksburg in September, 1792, of John Yates, the second son of his brother, John Orfeur Yates.

As John Yates now comes upon the scene, it will be convenient to give here some account of the Aglionbys, for his mother was the youngest daughter of Henry Aglionby, of Nunnery, and Anne Musgrave, his wife.

The family traces its origin to Walter d'Aguilon, a soldier of William the Conqueror, to whom land was assigned in Cumberland, including the manor of Aglionby, a village near Carlisle and Drawdykes Castle, between that city and the border. The family found it safest to live in Carlisle, where it wielded much influence, no less than eleven of its members having been returned to Parliament for the city between the 42d year of Edward III. and the 8th of George I. A William Aglionby followed King Richard I. on his crusade to the Holy Land.

The Aglionbys were connected by marriage with many other ancient families in the country—the Blennerhassets, the Skeltons, the Saltelds, the Gilpins, the Patricksons, the Richmonds, the Fletchers, the Lawsons and the Musgraves.

A branch of the family settled in Warwickshire, one of whom, Edward Aglionby, was M. P. for Warwick and held important posts under Henry VIII. As Recorder of Warwick, he welcomed Queen Elizabeth on her visit to Kenilworth and is mentioned by Sir Walter Scott in his novel.

In the next generation a noted member of the family was Dr. John Aglionby, Fellow of Queen's College, Oxford, and Principal of St. Edmond Hall, chaplain to Queen Elizabeth and King James I., and one of the translators of the Bible. His son George Aglionby was educated at Westminster School and Christ Church, Oxford, where he was buried. He was tutor to the son of George Viliers, Duke of Buckingham, and a friend of the Philosopher Hobbs. He became Dean of Canterbury in 1643.

The Aglionbys were loyalists during the Civil Wars. John Aglionby, of Carlisle, was taken prisoner by the Parliamentary forces after a vigorous defence of the city and sentenced to death, but made his escape the night before he was to have been executed.

The Neale line of the family became extinct by the death of Christopher Aglionby at Nunnery in 1786, where his great-great-grandfather, John Aglionby, had settled in 1696. He left four sisters, the youngest of whom, Mary, married John Orfeur Yates, of Skirwith Abbey. Their son John Yates, a boy of 14, joined his uncle, Charles Yates, at Fredericksburg. He was educated at Princeton and studied law at William and Mary College. In 1803 he married Julia, daughter of his uncle's friend and partner, William Lovell. They lived for several years at Fox Neck, near Germanna, then in Culpeper county, at the junction of the Rapidan and the Rappahannock. At the desire of his uncle he removed to Walnut Grove, then in Berkeley county. There he lived for nearly forty-four years, rearing a large family and winning for himself the esteem and veneration of his friends and fellow citizens. He had much to do with the establishment of the free school system in the county.

The Virginia Free Press spoke of him at his death as being universally lamented.

During nearly sixty years he had kept in touch with his English relations, whose letters were carefully preserved, and notably those of his mother, Mary Yates, up to her death in 1816. She was a woman of strong sense and fine intellectual powers. These letters he commended to his children, and a few years ago they were collected and printed, together with other letters by his granddaughter, the late Miss A. E. Terrill. They give a continuous family chronicle extending over some seventy years. They are aptly described by the words of a poet, who speaks of "Those fallen leaves which keep their green, the noble letters of the dead."

John Yates had an unquenchable desire to revisit his native country, and, although enfeebled by age and disease, he sailed from Philadelphia in May, 1851. He was accompanied by his grandson, John Yates Beall, a youth of sixteen.. They reached Liverpool after a voyage which greatly exhausted the aged traveller and pushed on at once to Nurney, near Penrith, where he was lovingly welcomed by the widow of his brother, Major Francis Aglionby (formerly Yates) and his own cousin. He lingered for three weeks and passed away in peace on July 6. He was laid to rest beside others of his kindred beneath the chancel of Ainstable Church. His widow, Julia Yates, survived until the year 1866, when she fell asleep in the presence of many children and grandchildren, leaving behind her a memory of rare worth and loveliness.

It remains for me to give a very brief sketch of the children of John and Julia Yates, whose careers and characters would in not a few cases, afford material for a series of articles.

Their sons were Charles, William, Francis and John Orfeur; their daughters, Janet, Mary, Anne, Elizabeth and Julia.

The sons: 1. Charles, born at Fox Neck 1807, educated at Princeton and inherited the portion of his brother's estate known as Mt. Pleasant. He married in 1844, Fanny, daughter of old James W. Walker, of Madison County, Va., by whom he had a large family. In 1854 a portion of the Nunnery property in England came to him by the will of his great aunt, Mrs. Bamber, nee Aglionby, in accordance with whose will he took the name of Aglionby. He died January 30, 1891; his widow still survives, the last of her generation.

2. William Yates, born 1809 at Walnut Grove, studied medicine and practiced in Charles Town. He married Anna S. Daugherty and died January 30, 1840.

3. Francis, born in Walnut Grove 1811, married in 1840 Anne Burwell, daughter of Bacon Burwell, of Jefferson county, by whom he had a large family. In 1863 he married a second time Sydney Virginia Rocker, of Charles Town, who had one daughter and survived him several years. He died January 1, 1892. He served as a member of the Virginia Legislature and was a colonel of militia. His eldest son, John Orfeur Yates, fought in Co. B., Twelfth Virginia Cavalry, during the war of secession, and died in 1899.

4. John Orfeur Yates, born at Walnut Grove, 1813, graduated

in law at the University of Virginia and practiced for several years in Charles Town. A career brilliant in promise was cut short by death at Pensacola, in Florida, where he had gone for his health, March 28, 1839.

The daughters of John Yates and Julia Lovell were as follows:

1. Janet, born at Fox Neck 1804, married 1826 George Brook Beall, of Jefferson county, and had a large family of sons and daughters. They lived near the old homestead at Walnut Grove; he died August, 1854, and she February, 1875. Their second son John Yates Beall, who accompanied his grandfather to England in 1854, entered the Confederate service and became a captain in the navy. He died for his country at New York in February, 1865. A memoir of him was published in 1866 by Judge D. B. Lucas.

2. Mary, born at Fox Neck 1805, married in 1826 Humphrey Keyes, of Charles Town and died in 1827.

3. Anne, born at Walnut Grove July, 1815, married 1847 the Rev. William Thomas Leavell, of Charles City county, Virginia, and died in Madison county 1858. They had a family of sons and daughters. The Rev. W. T. Leavell closed a long ministerial life at Hedgesville, Berkeley county, West Virginia, in August, 1899.

4. Elizabeth, born at Walnut Grove 1817, died unmarried in October, 1844.

5. Julia, born at Walnut Grove July, 1819, married William Lovell Terrill 1839, had three children. Her only son John Uriel, served in the Confederate Army, first in the Second Virginia Infantry, Stonewall Brigade, and afterwards in Co. B., Twelfth Virginia Cavalry. He died in November, 1878.

Anne Elizabeth Terrill, the eldest child of Julia and William Lovell Terrill, compiled the volume of Family Memorials, to which the writer of this article is so greatly indebted. She died in February.

It has only been possible to record with austere brevity the names, marriages and deaths of the children of John and Julia Yates. It would have been beyond the scope of this article to recount the things concerning so many of them which were "true, honest, just, pure, lovely and of good report," an omission which those in whose hearts their memories are still green will be able to supply for themselves.

This account of a family which has abounded during so many centuries in those who did their duty toward God and their fellow men acceptably and honorably, has its lessons for all, but more particularly for its living members. It is for these to strive that they may transmit to posterity the traditions of so goodly a lienage, with the added lustre which only pure, upright, strenuous, unselfish lives can give to them, and so to glorify Him who is "the God of the families of the earth."

F. K. AGLIONBY.

London, 1902.

————

279